The Discovery of
EGYPT

The Discovery of
EGYPT

Vivant Denon's Travels
with Napoleon's Army

Terence M. Russell

SUTTON PUBLISHING

First published in the United Kingdom in 2005 by
Sutton Publishing Limited · Phoenix Mill
Thrupp · Stroud · Gloucestershire · GL5 2BU

British Library Cataloguing in Publication Data
A catalogue record for this book is available from the British Library.

ISBN 0-7509-4145-6

Half Title Page: Study of the head of a camel by Dominique-Vivant Denon.

'In the desert one's respect is redoubled for the camel, that worthy animal. However hard is
his condition, he knows it and conforms to it without impatience. He is a truly bountiful gift
of Providence and nature has set him down in a country in which his place could not be
supplied, to the service of man, by any other animal whatever.'

Dominique-Vivant Denon

Dedication: Dominique-Jean Larrey after the painting by Madelaine Benoist.

Typeset in 11/14pt Garamond.
Typesetting and origination by
Sutton Publishing Limited.
Printed and bound in England by
J.H. Haynes & Co. Ltd, Sparkford.

To the memory of Baron Dominique-Jean Larrey,
Chief Surgeon to the French Army:
'The most virtuous man I have known.'

Napoleon Bonaparte

And to those who care for others today in the field of medicine –
'The noblest of the healing sciences.'

Connections formed amidst the hardships and dangers of an expedition, such as that of Egypt, become unchangeable.

Nothing but death can put an end to valour combined with gaiety. The greatest misfortunes can do nothing towards it.
Dominique-Vivant Denon

Contents

List of Illustrations and Maps

The maps are reproductions from the 1803 London edition of Denon's *Travels in Egypt*.
The fine dotted lines mark the route taken by Vivant Denon in the company of General
Desaix and the French army. The spelling of the names shown in the maps is that
adopted by the French translators who accompanied Bonaparte on the Egyptian
Campaign. The scales of the maps are shown in French leagues and British miles.

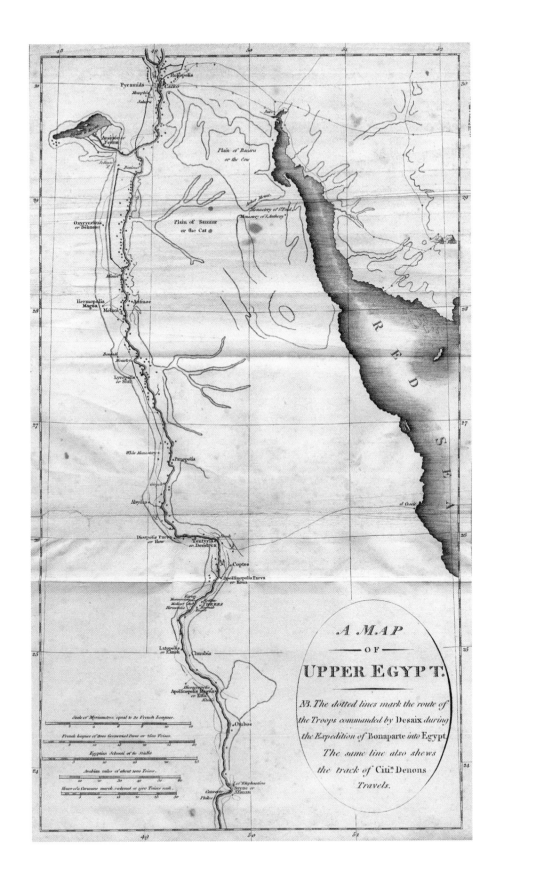

Heliopolis
Pyramids · CAIRO
Memphis
Sahara

Plain of Bacura
or the Cow

Arsinoe or
Fyoum

Oxyrnchus
or Behnese

Plain of Samut
or the Cat

Arbor Mount
Monastery of St Paul
Monastery of St Anthony

Hermopolis
Magna
Melaui

Antinoe

Benisch
Mounts
Lycopolis
or Siut

White Monastery · Panopolis

Girgeh

Abydus

Diospolis Parva
or How

Tentyris
or Dendera

Coptos

Apollinopolis Parva
or Kous

Karnak
Monuments
Medinet Abou THEBES
Hermontis
Luxor

Latopolis
or Esneh

Chmubis

Hierasonolis
Apollinopolis Magna
or Edfu

Osibos

R   E   D   S   E   A

el Cosir

Scale of Myriametres, equal to 20 French Leagues.

French leagues of 2000 Geometrical Paces or 2500 Toises.

Egyptian Schoeni of 60 Stadia

Arabian miles of about 2000 Toises.

Hours of a Caravans march, reckoned at 1500 Toises each.

Cataracts
Syene or
Philœ · Assuan

Les Elephantine

A MAP
— OF —
UPPER EGYPT.

NB. The dotted lines mark the route of
the Troops commanded by Desaix during
the Expedition of Bonaparte into Egypt.
The same line also shews
the track of Citn. Denons
Travels.

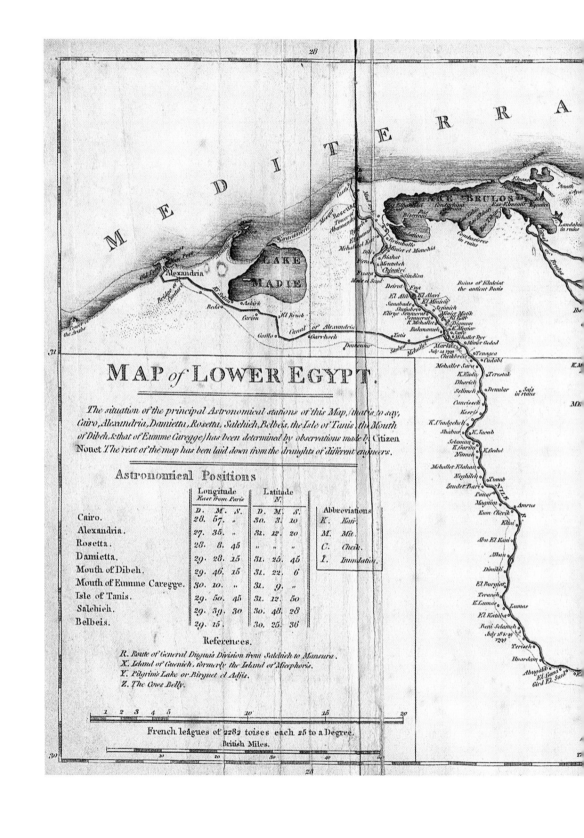

MEDITERRA

LAKE BRULOS

LAKE MADIE

Alexandria

MAP of LOWER EGYPT.

The situation of the principal Astronomical stations of this Map, (that is to say, Cairo, Alexandria, Damietta, Rosetta, Salehieh, Belbeis, the Isle of Tanis, the Mouth of Dibeh, & that of Eumme Caregge) has been determined by observations made by Citizen Nouet. The rest of the map has been laid down from the draughts of different engineers.

Astronomical Positions

	Longitude East from Paris			Latitude N.			Abbreviations	
	D.	M.	S.	D.	M.	S.		
Cairo.	28.	57.	"	30.	3.	10	K.	Kafr
Alexandria.	27.	35.	"	31.	12.	20	M.	Mit
Rosetta.	28.	8.	45	"	"	"	C.	Cheik
Damietta.	29.	28.	15	31.	25.	45	I.	Inundation
Mouth of Dibeh.	29.	46.	15	31.	22.	6		
Mouth of Eumme Caregge.	30.	10.	"	31.	9.	"		
Isle of Tanis.	29.	50.	45	31.	12.	50		
Salehieh.	29.	39.	30	30.	48.	28		
Belbeis.	29.	15.	"	30.	25.	36		

References.

R. Route of General Dugua's Division from Salehieh to Mansura.
X. Island of Guenieh, formerly the Island of Micephoris.
Y. Pilgrim's Lake or Birquet el Adjis.
Z. The Cows Belly.

French leagues of 2282 toises each 25 to a Degree.
British Miles.

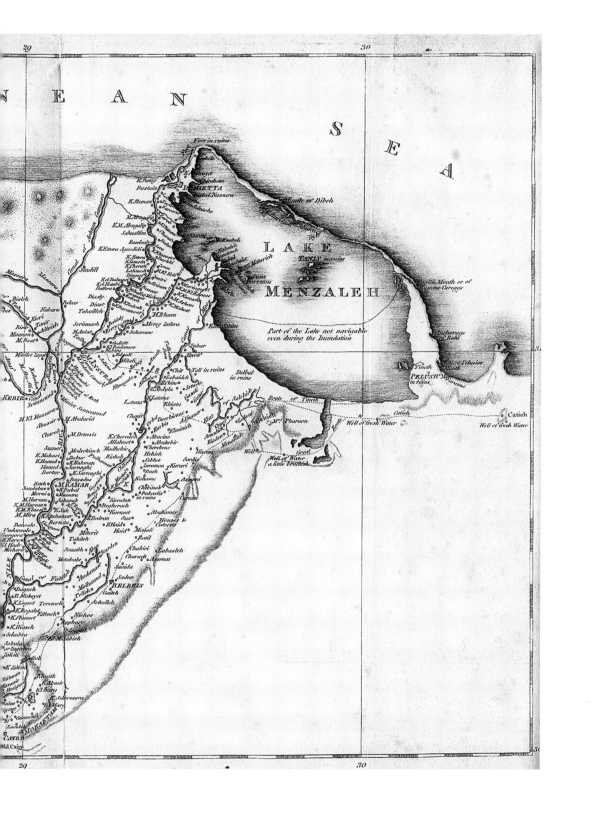

Preface: Dominique-Vivant Denon

This book is an account of the travels in Upper and Lower Egypt made by Dominique-Vivant Denon with the army of Napoleon Bonaparte. Denon's exploration of the Nile Valley to study the antiquities of Egypt is one of the great journeys of discovery of the nineteenth century. Through a combination of personal courage, vivid powers of description and remarkable artistic ability, he systematically recorded and described the treasures of Egypt. Others had journeyed into Egypt before him and had written descriptions of what they had seen, but Denon was the first to present a scholarly record of the ancient monuments combined with informed observations on the people of Egypt and their customs. Denon's pioneering work inspired Napoleon Bonaparte to commission and publish a comprehensive survey of the culture of Egypt, the influence of which on European architectural and ornamental design was far reaching.

Denon was a man of many accomplishments. At various times in his life he was a diplomat, artist and engraver, collector of antiquities, director of museums and minister for the fine arts. He was also a likeable man who got on well with others and was valued for his company and engaging conversation. Moreover, he was possessed of considerable energy and a sense of daring – qualities that were to serve him well in Egypt as Bonaparte's adviser on artistic matters.

Dominique-Vivant Denon was born into a wealthy family on 14 January 1747 near Chalon-sur-Saône in central France about 50 kilometres south of Dijon. He was educated privately and soon revealed an inclination to history and literature combined with an aptitude for drawing. In his early twenties he moved to Paris where he first studied law and then the technique of engraving in the studio of Noël Hallé. During this period he frequented the salons where his personal charm and intelligence came to the notice of influential ministers and court officials. Through these acquaintances, and in recognition of his abilities, he was invited by Louis XV to be keeper of the cabinet of carved gems he had inherited from Madame de Pompadour.

Denon was too active an individual to be constrained for long by life at court and, between 1772 and 1787, he secured diplomatic appointments in various countries. Most formative for his development, as an artist and man of letters, was his time in Naples where he was secretary to the ambassador and Chargé d'Affaires. He travelled extensively and accompanied an expedition to Sicily following which he published his researches as *Voyage en Sicile* in Paris in 1788. Throughout this time he continued to draw and etch portraits of members of society and people of standing, including the philosopher

Voltaire. For this work he was elected a member of the Académie de Peinture, earning the citation 'engraver-artist of diverse talents'.

In France this was the period Charles Dickens was to describe as 'the best of times . . . and the worst of times'. The Terror had been unleashed and the Revolution was on the march. Wishing to return to his homeland Denon, an aristocrat, had to seek the protection of the eminent painter Jacques-Louis David whose art was at the service of the new social and political regime – David was the first to paint Consul Bonaparte and later Emperor Napoleon. Settled again in Paris, Denon once more frequented the salons where he now came to the attention of the youthful Napoleon Bonaparte whose star was in the ascendant.

Bonaparte had seen a report from Ferdinand Magallon, the French Consul in Egypt (1793–7), drawing to the attention of the Directory in Paris the economic and military benefits for France were Egypt to become a French colony. Bonaparte's imagination was seized and the Egyptian Campaign was conceived. Only a few months later, on 19 May 1798, a huge armada of battleships and support vessels departed from Toulon. They carried some 34,000 troops, sailors and marines with more than 1,000 heavy guns, about 600 field carts, 700 horses and 100,000 rounds of ammunition. The rest of the French fleet comprised more than forty frigates. Bonaparte's strategy was to consolidate his forces on the way to Egypt with additional men and equipment sailing independently from Ajaccio, Civitavecchia and Genoa. When united, this would give Bonaparte a fighting force of 55,000 men.

To give legitimacy to the invasion of Egypt, Bonaparte planned his Egyptian Campaign as one of liberation – to free Egypt from Ottoman rule. By establishing a French presence in the East, with Egypt as a colony of France, Bonaparte could threaten British India and the balance of power in Asia. Moreover, this was the Age of Enlightenment. Bonaparte had read widely and was aware that the antiquities of Egypt awaited rediscovery. Hence, the Egyptian Campaign, although primarily a military adventure, would also be one of exploration and discovery.

To survey and record the treasures of Egypt, Bonaparte took with him a second 'army' consisting of 165 men of letters – savants. They were selected from all spheres of learning and included archaeologists, architects, artists, astronomers, botanists, cartographers, chemists, engineers, geologists, mathematicians, musicians, naturalists, pharmacists, physicians, printers, shipbuilders and surgeons. Together they formed Bonaparte's Commission of the Sciences and Arts. Although not a member of the Commission, Vivant Denon served as the Commander-in-Chief's adviser on artistic matters. In this capacity, Denon was the first to record and illustrate the ancient monuments of Egypt and inspired much of the later work of Bonaparte's Commission. Thereby, the science of Egyptology was born.

When the expedition to Egypt set sail, Denon could scarcely contain his excitement: 'I would be the first to see without prejudice, and to make researches in, a part of the earth hitherto covered with the veil of mystery and for two thousand years shut out from the curiosity of Europeans.' Once established in Egypt Denon was surrounded by a superfluity of wonderful things – a veritable *embarras de richesses*:

With my pencil in my hand I passed from object to object distracted from one by the inviting appearance of the next. Constantly attracted to new subjects – and again torn from them – I wanted eyes, hands and intelligence vast enough to see, copy and reduce to some order the multitude of striking images that presented themselves to me.

Although Denon benefited from the protection of the military, he was constantly embroiled in conflicts and on several occasions was fortunate to escape with his life: 'I now saw death close at my side. In the short time of ten minutes, that we stopped, three persons were killed while I was speaking to them.' These encounters affected him deeply, impelling him to exclaim: 'Oh war! Thou art brilliant in history but frightful when viewed with all thy attendant horrors, naked and undisguised!'

Having survived the Egyptian Campaign, Denon returned to France with Bonaparte where he set about ordering his *Journal* and the hundreds of sketches in his portfolio. Working feverishly and with the assistance of the best engravers in France, he published his researches as *Voyage dans la Basse et la Haute-Égypte pendant les campagnes du Général Bonaparte* (Paris, 1802). His book was an immediate success and went through numerous editions and reprints. It was translated into several languages, an English edition appearing as *Travels in Upper and Lower Egypt during the Campaigns of General Bonaparte* (London, 1803).

There is much to admire in Denon's account of his travels in Egypt. His *Journal* is written in an accessible style that has the power to captivate the reader. He makes us feel we are by his side experiencing the very events he is reporting. Moreover, Denon shares with us the insights of an accomplished artist and scholar. His commentaries are informed and reveal an expert's understanding of the art and architecture of the Egyptians; he is the first writer to convey, with aesthetic sensibility, the majestic scale and beauty of the antiquities of Egypt. With some justification Denon has been described as 'The first Egyptologist' and 'Discoverer of the Empire of the Pharaohs' (Raoul Brunton, *Musée de l'Empire*).

We admire Denon's humanity, as conveyed by his scenes of everyday life in Egypt and his observations on the people and their culture. And, as we read his account, we are mindful of the personal risks to which he subjected himself, in an occupied country, to enrich his *Journal* and portfolio. He also had to endure extreme temperatures when making his observations, often having marched many miles to reach the subject of his research.

The military conflict amid which Denon undertook his investigations imposed considerable restraints. He had to work mostly under the protection of an armed escort and time was always inadequate. Sometimes he was not even allowed to stop at the site of an ancient temple or antiquity and had to be content with improvising a sketch – seated on the back of a camel. In many ways Denon was the precursor of the modern-day war-artist. By any standards he was a courageous and gifted man.

The French savants who accompanied Denon into Egypt made their own researches of the ancient monuments and experienced the same hardships and personal tribulations as he. However, they remained in Egypt for about two years longer and were therefore able to undertake more detailed and comprehensive surveys than Denon of Egypt's antiquities and culture. These circumstances are discussed in our closing pages. To give the reader a fuller insight into the French exploration of Egypt, Denon's account is here supplemented with a selection of images from the work of his fellow artist-illustrators.

The French survey of the monuments of Egypt inspired others to follow in their footsteps. Notable among these was the Scottish artist David Roberts (1796–1864). He travelled in Egypt and recorded several views that were published, to universal acclaim, in the then relatively new medium of lithography. A number of Roberts's views are included in the selection of images. Doubtless, Denon would have heartily approved since he was himself a pioneer of lithography in France.

Although the epochal events that form the subject of this book took place two hundred years ago, the fluency of Denon's narrative style lends them an immediacy that has the capacity to enthral us today. It is fitting, therefore, that we should commend our account of Denon's remarkable travels of exploration and discovery with his own words:

> I shall esteem myself happy if, by my zeal and enthusiasm, I have succeeded in giving my readers an idea of a country so important in itself – and in the various recollections that are associated with it – if I have been able to portray with accuracy its characteristic forms, colours and general appearance and if, as an eyewitness, I have described with interest the details of an extended and singular campaign that formed [so] prominent a feature in the vast conception of this celebrated expedition.

Terence M. Russell
Edinburgh 2005

Acknowledgements

I have tried, wherever possible, to create this book from original sources and contemporaneous materials. This has given me the privilege of working with Vivant Denon's two great folio volumes, the majestic folios of *Description de l'Égypte* and the no less splendid folios of David Roberts. The experience has also brought me into contact with many kind and helpful people.

I am grateful to Michelle Gait and her colleagues at the Special Collections Library at the University of Aberdeen for permission to consult Denon's *Voyage dans la Basse et la Haute Égypte pendant les Campagnes du Général Bonaparte* and for consent to reproduce the maps of Bonaparte's Egyptian Campaign published in Arthur Aikin's 1803 London edition of Denon's *Travels*. I am similarly grateful to my colleagues in the Special Collections Library at the University of Edinburgh. They have provided me with access to their copy of Arthur Aikin's *Travels* and several of the folios from *Description de l'Égypte*. Concerning the latter, I have been privileged to consult the magnificent edition of *Description de l'Égypte* housed in the National Library of Scotland – still resplendent in its original Napoleonic bindings and shelved in its purpose-made bookcase.

The British Library has provided me with photographic reproductions from Denon's *Voyage* and David Roberts's *Egypt and Nubia*. For their care in undertaking this part of the work I wish to acknowledge the efforts of the British Library staff at Boston Spa and London. For the portrait of Bonaparte I am grateful to the British Museum (Department of Prints and Drawings). I have to thank David Taylor of the National Maritime Museum, London, for permission to reproduce the images of the Battle of the Nile. For providing me with a copy of Madelaine Benoist's painting of Dominique Larrey I have to thank Jean-Marie Milleliri, Médecin Principal of the Institut de Médecine Tropicale, Marseilles. I am particularly grateful for the care taken by the staff of the photographic departments at the University of Aberdeen, the University of Edinburgh, the National Library of Scotland and the British Library. It requires considerable skill to make accurate images from the pages of heavy, large-format folios. For financial support in helping to meet the costs of this part of the work, I am indebted to the Research Awards Committee of the School of Arts, Culture and Environment of the University of Edinburgh.

A NOTE ON SOURCES

Throughout the text I have identified the origin of each illustration together with the name of the artist. In a few cases I have identified works that have been reproduced from my own collection. For these I am indebted to the kindness and generosity of the late Mr and Mrs Nelson, former antiquarian book and map dealers in Edinburgh.

The 1802 edition of the text of Vivant Denon's *Journal* was published as one continuous narrative; it has no individual chapters or any form of textual subdivisions. This presents a challenge to the reader in grasping the structure of Denon's text and finding a way through his 265 closely printed pages. Doubtless mindful of this, when Arthur Aikin published the London edition of Denon's great work in 1803, he retained the spirit of Denon's text faithfully – in a splendid and lively translation – but recast the format of the text into twenty-one chapters. He did not give these titles but simply numbered them together with a list of their principal subjects. I have followed Aikin's plan with the addition of chapter titles appropriate to the subject matter under consideration. The passages of Denon's text that I have translated are faithful to the original but are sometimes presented in the style of free adaptations so as to make the meaning more accessible to the modern-day reader – some of Denon's sentences are almost a page long! In order not to interrupt the flow of my text, I have kept editorial intrusions to a minimum and have done without the use of footnotes. I have retained Denon and Aikin's references to the mile when referring to distances since the mention of kilometres, in events that took place two hundred years ago, would look out of place. Similarly, I have retained Denon's frequent reference to leagues. In the late eighteenth century the league was a formal unit of linear measure denoting about 3 miles. Where the context to which I refer is a contemporary one – say the distance of a town or monument from Cairo – I make reference to kilometres. Interestingly, the French editors of *Description de l'Égypte* adopted the metric system that had then been newly introduced to France together with other reforms of the post-Revolutionary era.

For accepting this book for publication I wish to warmly acknowledge the support I have received from Sutton Publishing Limited. In particular, I am grateful for the enthusiasm of Christopher Feeney, Senior Commissioning Editor (History), and that of his colleagues who have helped me to create this book. In particular I wish to thank my Project Editor Clare Jackson for her skill in manipulating my text and images into their final form.

CHAPTER 1

The French Armada

Dominique-Vivant Denon opens the account of his adventures with the French army with the observation that he had longed to travel to Egypt from his earliest years. When the opportunity to do so arose, he seized it eagerly:

> I had from infancy wished to make a voyage to Egypt but time, that softens every impression, had weakened this desire. When the expedition which was to render us masters of that territory was in hand, the possibility of executing my old project awakened the wish to undertake it. In a word, the hero who commanded the expedition [Bonaparte] decided on my departure. He promised to take me with him and I had no anxiety about my return.

It was a courageous decision. At fifty-one years of age Denon was twice as old as many of the soldiers in Bonaparte's Army of Egypt and like them he was venturing into a little-known country. Just how little known can be inferred from the fact that the loved ones of many of the military sent their men on their way with warm winter clothing to supplement their heavy uniforms. They could not have imagined that within a few weeks their men would be throwing off these uniforms in a desperate bid to keep cool and would be fighting each other to gulp a mere mouthful of muddy water at a brackish oasis. Yet, these men would also experience the adventures of a lifetime and stare in wonderment at the majestic ruins on the bank of the River Nile, calling out 'Hurrah!' But this is to anticipate events. For the present we need to trace Denon's departure from Paris.

First, he made his preparations. These entailed gathering together the artists' materials he needed to measure and record the ancient antiquities, including supplies of paper, pencils, drawing instruments and the portfolio that accompanied him everywhere. His next task was to fulfil his obligations to his family. He made the necessary provisions for their well-being and then strove to calm himself for the project in hand: 'I became tranquil as to what was past and devoted myself to the future. I no longer reflected on the obstacles that were in my way. I felt within myself all that was necessary to surmount them.'

Although outwardly serene, the enormity of Denon's project preyed on his mind. He experienced palpitations without being sure whether this was from the joy of anticipation of the adventures that lay ahead, or from the apprehension of leaving loved ones behind. For some days he was agitated. He shunned contact with others and busied himself with his preparations.

Baron Dominique-Vivant Denon depicted in bronze by the artist-sculptor Pierre Cartellier, Paris, cemetery of Père-Lachaise. We have to imagine Denon on the Egyptian Campaign, when he was thirty years younger – with broad shoulders, upright posture and a mass of flowing hair. Ever courageous, energetic and intellectually alert, he was Bonaparte's eyes. His survey-work and drawings inspired his younger colleagues and together they established the science of Egyptology. *(Image, Dr Graham Harris)*

Denon's journey from Paris to the port where he was to embark was uneventful. He and his travelling companions arrived at Lyons without quitting their carriage, and from there they journeyed down the Rhône to proceed to Avignon. Staring at the river banks Denon reflected that in Russia he had seen the Neva, in Italy the Tiber and now, venturing to Egypt, he was to go in search of the Nile. He spent a day at Marseilles from where he set out on 13 May 1798 for Toulon.

The following day he embarked the frigate *La Junon* which, in company with two others, was to reconnoitre ahead of the main French fleet. The wind was foul and the small ships quitted the port with difficulty. Towards the evening of the 16th, the main fleet was sighted and was deployed in order of battle to leeward of *La Junon*. This situation enabled Denon to gain insights into eighteenth-century naval procedures in times of war. Guns were manoeuvred into position. Silence and terror, the preparatives for slaughter, gripped the men.

Night came on but did not restore the tranquillity of Denon and his fellow savants. Their position as men of letters did not relieve them from being allocated duties by their naval and military commanders. The scientists in the group were considered to be the most useful to the expedition and were given the rank of senior officers. Their engineer-companions were accorded the status of lieutenants, which was the cause of some resentment. The most senior of the savants enjoyed the privilege of dining at the captain's table; others took meals with the generals. The most junior of the non-combatants had to rough it with the rest of the crew – and suffer their indifference and occasional caustic remarks.

At daybreak the frigates took advantage of the wind. Distant vessels were sighted but were so remote that Denon could not make out if they were French ships of the line, fighting ships, or, like *La Junon*, small frigates. In the cold morning air he occupied himself by looking about his ship. He noticed how much of the deck was encumbered with artillery – a chilling reminder that he, an artist and man of letters, was now embroiled in a great military expedition.

On the morning of the 19th, the main French ships of the line and the convoy of support vessels quitted port. By noon the sea was covered with vessels. How grand a spectacle that must have been! Denon was captivated: 'Never can any national display give a more sublime idea of the splendour of France, of her strength and of her means'. He had reason to feel proud of his country and the great armada that, incredibly, had been assembled in only a matter of months. Moreover, the thousands of men taking part in the expedition – soldiers, cavalry and support personnel – had all had to make their own way to the ports from numerous locations throughout France. And all were ignorant as to their destination. They had left behind wives, children and friends to follow Bonaparte.

The next day the French flagship *L'Orient* put out to sea with her accompanying vessels taking station in their order of sailing. The squadron of frigates was ahead. Next came the Commander-in-Chief with his advice-boats and then the line of battleships, which extended for a league and a half. The circle formed by the convoy was no less than 6 leagues in extent. *L'Orient* had three gun-decks, each equipped with forty cannon. She

Admiral Nelson (1758–1805) after the painting by William Beechey. His prowess and judgement at the battle of the Nile (Abukir Bay) resulted in the near total destruction of the French fleet. He was rewarded with a peerage and adopted the title Lord Nelson, Baron of the Nile. *(National Maritime Museum)*

was a veritable floating fortress. Bonaparte was on board *L'Orient* and looked intently at each of his vessels as they passed by his flagship. They saluted and went on their way, unsure of their ultimate destination; it was known only to Bonaparte and the senior officers in whom he had confided his plans.

The destination of the French convoy was Egypt. The route taken by the majority of the French ships was: Toulon, the west coast of Corsica and Sardinia, the Straits of Sicily, the Malta Channel, the Mediterranean Sea and Alexandria. Other French ships sailed independently from Ajaccio and the Italian ports of Civitavecchia and Genoa. They later united with the main fleet in the vicinity of Malta.

Perhaps some men thought they were destined for England, where the prospect of a French invasion was the subject of fevered conversation. Such was the fear of a French incursion on to English soil that the British government had recommended London's principal streets be barricaded and its houses fortified. At the same time the Admiralty ordered a squadron to embark for the Mediterranean to gain information about French naval activity in Toulon, a task entrusted to Admiral Sir Horatio Nelson. He set sail on 2 May with three battleships, two frigates and a sloop. Nelson was then more than ten years older than Bonaparte and had already lost an eye and his right arm. His naval forces

The youthful General Napoleon Bonaparte, from the portrait by Andrea Appiani. Not yet thirty years of age, he led an army of 55,000 troops into Egypt and conceived the French Commission of the Sciences and Arts. The latter's achievements proved to be the durable legacy of the Egyptian Campaign. *(British Library, Prints and Drawings)*

were later augmented with eleven more ships of the line providing a fighting force that included thirteen battleships, each equipped with seventy-four guns and one with fifty giving a combined firepower to rival that of the French.

Observing the movements of the French ships, Denon counted 160 vessels 'without being able to reckon the whole'. About 180 ships are thought to have departed from Toulon. On the morning of the 24th, the frigates were off the eastern coast of Corsica, opposite Bastia. Next in sight came the island of Elba which seemed to Denon like 'a rock of ferruginous earth whose crystal portions presented all the colours of the prism'.

At five in the afternoon the island of Pianose could be seen to the east, its flat low-lying terrain presenting a hazard to an unwary captain. Denon observed how the bleak landscape appeared to be abandoned to wild goats. The wind died away and the sluggish convoy, laden to the gunnels with ordnance, made slow progress. This state of torpor provided Denon with an opportunity to contemplate his fellow voyagers. The ship's crew were brave lads but, to his Parisian sensibilities, they were a rough lot. Reduced to sloth,

The hapless and courageous French Admiral Count de Brueys, after the engraving by Alexander Lacauchie. Despite having his legs shot from under him, he continued to direct the French response to the British onslaught until he and his flagship *L'Orient* were blown to smithereens. *(National Maritime Museum)*

they voiced their complaints and demanded double their allowance of water and provisions. Things grew worse: 'The most greedy among them sold their effects or disposed of them by way of lottery. Others, with a strong propensity to gamble, played and lost more in a quarter of an hour than they could pay in their lifetime. Those who had lost their money staked their watches, six or eight of which I have seen depending on the chance of a dice.' When night came on it put an end to gaming and a matelot played his fiddle. An indifferent singer did his best to entertain the men who, in response, cleared a space on the decks and made merry. Then it was the turn of a storyteller who held his audience with the tales of the prodigious valour and marvellous adventures of *Tranche-Montagne,* a tale similar to 'Jack the Giant Killer'.

On the evening of 31 May the fleet was joined by the *Bodine.* Reassuring information was obtained. The French captains were advised they would reach Cagliari Point without being intercepted by the English navy that was thought – correctly – to be searching for them in the vicinity. Nothing much occurred over the next few days but, by 4 June, the ships' provisions were nearly exhausted and the water had become so fetid as to be scarcely drinkable. Denon wryly observed: 'The useful animals had disappeared while those that fed on us were multiplied a hundred fold!' The following day orders were received to form a fresh line of battle in anticipation of enemy action. *La Diane* led and made signals to *La Junon* that were relayed to the supporting sister-ships *L'Aquilon*, *L'Alceste* and *La Sportine.* In effect, these ships were a form of 'flying squadron' whose role was to hasten and crowd the enemy should she show her sail. Amid these dramatic developments Denon's roving eyes cast a glance overboard:

> We saw several small dolphins playing before the head of the ship. To our mortification they disappeared while we were preparing to harpoon them. I had a close view of them. Their progress resembles the pitching of a vessel. They leap out of the water and dart forward twenty feet. They are elegantly shaped and their rapid movements rather resemble a sportive gaiety than announce the voracity of an animal in quest of its prey.

In the evening the wind picked up and, shifting round from east to west, it collected the convoy in such a way that the many ships' lights crowded together like stars, prompting Denon to record: 'I fancied I saw Venice hovering on the waves'. At sunset Martimo was discerned and orders were received for the convoy to close-form and to pass the night as a floating fortress and thereby be better prepared for any surprise attack. The night, however, passed uneventfully.

On 6 June the order of sailing was resumed. Martimo was still in sight and to Denon it resembled 'a mole at the western point of Sicily'. This was one of the locations in the Mediterranean where the English might be expected to rally their fleet and therefore a place to be navigated with some trepidation. A freshening wind stepped up the French ships' rate to 'two leagues an hour'. Good progress was made and the danger passed. The men's spirits rose and Denon mused: 'Under such circumstances as these the inconveniences of sea life are forgotten and nothing is felt but the advantage of having such an agent as the sea, for the transport and conveyance of forty thousand men.'

The fleet was now off Martimo. Favignana could be made out as a mere rock situated before Trapani and Mount Erice that overlooks the city. In antiquity, a temple was raised there to Venus and was celebrated for the sacrifices made to her. Denon spied the coast of Sicily through his telescope. He judged the land to be 'agreeable, productive and well cultivated'. The scene held other enchantments for him. It called to mind his youthful wanderings in Sicily and in his imagination he fancied he saw Marsala, formerly Lilybaeum, from where the Greeks and Romans discerned the fleets sent out from Carthage to attack them. More distant was the aspect of Selinuns with its temples and still upright columns resembling 'so many towers'. Now strengthening wind bowled the fleet along 'at three leagues an hour'.

The ensuing night was fine and the diminutive *La Junon* found herself in the midst of the great fleet. Denon rose early the next morning and was soon on deck. He watched dawn break and observed the convoy begin its complex series of co-ordinated manoeuvres to leave the security of the shoreline and put out to sea. The French vessels were soon making good progress for Malta. Sicily was passed and, to the south-east, Denon fancied he could see the volcanic island of Pantelleria shrouded in the thick clouds in which it is frequently enveloped. It was there the Romans banished prominent persons and errant members of the imperial family.

The night of the 7th was clear but the wind slackened and the rate of progress of the fleet slowed. Calm weather prevailed and little distance was made the next day but the monotony was relieved by the sight of Mount Etna towering above the horizon to the north. Smoke could be seen issuing from its eastern slopes and the crew became excited at the prospect of witnessing an eruption – of which Denon's account, however, makes no mention. Denon estimated the volcano to be some fifty leagues distant and noted that it so commanded the horizon that it appeared to be 'taller than mountains only twelve leagues away'. At six in the evening the island of Gozo, still some seven leagues distant, came into view bathed in the reddening glow of sunset.

La Junon and her sister ships laid to and waited for the heavily laden convoy to catch up. Denon could not resist taking out his telescope to have another look at Etna, reckoning her smoke pall hung in the air for a distance of more than twenty leagues 'like a long sheet of vapour'. In due course the men-of-war passed under the stern of the vessel of the Commander-in-Chief. A course was then steered towards the north side of the island of Gozo. Although the coastline was forbidding, Denon thought he could see cotton under cultivation in the fields and considered that the valleys resembled 'so many gardens'. At eight the next morning a signal was made that several unidentified ships had been sighted at a distance – perhaps as many as thirty sail. Was this the English enemy reconnoitring? There was a moment of alarm until it was realised that they were the anticipated contingent of French ships sailing to meet them from Civitavecchia. On board was General Desaix's military division complete with field guns, small arms and equipment, this impressive convoy having crept along the coast of Italy, passed through the Straits of Messina and reached the waters off Malta before Denon and his companions. The French fleet was now united and in Denon's eyes constituted an awesome force: 'As an impetuous torrent, that has increased its bulk in passing over mountains covered with snow, threatens in its course to sweep away forests and cities, so our fleet now became immense [and] unquestionably spread terror and dismay wherever it was descried.'

The first stage of the Egyptian campaign had been achieved without major incident. By good fortune the French armada had run clear of the English men-of-war. The French had even departed from Toulon unnoticed by Nelson. His ships had suffered the effects of heavy weather and did not arrive at Toulon until eight days after the French fleet had slipped away. For the moment the combined French naval and military forces were safe. They now faced their first major challenge. They must secure Malta in order to achieve naval supremacy in the Mediterranean.

CHAPTER 2

The Conquest of Egypt

At five in the afternoon on 9 June 1798 the French fleet was off Comino and Cominotto, the two islets lying between Gozo and Malta. At the time of the French conquest of Egypt these islands constituted the dominion of the Knights of Malta, the former Knights Hospitaller of St John of Jerusalem. They were renowned for their courage, chivalry and splendid uniforms. The brotherhood of knights, which dated from around the time of the first crusade (1096–9), was presided over by a Grand Master. If the French were to take Malta, which was a prerequisite for conquering Egypt, the brotherhood and their allies would first have to be won over – or be subjugated.

Bonaparte held the Knights Hospitaller in contempt. Notwithstanding his sense of history, he regarded them as an anachronism in the modern era. Storming their fortress, though, was another matter. In the late eighteenth century a number of fortresses defended the Mediterranean islands around Malta, and Malta herself was – and remains – strongly fortified by the formidable fortress of St Elmo that defends the township of Valletta at its coastal promontory. The principal marauders in the eighteenth century were the infamous pirates who plagued the Barbary Coast and the defensive works had been constructed to prevent them acquiring a base from which to threaten the Maltese galleys. These same defences, equipped with cannon, now faced the French fleet.

The fleet itself must have looked awesome to those who contemplated it from the fortress ramparts. More than four hundred ships of all sizes, crowded with men and equipment, covered a vast expanse of sea 'like a forest'. Bonaparte did not want blood to be shed and had initially decided on a strategy of cordiality to secure Malta. His plan was to request permission for the French fleet to be given supplies of fresh water with the reassurance that 'the religion, customs and property of the Maltese would be scrupulously respected'. A small French barque was sent out to obtain permission to disembark peaceably – but a landing was refused. To Bonaparte's dismay unacceptable conditions were imposed. Only a few ships at a time were to be allowed to renew their supplies. The sole concession to the French was in the form of two paltry rowing boats bearing cargoes of tobacco. This was scarcely the welcome – even less the gesture of acceptance – that Bonaparte was expecting. Napoleon grew indignant and on 10 June, on board *L'Orient*, he drafted a letter to the Grand Master Ferdinand von Hompesch, the gist of which stated: 'Bonaparte is resolved to procure with force that which should be accorded to him following the principles of hospitality which are the basis of your Order'. Conflict was inevitable.

Sketches of Valetta's defensive works as viewed by Denon through his telescope from on board the frigate *La Junon* as it approached Malta with the French fleet.
Upper: Entrance to the harbour with the township to the right and Fort St Angelo to the left.
Middle: View from within the harbour. A vessel lies part submerged – testimony to the fierce conflict for possession of the island.
Lower: The Fort of St Elmo with Valeta in the distance. French ships are entering the harbour following the capitulation of the Knights of St John. *(Denon, British Library)*

The evening drew in and there was not a single light to be seen on the mainland of Malta – all had been extinguished to frustrate the enemy. A French frigate was stood off the entrance to the port within less than a gunshot of Fort St Elmo. Orders were given for the loading of troops into barques preparatory to attempting a landing on the island and at nine o'clock a signal was made for the ships to take up their stations. There was little or no wind. The ships of the line, the principal ships of war, made night signals to each other to establish their relative positions and to make their movements known to the rest of the convoy. Rockets were let off and signal guns were fired.

The main fleet found itself to the leeward of the island as a consequence of the strong prevailing currents. Having drifted somewhat to the east, calm waters were found enabling the French to consolidate their position. Denon took advantage of this lull in the proceedings to set about making drawings of the island of Malta – as well as he could observe it from on board ship. A gentle breeze sprang up of which the battleships, acting in unison, took advantage to form a threatening semi-circular line whose extremities extended from St Catherine's Point to a league beyond Valletta and her port. The centre of the fleet was stationed off the forts of St Elmo and St Angelo, while the convoy bearing the soldiers and equipment required for the invasion of Egypt was held at anchor between Comino and Cominotto.

The intimidating scene confronting the Knights of Malta instilled in them the utmost fear despite the near impregnability of their great fortress. Nonetheless, it was they who opened the hostilities, firing shots from Fort St Catherine at the French barques attempting to approach the shore and at the troops making a landing under the command of General Desaix. Instantly, further shots were fired from the ramparts of the fortress commanding Valletta. At the same time the standard of the Knights of Malta was raised in defiance. The batteries of all the forts rained down their fire on the French fleet and the small boats from which the foot soldiers were attempting to disembark. A steady fire was maintained until evening but, according to Denon, 'the Knights progressively betrayed more fear and confusion than military strategy'. By ten o'clock detachments of French troops had ascended several of Valletta's defensive works – no mean achievement under heavy fire – and others attacked the rear walls of the city. The townsfolk were in mortal dread.

At the same time two Maltese galleys anchored off the entrance to the port maintained aggressive opposition to the French battleships, inducing the captain of *La Junon* to move his frigate to the protection of the main fleet. This provided Denon with a better view of the battle. Initially there was military order within the citadel but this gradually collapsed under the relentless discipline of the superior French forces. Viewing events through his telescope, Denon observed:

> They kept up this fire until evening with an imprudent precipitation that betrayed their fears and confusion. The first day the Knights were in full uniform and a constant communication was kept up between the city and the forts into which provisions and ammunition of every kind were thrown. Everything in short indicated hostility. On the second day, the movements were confined to an agitated state. A part only of the Knights were in uniform. They disputed with each other but ceased to act.

By daybreak on 11 June resistance from the fortress was almost over and only a slow and insignificant fire was put up in opposition to the French advance. Soon after, General Reynier assumed command and became Master of Gozo. His first act was to have several prisoners despatched to Bonaparte on board *L'Orient*. Bonaparte sent them back to the island with the withering remark: 'You should have known how to die'. At about this time a small boat was seen quitting Malta with a flag of truce. On board were several Knights. Under interrogation it was discovered the Maltese had few resources left, something which Denon himself was able to confirm. By four in the afternoon *La Junon* was within half a gun-shot of the island, affording Denon a distinct view of the forts in which he records he could see 'few men and guns'. A little later a deputation of twelve Maltese commissaries went on board *L'Orient* to parley with Bonaparte. There was little to negotiate. The French were outright victors:

> On the 12th, in the morning, we were informed the inhabitants had favourably received the General's aide-de-camp. At half after eleven the barque that had brought the flag of truce, and

which had remained under her stern during the night, left *L'Orient*. At the same time we received orders to hoist our colours [above the fortress of St Elmo] and a moment after the signal was made that Malta was in our possession.

It was a remarkable victory and gave the French an advantageous position in the Mediterranean. At five o'clock on 12 June 1798 the French troops took possession of the forts and were hailed by their fleet with a 500-gun salute. During the next few days Bonaparte immersed himself in a frenzy of activity dictating dozens of military orders and commands. He decreed that the tricolore should be displayed and that prominent citizens should demonstrate their loyalty to France by adorning themselves with cotton armbands in white, red and blue. Slavery was abolished and some Knights of French origin were recruited for the Egyptian Campaign.

On the fourth day after landing Bonaparte gave a supper to which he invited the newly constituted authorities who were to preside over Malta. Denon was one of the guests and left the following description of the impression made by Bonaparte and his generals on the vanquished enemy: 'They saw, with equal surprise and admiration, the mortal elegance of our generals and the assemblage of officers on whose countenances beamed health and vigour, hope and glory. They were struck by the noble physiognomy of the Commander-in-Chief whose expression seemed to augment his stature.'

Denon satisfied his artistic inclinations by exploring Valletta, which he found to be a fine city. The soldiers secured the forts and bastions and armed the fortifications with French cannon. A few days later they were summoned back to their ships. Strong winds initially delayed the fleet from sailing and Denon busied himself with making drawings of the Old Port. On the morning of the 19th, *L'Orient* sailed out of the harbour. Under the command of General Vaubois, 4,000 men were left behind to secure the island of Malta together with officers, artillery and engineers.

On 19 June the day was spent in collecting into order the fleet of the line of battleships, the squadron of frigates and the convoy – no small undertaking amid the turbulence of the Straits of Malta. At six in the evening the signal was made to observe the order of sailing. The convoy of supply ships was stationed ahead with the armed ships of the line placed defensively at the rear. On the two days following the weather held fine and the prevailing wind would have bowled the fleet along as far as Crete had it not been for the heavily laden transports in the convoy weighed down with field guns and equipment.

Unknown to the French the English fleet was in the vicinity of Malta, searching the horizon for a sight of their ships. Had Nelson set his telescope upon them, there is little doubt that his heavily armed battleships would have picked off the handicapped French vessels at will and there would have been no French invasion of Egypt – and the course of European history would have been changed. Unaware of the presence of the French ships, Nelson sailed unwittingly by them assuming they were on course for Alexandria.

From his cabin on board *L'Orient* Bonaparte issued a sequence of military commands. With the Egyptian Campaign now foremost in his mind he gave instructions to his Commanders Bon, Cheval, Desaix, Kléber, Menou and Reynier listing the brigades, divisions and cavalry for which each would have responsibility when the landing in

Egypt was achieved. Bonaparte then turned his attention to his soldiers and issued a stirring Proclamation & Articles:

Soldiers!

You are going to undertake a conquest the effects of which, on the civilization and the commerce of the world, are incalculable.

You will bring to bear on England a certain and most sensitive wound, while waiting to give her the death blow.

We shall make fatiguing marches; we shall engage in several battles; we shall succeed in all our undertakings; destiny is with us.

The Mameluke beys, who exclusively favour English trade, who have snubbed our merchants and tyrannised the unfortunate inhabitants of the Nile [Valley], will – a few days after our arrival – no longer exist.

The people with whom we go to live are Mohammedans; their first article of faith is this: 'There is no other God than God and Mohammed is his Prophet'.

Do not contradict them; act with them as we have acted with the Jews [and] with the Italians; have respect for their muftis and their imams as you have for rabbis and bishops.

Have the same tolerance for the ceremonies prescribed by the Koran [and] for the mosques that you have for the convents, synagogues and for the religion of Moses and Jesus Christ.

The people, to whose country we go, treat their women differently to ourselves; but, in all countries, he who violates them is a monster.

Pillage enriches only a small number of men; [but] it dishonours [all of] us; it destroys our resources and it renders enemies of the people whom we are interested in having for our friends.

The first town we are going to encounter was built by Alexander. We shall find, at each step we take, souvenirs of deeds to inspire emulation by the French.

The sentiments in Bonaparte's Proclamation & Articles are high-minded. They were upheld by many French soldiers who behaved with extraordinary chivalry and made personal sacrifices to help women and children. But there were also many atrocities.

During the months of June, July and August, the north and north-east winds are the trade winds of the Mediterranean making navigation propitious in the era of the sailing ship. Consequently the French fleet made good progress and on 24 July a distance of 48 leagues was achieved 'with a breeze that bordered on a gale of wind'. This wind was even more favourable to the English fleet. Progressing at twice the speed of the heavily laden French convoy it overtook the French ships. Since the weather was foggy neither fleet was aware of the other despite their being separated by only a few miles. Nelson was then in the paradoxical position of hastening to Alexandria, thinking he was going to intercept Bonaparte's armada, when all the while he was leaving the French warships and support vessels in his wake. Three days later Nelson reached the Egyptian coast only to find the harbour of Alexandria deserted. His response was to sail along the coast of Palestine. Failing to discover the French ships, he doubled back on a westerly course to continue his search.

Unaware of Nelson's activities the French continued on their way. Candia on the island of Crete came into view. Candia was the ancient Herakleion (modern-day Iraklion) which is rich in Greek mythology, a fact that was not lost on the scholarly Denon who, through his telescope, fancied that: 'At the distance of twenty leagues I could distinguish mount

Ida, the birthplace of Jupiter and the country of almost all the gods'. Two days later, at five in the morning, the French caught sight of the English fleet, no less than 6 leagues distant, steering to the west in quest of them. Thick fog denied the English the encounter they were seeking and the French proceeded without challenge. A short passage then occurs in Denon's *Journal* that is often quoted. It captures perfectly what it must have been like to have been on board Bonaparte's flagship in the midst of the great French fleet:

> It would be difficult to convey a precise idea of the sensations of power, dictating its decrees amidst three-hundred sail of vessels, in the still silence of the night. The moon afforded to this picture just as much light as was necessary to the enjoyment of it. Five hundred persons were on our deck and the flapping of a bee's wings might have been heard. Our very respiration was suspended.

A message was received from the captain of *La Junon* instructing his men to detach from the main fleet and proceed without delay to Alexandria. The plan was to seek advice from the French Consul then resident at the ancient Egyptian port, and to learn from him if the Egyptians were well disposed towards the French. It would therefore be their destiny to be the first of the French fleet to reach African soil.

Bonaparte continued to direct military affairs from his cabin on board *L'Orient*. To the consternation of his admiral and chief naval officers, he also took a keen interest in naval matters and plagued those around him with questions concerning the ship's progress and her manoeuvres. The savants were also caught up in Bonaparte's all-encompassing enthusiasm. Bonaparte commenced what he called his *Institutes* or after-dinner discussions. Sometimes these were formal occasions held in his cabin around the dinner table; on others they took place while he strolled on deck. All manner of subjects were discussed – religion, science, politics, travel, geography – in fact anything Bonaparte considered worthy of reflection. There were times when he himself would initiate the conversation; at others he would nominate one or other of the men of letters to lead the debate. These discussions were of no great importance in themselves but they were significant insofar as they formed a precursor to the activities of the Institute of Egypt which Bonaparte later established at Cairo.

La Junon set full sail to accomplish as speedily as possible the 60 leagues remaining to make landfall. However, during the night the unpredictable wind fell and for several hours there was only a gentle breeze to send her on her way. On landing their orders were to warn the French Consul and his fellow countrymen to be on their guard after which they were to return to the main fleet. Then a fair breeze arose to carry them on their way and at daybreak on 29 June the coast of Egypt could be seen, stretching like a white ribbon over the blue horizon.

Although the weather was fine, the captain of *La Junon* was mindful he was skirting along a coast that could be dangerous in stormy weather and no less so during fog when the low-lying shoreline could all but disappear from view. So hazardous was the sea route to Alexandria that in antiquity the great lighthouse at Pharos, one of the Seven Wonders of the ancient world, had been built to cast its beacon to aid voyagers approaching the port.

The New Harbour of Alexandria from the burial ground separating it from the Old Harbour. On the western promontory is Fort Qaitbey or Castle of the Pharos from which the French tricolore flutters triumphantly in the breeze. This is the site of the famed Pharos lighthouse, one of the Seven Wonders of the ancient world. *(Cécile, National Library of Scotland)*

As *La Junon* progressed, the countryside that came into view appeared arid, prompting Denon to observe: 'To the right and left of us our Promised Land seemed more sterile than that of the Jews'. He added, with a touch of humour, that if it had rained on them 'manna from heaven and quails ready roasted' it would have done little to raise their estimation of the bleak scene confronting them. At that moment a landing place was sighted and at one o'clock a lieutenant was sent on shore. Through his telescope Denon could see the tricolore flag displayed over the French Consul's house.

Denon did not spend long in contemplation; the artist and scholar stirred within him. He was mindful that the great port of Alexandria, with its associations of learning and antiquities, was but a few miles distant. Taking out his telescope and scanning the horizon, he observed the scene before him. He started to make notes for his *Journal* and sketches for his portfolio but was roused from his occupations by the firing of a gun from his frigate. It was the signal to call on board the French Consul who duly arrived with a local man and an interpreter. They had weighty news. An English fleet of fourteen heavily armed ships of the line had visited Alexandria in expectation of finding the French and had only quitted the port the evening before to resume their search. Moreover, the local people had mistaken the English ships for French, a circumstance that had created considerable agitation. As a consequence they had resorted to arms. In addition the shoreline strongholds had been fortified, the militia had been reinforced

with additional troops and an army had been improvised from a tribe of wandering Bedouin.

This was disturbing news. It was evident from the combative attitude developing at Alexandria that the French forces would be assured a hostile reception when they eventually landed. That evening Denon, a non-military man, confided to his *Journal*: 'From that moment I became a fatalist and commended myself to the star of Bonaparte'.

La Junon duly departed the coast of Alexandria to be reunited with the main French fleet which was discovered at daybreak the next morning. By seven o'clock in the evening

The Old Harbour of Alexandria from the shoreline looking across the bay. The French support ships disembarked their troops after the capture of Alexandria. The men-of-war sailed on to the deeper waters of Abukir Bay where Nelson destroyed them at the battle of the Nile. The view shows the harbour forty years later, resplendent with the Egyptian fleet. *(Roberts, British Library)*

the frigate was within hailing distance of *L'Orient*. It fell to Denon, a close confidant of Bonaparte, to accompany the French Consul on board the flagship. The Consul's message was brief and to the point. The English had been seen and they might return at any moment.

As if in response to the bleak news a gale sprang up that caused confusion among the French fleet. The convoy of military transports, heavily laden and slow to respond, mingled dangerously with the warships. There was a risk in all quarters of ships' rigging becoming entangled. Denon grew alarmed and reflected that should the enemy appear amidst their confusion, the French would suffer a terrible defeat. Throughout these dramatic episodes he was by the Commander's side and he remarks: 'I watched the General's countenance that did not change in the slightest degree'.

Bonaparte, decisive as always, ordered his troops and equipment to be landed – despite the hazards. The sea was worsening and rocks and perilous reefs obstructed the coast. New dispositions of the ships were signalled so as to bring the convoy as near to land as possible. To offer protection from the enemy, the men-of-war formed a circle of defence on the outside of the fleet. Their sails were taken in and their anchors released. The three military divisions of Generals Desaix, Menou and Reynier were on board the transport vessels moored about 3 miles from the shore. The soldiers had to make their way to land in longboats. The two remaining divisions of Generals Kléber and Bon were on board the battleships that formed part of the outer defensive ring, and were therefore required to make an even longer journey by longboat to reach the safety of the shore.

For the thousands of soldiers waiting to set foot on dry land the order to disembark, although welcome insofar as it would put an end to their ordeal at sea, must have been received with feelings of dismay. The men had already endured a long sea voyage, many were weakened by seasickness and few knew how to swim. Most were already bruised and light-headed with fatigue. And now they were to be packed into longboats in a bid to make for the shore – in full dress uniform, weighed down with arms and ammunition. Little wonder that, according to Denon, 'many of the men – abandoned to their basic instincts – were heard wailing like children above the sounds of the raging wind and the crashing waves'.

The landing of the soldiers took several hours. Bonaparte himself had to endure the same conditions as his men and eventually reached the shore by longboat in the company of Generals Berthier, Caffarelli and Damartin. By six o'clock in the morning on 1 July 1798, several thousand French troops had landed, against all the odds, on an insignificant little beach near a place called Marabou. Momentous events had occurred. The French army had arrived on Egyptian soil and the tricolore was hoisted for the first time in North Africa. The first stage in the conquest of Egypt had been achieved.

CHAPTER 3

The Storming of Alexandria

The perils the French army had experienced in making the sea landing on the coast of Egypt were bad enough, but worse was to follow. Fatigued by a voyage that had lasted several weeks, burdened by their weapons and having had little to eat, the army now faced the prospect of trekking through the Libyan desert to secure Alexandria – in the searing heat of the North African sun.

Early in the morning of 2 July 1798, Bonaparte made a show of reviewing those of his troops who had so far made it to the shore, about five thousand men. He then set out for Alexandria at the head of three divisions led by Generals Bon, Kléber and Menou, leaving two divisions behind to secure the beachhead under the command of Generals Desaix and Reynier. Once on the march the men had no option but to stagger on. The alternatives were to perish from heat and thirst or to be taken captive by the marauding Bedouin who threatened stragglers with their spears and small arms. The march to Alexandria was truly harrowing but was eventually achieved out of sheer desperation. Denon provides the following account:

> We got under way and perceived that the beach was filled with our soldiers. By noon they were under the walls of Alexandria, the centre being stationed at Pompey's Pillar behind some small hillocks formed by the ruins of the ancient city. The old walls presented a succession of breaches to the valour of our soldiers. As soon as one of the columns was in motion the others drew up in battle array, marched and attacked at the same time.
>
> A heavy fire, kept up by the besieged, surprised our troops for a moment but did not check their impetuosity. Our troops stormed. Generals Kléber, Menou and Lescale were wounded by the enemy's fire and by the collapse of pieces of wall.
>
> Our adversaries maintained their ground. We were under the necessity of putting the whole of them to death, at the breach, where two hundred of our soldiers fell.

Denon enjoyed the privilege of journeying to Alexandria by boat where his frigate, *La Junon*, was ordered to moor and offer protection for the eventual entry of the French convoy into the Old Port. As he set foot on land he recalled a prophecy. It foretold that as soon as a French vessel should enter the Old Port, Alexandria would cease to be in the possession of the Muslims. The presence of *La Junon* seemed to fulfil this prediction – at least for the moment.

Denon was eager to enter Alexandria where in ancient times culture had so flourished that scholars had journeyed from far and wide to consult the books and manuscripts

Harrowing military scenes witnessed by Denon on his marches with the army.
Above: A soldier tries to comfort his dying companion as the French troops march on. Another covers his head so as not to see the death that awaits him from the charging Mamelukes.
Below: A soldier drags a wounded comrade from the charge of the enemy cavalry. He calls out: 'Leave me! Save yourself! I shall perish!' Denon remarks: 'Such valour was expressed a hundred times'.
(Denon, British Library)

stored in profusion in her great library. However, the sights that met his gaze fell short of his romantic imaginings:

> It would be impossible for me to describe what I felt on landing at Alexandria where there was no one to receive us or to prevent our going on shore. All the houses were shut. Those who had dared to fight had fled and those who had not been killed in the combat had concealed themselves for fear of being put to death according to the oriental custom.

> Everything was new to our sensations [including] the soil, the form of buildings, the persons, customs and the language of the inhabitants. The first prospect that presented itself to

our view was an extensive burial ground covered with innumerable tombstones of white marble on a white soil. Among these monuments were seen wandering several gaunt women, in long tattered garments, resembling so many ghosts. The silence was only interrupted by the screeching of kites that hovered over this sanctuary of death. We passed from thence into narrow and deserted streets.

Alexandria still had to be secured and Bonaparte, halting with his generals before the city's defensive works, attempted to parley with the hordes of combatants menacingly arrayed on the ramparts. The French salutations were greeted with a hail of bullets and abuse from the courageous, if somewhat foolhardy, defenders. Below them was assembled the finest and most disciplined fighting machine in Europe. The French response was to attack the fortifications. The French charged like tigers. The soldiers, weary from their marching and desperate with thirst, were more than eager to take Alexandria in order to put their personal miseries to an end. Many died as they tore their way through the fortifications.

The defences breached, street fighting took place across the city. Men, women and even children were put to the sword. Bonaparte eventually received a deputation and a truce was secured at his encampment before the monument known as Pompey's Pillar. He then made an inspection of parts of the city in the company of several guides. This was almost Bonaparte's nemesis; he only narrowly escaped a sniper's bullet. The would-be assassin was located and summarily shot. Bonaparte, unharmed, proceeded on his way to take up residence in the house of the French Consul.

Denon paid a visit to Bonaparte's headquarters. There he found the Commander-in-Chief surrounded by the grandees of the city and various members of the old government of Alexandria. From all of these Bonaparte demanded an oath of fidelity. He addressed himself in the following terms to their leader Sheikh Koraim: 'I have taken you in arms and I might treat you as a prisoner. As you have however behaved honourably, I give you back your arms and I trust you will be as faithful to the Republic as you have been to a bad government.' Denon noted the effect these words had on the countenance of this able and important man. Initially Koraim was neither shaken nor even subdued by the words of the Commander-in-Chief. However, some time later, when he saw 30,000 Frenchmen with their heavy ordnance and field guns, his demeanour changed. According to Denon: 'He endeavoured to captivate the good graces of Bonaparte, was never absent from his headquarters and was in the ante-chamber before the Commander in Chief was out of bed'!

At the same time as Bonaparte was imposing his authority and personality on the impressionable Sheikh Koraim, he ordered a Proclamation & Articles to be issued that spelt out in uncompromising terms what he expected of the Egyptian people:

2 July 1798

People of Egypt, they will tell you I have come to destroy your religion. Do not believe it! Reply that I have come to restore your rights, to punish the usurpers and that I respect, more than the Mamelukes, God, His Prophet and the Koran.

Tell them that all men are equal before God. Wisdom, ability and virtue alone demarcate the difference between them.

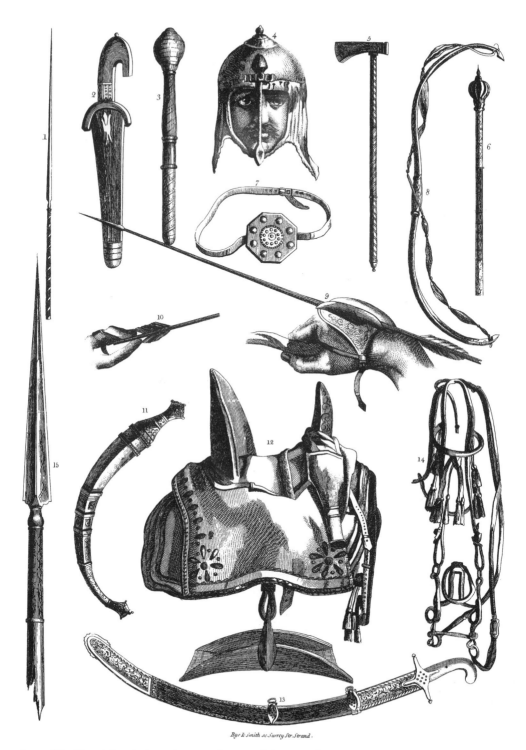

Arms of the Mamelukes. Arab warriors were fearsome fighting machines equipped with an array of formidable weapons. Lances (1, 15); helmet with protective nose piece (4); daggers and a Damascus-bladed scimitar (2, 11, 13); battle axe (5); truncheon and mace (3, 6); whalebone bow with silk cord from India (8); arrows and methods of releasing them (9, 10); magnificent saddle and bridle (12, 14); and a decorative motif worn by the combatant (7). *(Denon, University of Edinburgh)*

Now, what wisdom, ability and virtue distinguish the Mamelukes for them to have exclusively all that renders life so agreeable and pleasant . . . ?

You once had in your midst great towns, large canals and plentiful commerce. What has destroyed all this, if not the avarice, the injustice and the tyranny of the Mamelukes?

Kadis, sheikhs, imams and [other notable persons] tell the people [of Egypt] that we are the true friends of the Muslims.

Thrice happy shall be those who are with us! They shall prosper in their fortune and their rank. Happy shall be those who are neutral! They shall have time to learn about and understand us and move freely among us.

But misfortune, thrice misfortune, to those who take up arms with the Mamelukes and fight against us! They shall perish.

To his Proclamation Bonaparte appended a series of Articles, the military gist of which was as follows. First, all villages situated within 3 leagues of the route taken by the French army were to send a deputation informing the general commanding the troops that they were obedient to his will and to display the tricolore. Second, all villages taking up arms against the army were to be burned.

Several thousand copies of the Proclamation and its Articles were distributed among the local villages and beyond. In some places it was reported to have produced 'a great effect'. Elsewhere it was received with disdain.

The first drawing Denon made in Alexandria was of the Old Port. He created this when walking out to a sandbank near the quarter occupied by the Francs. In the time of Cleopatra this had been a delightful place; here she had built her palace and here the Theatre of Alexandria had once stood. The next day Denon had a further opportunity to see the sights, spending the morning in the company of the Commander-in-Chief who was anxious to visit the forts and military installations. They turned out to be little more than a collection of clumsy buildings in a ruinous state. Worn-out guns rested on stones that served for carriages. The Commander's orders were to demolish whatever was unserviceable and to repair what might be useful to prevent the approach of the Bedouins. He paid particular attention to the batteries for the defence of the harbours, aware of the threat posed by Nelson's fleet.

Of greater interest to Denon was the opportunity he had of paying a visit to Pompey's Pillar. At the time of the French invasion this free-standing column was Alexandria's most prominent landmark and the imposing structure still stands to the south-west of modern Alexandria. 'Pompey's Pillar' is the colloquial term for the giant column, surmounted by a Corinthian capital, that was erected in AD 300 in honour of the Roman emperor Diocletian (Gaius Diocletianus). It is believed that Pompey's Pillar is the single remaining column from the portico of the Temple of Serapis and that in Roman times the column, almost 30 metres high, was surmounted by a great equestrian statue of the emperor Diocletian, now lost.

When Denon was at liberty to make further explorations of Alexandria's architectural legacy, he was dismayed to discover the extent to which so many ancient monuments had either disappeared or had been used as a source of building materials:

The defensive works are built from [ancient] ruins and these edifices bring increasingly to mind destruction and ravage. The jambs and lintels of the doors of the dwelling houses and fortresses

Care of the wounded on the field of battle. Chief surgeon Dominique-Jean Larrey, his case of surgical instruments nearby attends an Arab soldier whose shattered lower-leg he has just amputated. A 'camel-ambulance' waits to take the man to a field hospital. The lives of many soldiers were saved by Larrey's expedient surgical skills, often deployed at considerable personal risk.

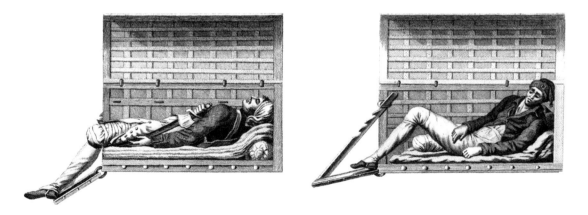

Details of the ambulance; a camel could transport two wounded men.

consist entirely of columns of granite that the workmen have not taken pains to shape to the use to which they have applied them. They appear to have been left there merely with a view to attest to the grandeur and magnificence of the [ancient] buildings, the ruins of which they are.

The Turks, more especially, adding absurdity to profanation have not only blended [modern materials] with the [ancient] granite bricks and calcareous stones, but even logs and planks. From these different elements which have so little analogy with each other, and are so unharmoniously united, they have created a monstrous assemblage of the splendour of human industry with its degradation.

Later Denon paid a visit to the outskirts of Alexandria where he viewed the Arabic walled enclosures. At the time of his inspection these resembled little more than an encroachment of the desert. However, at the season of the inundation of the Nile, they were transformed as though by magic into productive gardens resplendent with fruit and vegetables in proportion to the size of the irrigation system with which they were provided. The water cisterns to these enclosures were the source and principle of their existence. When they dried up the gardens once more reverted to an arid terrain of sand and rubbish.

At the gate to each of these gardens, Denon noticed monuments that imparted a benevolent and charitable feeling and were frequently decorated with large colourful inscriptions from the Koran. These monuments were erected above the water-supply cisterns that irrigated the gardens. The cisterns also served to supply drinking fountains and basins for the benefit of the weary 'to satisfy his most pressing want in this burning climate – thirst'.

Water was fed into the cisterns by irrigation channels or, if this was not possible, camels transported it there in large leather-skin bags. The monuments and water fountains were erected and maintained by wealthy civic dignitaries, or by charitable foundations, by whose names they were known. In Cairo there were no fewer than 300 such watering places, some of which were embellished with marble columns and ornate roofs. Denon, with his keen eye for everything of interest, recorded in his *Journal*:

> The conduits of the cisterns are to be seen everywhere, communicating with each other, and have their openings covered by the base or capital of an ancient column, hollowed out in the centre, which answers the purpose of the stone that surrounds the mouth of a well. For the construction of a new cistern it is sufficient to dig and bank-in reservoirs, of different depths, and afterwards to cut a drain carrying it until it meets with another excavation. In this way it receives the common benefits of the inundation which, by the level that the water seeks, fills the whole of the vacuum presented to it.

Denon traced his way to the most famous of the architectural monuments then surviving at Alexandria – namely, Cleopatra's Needles. This popular name describes two great rose-red, granite obelisks that had originally been quarried hundreds of miles further south near Syene. When Denon saw them only one was standing. Its companion had toppled to the ground following an earthquake and it lay almost buried in the sand.

The obelisks, to use their correct designation, had been erected at Heliopolis by the Egyptian king Tuthmosis III, in 1500 BC, to honour the sun god Re-Horakhti. They had been subsequently transported to Alexandria by the Roman emperor Caesar Augustus to adorn the Caesareum in honour of the deified Julius Caesar. Their original excavation from the living rock, and later removal, must have been a Herculean task since each is estimated to weigh about 200 tons (over 200,000 kilograms). Afterwards they were intended as a tribute by the Roman general Mark Antony to the beautiful Queen Cleopatra, from which their popular name derives.

Denon could not resist speculating how fine a show these great symbols of Egyptian art would make at home: 'They might be conveyed to France without difficulty and would there become a trophy of conquest – and a very characteristic one – as they are in themselves a monument'. His words were prophetic, although not quite as he had intended. In 1871 the British engineer James Dixon removed the fallen obelisk to London where it now adorns the Thames Embankment. In 1880 the upright obelisk was removed to New York City where it now stands in Central Park. Nor were the French denied their – dubious – honour of acquiring an Egyptian obelisk. In 1836 they removed one of the two obelisks from the great Temple of Luxor. It now stands in the Place de la Concorde in Paris.

The standing obelisk, one of a pair known as 'Cleopatra's Needles', now sited in Central Park, New York. Half-buried in the sand is the fallen obelisk now sited on the Thames Embankment, London. They were originally raised by Tuthmosis III, at Heliopolis, in 1500 BC to honour the sun-god Re-Horakhti. Intended as a tribute by Cleopatra to Mark Anthony, they were moved to Alexandria in 14 BC by Caesar Augustus to adorn the Caesareum in honour of the deified Julius Caesar. *(Cécile, Author's Collection)*

After Denon had satisfied his curiosity about the great obelisks of Tuthmosis III, he went in search of fresh discoveries in the vicinity of the Old Harbour. In ancient times this had been dominated by the famed Pharos. While inspecting the harbour he discerned many ruins beneath the waves. Doubtless, the Mediterranean Sea was clearer at the time of Denon's visit and, moreover, there would have been less silt covering any architectural remains than is the case today. These circumstances would have allowed for a better view of what lay below the surface. Denon comments:

In returning to the lower part of the harbour by the seashore, ruins of edifices of different ages are to be found having suffered alike from time and from the waves. Vestiges of baths are to be

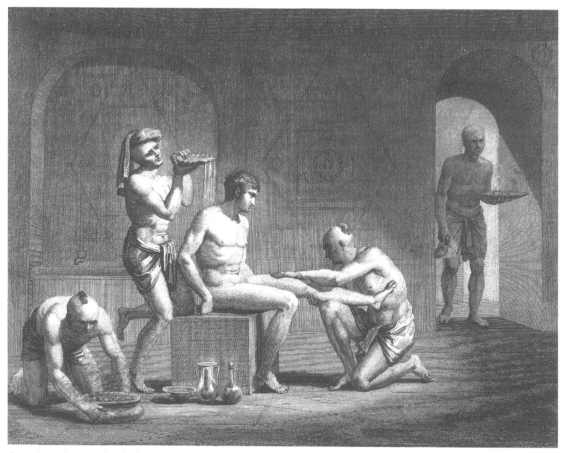

Scene in an Egyptian hot-bath. A young man – possibly a French officer – is seated on a marble slab accompanied by his attendants. One rubs his skin with a gloved hand – the friction assisted perspiration; another pours warm water; a third fills the room with fragrant odours; and a fourth brings coffee. Denon spent 'many delicious hours' in the baths. Women also had their baths where they 'shared their intrigues and displayed their ornaments'. *(Denon, British Library)*

distinguished. Several apartments still exist having been fabricated in the walls of more remote antiquity.

Their immense number is evidence of the magnificence of the palaces they once decorated.

The Graeco-Roman city of Alexandria benefited from its location, on the western extremity of Egypt's border, and, more importantly, from its position on the coast of the Mediterranean Sea. Alexandria became an important port during the Ptolemaic and Roman periods and for a time the township even supplanted Memphis as the capital of Egypt. It was at this epoch that the celebrated Library of Alexandria flourished, housing all the recorded learning of the ancient world. As Alexandria prospered, buildings and monuments were erected and were often ornamented with precious antiquities plundered from ancient monuments. Later, Arab conquerors also left their mark on the face of Alexandria in the form of religious buildings, defensive walls and towers. However, at the time of the French occupation of Egypt, Alexandria's charms had faded and the capital had centuries earlier been relocated to Cairo. Nonetheless, Alexandria's cosmopolitan origins were still evident, as Denon discovered in his wanderings about the town:

After passing the extremity of the harbour, large Saracen edifices are met which have an air of grandeur and a mixture of styles by which the observer is perplexed. [The Saracens were the wandering Syrian people of Roman times renowned and feared for the prowess of their army.] Friezes, adorned with Doric triglyphs [decorative ornaments], and surmounted by arched vaults would lead one to believe those edifices were constructed from antique fragments that the Saracens blended to adapt them to the style of their architecture. Behind this kind of fortress are Arabian baths most magnificently decorated. Our soldiers, who found them ready heated, had taken possession of them to wash their linen so that no other use could then be made of them.

Near the baths Denon came upon one of the principal mosques that was formerly a church dedicated to St Anthanasius. This edifice was in a ruinous state although its style could still be recognised as magnificent. He entered a small octagonal courtyard where, to his delight, he discovered an ancient Egyptian bowl: '[This was] of black marble, with white and yellow spots, [and] of incomparable beauty both on account of the substance of which it was formed and by reason of the innumerable hieroglyphic figures with which it was covered, both inside and without.' This was no doubt a sarcophagus that had been removed from an ancient funerary site. Despite Denon's personal objection to the removal of antiquities from their original locations, he could not resist yielding to such thoughts: 'It may be considered as a very valuable antique and one of our most precious spoils in Egypt with which it is to be wished our national museum may be enriched'.

Denon ascended the minaret of the mosque and from its gallery took a bird's-eye view for his portfolio of the port and New Harbour of Alexandria. On departing, he and his companions chanced upon three columns still standing which they reasoned must have come from another ancient temple. The scholarly side of Denon's nature was stirred and he reflected: 'It would be interesting to dig around their bases. The wide space they occupy would lead us to conjecture they are the remains of a large and magnificent edifice.' As so often during his travels in Egypt, the pressures of time did not allow for such investigations and, reluctantly, he continued on his way with his curiosity only partially satisfied.

A circumstance occurred that illustrates how Denon was touched by the barbarous effects of war. He was making his way to the city gate that led to Rosetta when he found evidence of the military conflict that had raged in Alexandria. The horrors of war were everywhere to be seen. To his amazement he came across an attractive young Frenchwoman, one of the few who had sailed out with the troops. She was in a pitiable state and quite forsaken:

A young woman, fair and with a ruddy complexion, was seated surrounded by the dead and rubbish on a fragment of a ruin still covered with blood. She was the picture of an angel of the Resurrection. Moved by a compassionate feeling, I testified my surprise at finding her in this forlorn state. She told me, with charming innocence, that she was going to pass the night in the desert [with her husband]. To her this was no difficulty. She was about to repair there to sleep

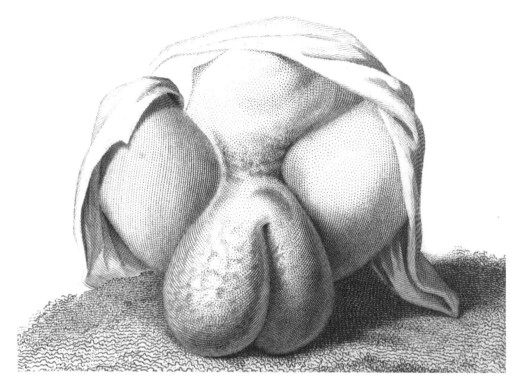

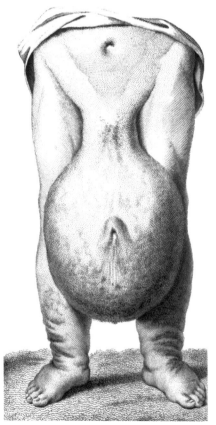

Medical case studies of advanced tumours. In their survey of the health and wellbeing of the people of Egypt, the French physicians discovered many harrowing individual circumstances. The following extracts are taken from the records of the expedition's Chief Surgeon Dominique-Jean Larrey:

Above: [This woman], aged about 30 years, [had] two enormous tumours that had afflicted her for several years. These were located each side of the vulva. They were about the size of the head of a child, were rough [at the front] and smooth at the rear and of a red-violet colour.

Left: This sightless boy was affected in both legs with elephantiasis and a gross tumour of the reproductive organs. His ankles were thicker than the thighs and the feet were monstrous. The skin was smooth, blotchy and traversed with varicose veins. His feet were covered in thick, yellowish crusts separated by deep ulcerated furrows.

Larrey planned an operation for these unfortunate people – without anaesthetic! – but was called away on a military expedition. (Engraving by Ingouff after drawings supplied by Larrey, National Library of Scotland)

with as little reluctance as if a down bed was to be her portion. From this anecdote, some idea may be formed of the lot which awaited the women whom love had inspired with the courage to follow their husbands on this expedition.

By 3 July all the troops, civilians, their horses and equipment had been landed at Alexandria. The greater part of the divisions quickly passed through the town to make camp in the very desert where the young Frenchwoman had hoped to find her salvation. Denon's fellow artists and men of letters had had a bad time of it. Left by their military commanders to fend for themselves, they had had to look after their own equipment with little, if any, help from the soldiers. They subsisted on the minimum of rations and were lodged in poor quarters. All this must have seemed a far cry from the delights they had been promised on visiting Alexandria, the famed city of classical antiquity. The truth of the matter is that for the French expedition their work was not a priority. For the present, Bonaparte and his generals had to concern themselves with military matters.

Bonaparte ordered that Alexandria's defensive works be strengthened. On the same day, aware of the sacrifices that had been made in securing the town, he instructed that the remains of those soldiers who had fallen in battle be laid to rest at the foot of Pompey's Pillar and their names inscribed on the monument.

The following day Bonaparte, who is credited with the remark that 'an army marches on its stomach', revealed his grasp of everyday necessities. He ordered four large ovens to be constructed to ensure the soldiers had their supply of bread.

Bonaparte's mind now turned to the next stage of his campaign. He intended to progress inland with the army as part of his strategy to capture Cairo – the stronghold of the Mamelukes and capital of Egypt.

CHAPTER 4

Rosetta and the Battle of the Pyramids

To secure Alexandria, the French armed a garrison with about two thousand soldiers and men from several of the ships' crews. The pressing need now, having made landfall in Egypt, was for Bonaparte to relocate his army to a more secure and advantageous position. To achieve this meant moving the divisions that were safely ashore as far south as possible – something in the order of eighteen thousand men. These tactics were necessary to lessen the advantage the Mamelukes might gain in assembling their own forces to oppose these advances. Since the ultimate military goal was the conquest of Cairo, Bonaparte elected to direct his army to El Rahmaniya on the western tributary of the River Nile. This is the so-called Rosetta branch of the Nile – the eastern tributary being the Damietta. Together these two great rivers irrigate the Delta region, making it lush and fertile. At the time of the French invasion, the Nile was at its lowest level and the stretch of country through which the troops had to pass was parched and desert-like. Military manoeuvres of any kind would be a severe ordeal for all concerned.

Bonaparte's divisions had to set out on foot, in full uniform, with all their equipment and without delay. Since drinking water for the troops was of the highest priority, Bonaparte issued the following command: 'Before leaving, [officers] will order that all those with jugs and bottles fill them with water and only make use of them when the greater part of the march is completed'. There were two problems with this command. Only a few soldiers had been equipped with drinking vessels and, by the time the order was circulated, several of the divisions had already commenced their march – largely ignorant of the severity of the terrain they were about to encounter and quite unprepared for the fierce heat of North Africa.

According to Denon an officer emboldened his division as they were about to depart with the encouragement: 'My friends, tonight you are to sleep at El Beydah – you understand – at El Beydah. This is all the difficulty you will have to encounter. Let us march, my friends!' And off the soldiers marched.

El Beydah lies a dozen miles south-east of Alexandria, on the route to Damanhûr, which is about half-way to El Rahmaniya, the first resting place of the army on its way to Cairo. This route, a journey of about 35 miles, was taken on 3 July by General Desaix's division. General Reynier's men followed on 5 July and three more divisions followed soon afterwards. Two of these divisions took the direct route to El Rahmaniya. General Kléber's division, under the command of General Duga, followed the coastal route

Mosque near Rosetta. This view is one of Denon's first architectural studies following his landing in Egypt.

The French quarters at Rosetta. General Menou lodged in the house from which a flag flies. The head sheikh stands by the doorway as the troops parade. Denon remarks: 'We never arrived at a village without a sheikh to whom honour was shown'. To the right is the Nile with French supply-boats. *(Denon, British Library)*

leading to Rosetta so they could provide military support to a flotilla of gunboats that was to sail south by way of the Nile.

The soldiers taking the route to El Beydah followed the long since dried up Canal of Alexandria, which in ancient times had provided direct communication with the Mediterranean Sea and the Nile. The men, and in some cases their women companions, staggered along this route as best they could, terrified of falling behind for fear of capture by the Bedouin. Many found it progressively more difficult to go forward as their strength gave out. Denon saw these events at first hand:

> They reached El Beydah . . . [where] they could find nothing but a well choked up with stones between whose interstices a little brackish muddy water was found. This water was collected in goblets and a small quantity was distributed to them as if it had been brandy. This was the first halt made by a part of our troops, in an unfamiliar quarter of the globe, separated [from home] by seas covered with enemies and surrounded by desert a thousand times more formidable still.

As the march progressed, a number of men succumbed to heat stress and several perished by the wayside. Some became so disoriented by the extreme heat and so tormented by mirages of great lakes of water that they shot themselves. To add to these woes there was the continual threat of being picked off by the armed tribes who pursued and harassed the wavering columns of soldiers. Denon again witnessed these harrowing circumstances:

> On the 5th and 6th of July, the army was in full march by Birket and Damanhûr. The Arabs attacked the advanced guard and harassed the main body insomuch that death was the fate of the straggler. General Desaix was on the point of being made a prisoner as a consequence of having remained fifty paces to the rear of the column. Le Mireur, an officer of distinguished reputation, was assassinated within a hundred paces of the advanced guard because of momentary neglect in complying with the request made to him to come up. Adjutant-General Galois was killed carrying an order to the Commander-in-Chief. Adjutant Delanan was made prisoner at a short distance from the army while crossing a ditch. A price was demanded for his ransom. The Arabs disputed the booty and blew out [his] brains.

On the second day's march, Denon had a horrific encounter. The troops were passing by El Beydah when they came across a young Arab woman whose face was covered in blood. In one of her arms she cradled an infant while holding out the other as though in self-defence. They were astonished and dismayed to find a young woman in such a harrowing condition in the desert with a young child. They approached her with an interpreter. Through her sobs they learned that her husband, in a fit of rage and jealousy, had pierced out her eyes. Such was her abject state she dared not complain but merely mumbled prayers for her child who appeared to the onlookers to be close to death. Observing these events Denon records:

> Our soldiers, moved by pity and contemplating her needs were more urgent, gave her part of their rations and lost sight of their own necessities. They had just deprived themselves of a small portion of water, which was extremely scarce and which they were about to be absolutely in need of, when they saw a madman approach. Feasting his sight on the spectacle of his revenge, he kept his victim constantly in view. He then snatched from the woman the bread and water she held in her hands – the last sources of existence which compassion had just granted to misery. [This man was her husband and he raged:] 'Forebear! She has forfeited her own honour and has tarnished mine. That infant is my disgrace. It is the offspring of guilt.'

The soldiers endeavoured to prevent him depriving the young woman and child of the succour they had just provided. His jealousy then became so inflamed that he too became an object of their pity. The man was clearly out of his mind. Before anyone could

Coastal defences at the mouth of the Nile. Following the loss of France's fleet at the battle of the Nile, Bonaparte authorised the strengthening of his batteries against further attack from Nelson's ships. While this work was in progress the Rosetta Stone was discovered. *(Balzac, Author's Collection)*

intervene he drew a dagger from his cloak and inflicted a mortal blow upon his wife. In the ensuing confusion he then seized the little child, held it for a moment in the air, and dashed it lifeless to the ground. His fury now expended, he stood motionless looking steadfastly at the soldiers around him as though in defiance of their vengeance.

Denon was appalled at this show of inhumanity and enquired of the interpreter whether there were Arab laws to punish such atrocious conduct. He was told the man had indeed done wrong to stab his wife. The interpreter then added, enigmatically, that if God had vouchsafed to spare her life, after the expiry of forty days she would have been received into someone's house and been kept on charity. Denon does not tell us the fate of the madman.

The soldiers continued on what became a nightmare of a journey. When a well was encountered they piled upon one another in their desperation to get a share of the muddy water. Some were crushed in the disorder and many could do little more than moisten their lips. It is said some cried out to their companions to end their misery with a bullet. General Reynier's men, however, fared better. By good fortune they found a cistern brimming with water – sufficient for all his troops. News spread through his ranks and the division was soon hysterical with joy. Men drank their fill until they were bursting with water. The commonest pleasure in life had become the most precious. General Kléber's division, under the command of General Duga, also had an easier time of it on the coastal route. Remarkably, these men found fresh water in wells close to the seashore and were consequently able to reach their destination in much better shape than their compatriots taking the more direct but inhospitable route to the south.

As the troops progressed further inland the heat became intolerable. To add to their torment was the phenomenon, previously mentioned, of the mirage. Denon experienced this chimerical provocation and gives the following description in what is one of the earliest accounts of a mirage by a Western traveller:

The Rosetta Stone (fragment). Found by the army-engineer Lieutenant Pierre Bouchard during excavations at Fort Julien, this was one of the most significant discoveries made by the French in Egypt. It was placed in the safe-keeping of his commanding officer General Menou, a man of learning, who realised its importance. The subsequent decipherment of the hieroglyphic inscriptions 'opened the door to the Egyptian mind' (see Postcript: The French Legacy). *(Jomard, University of Edinburgh)*

While they were a prey to thirst the image of a vast lake [was] before their eyes. This torment, of a new description, requires explanation as it results from an illusion peculiar to this country.

It is produced by the reflection of salient objects on the oblique rays reflected by the heat of the burning soil [sand]. This phenomenon has so truly the appearance of water that the observer is deceived by it over and over again. It provokes a thirst which is the more importunate as the instant when it presents itself to the view is the hottest time of day.

Mention has been made of the Bedouin tribes that harassed the French troops on their march out of Alexandria. As the columns approached Damanhûr a more menacing enemy materialised in the form of the Mamelukes. These were the usurper warrior-leaders of Egypt who were renowned for their fearless conduct in battle. Centuries earlier they had formed the core of the resistance to the crusaders. The Mamelukes were descended from Caucasian slaves and were introduced to Egypt by the caliphs of Baghdad. They became a military caste and initially ruled as Mameluke sultans and later as local governors or beys. At the time of the French conquest, the leaders – some twenty-four in number – together constituted a form of Turkish Viceroy and occupied all the important positions in Egyptian society. They retained their Turkish language and customs, were possessed of fabulous wealth and enjoyed a sumptuous way of life – including magnificent houses complete with harems.

When the Mamelukes appeared over the sand dunes with their armed men, it was to reconnoitre and size up the French forces. As they watched the French troops struggling along beneath them, they assumed that the inevitable battle between them and the French would be a mere formality. Denon puts it more eloquently:

Having observed our army was composed entirely of infantry, a description of soldiery for whom they had sovereign contempt, they assumed themselves certain of an easy victory and

Murad Bey, the most redoubtable and implacable of Bonaparte's enemies in Egypt, seated here at an open window overlooking a tributary of the River Nile. The most formidable of all the Mamelukes, his scarred countenance and piercing gaze intimidated anyone who had the misfortune to incur his wrath. Although his forces were scattered by the French at the battle of the Pyramids, he regrouped his men and continued to harass the French throughout the time of their occupation of Egypt. *(Dutertre, Author's Collection)*

forbore to harass our march. This was rendered sufficiently painful by its length, by the heat of the climate and by the sufferings of hunger and thirst.

This disdainful view of the French was shared especially by the leader of the Mamelukes, the redoubtable and implacable Murad Bey. The quintessential embodiment of the fearless Mameluke, he was always surrounded by an entourage of trusted followers and armed escorts, and could personally call upon a large army to oppose the French forces. On receiving a description of them he boasted that he would 'slice through the French as though they were gourds' – mere water pitchers.

The French infantry knew little of the history of the Mamelukes but they respected their reputation as fearless combatants. The sight of so many finely arrayed warriors, mounted on their magnificent horses, must have sent a shiver of apprehension down the spines of the beleaguered troops – what Denon describes as 'that uncertain emotion bordering on terror that is constantly inspired by an unknown enemy'. But the French troops were not easily intimidated. They had come a long way to do battle and many were seasoned veterans of Bonaparte's Italian Campaign. The Mamelukes would shortly discover their foreign invaders were no mere 'water pitchers'.

The French usually found the various villages they encountered on their march were abandoned, the inhabitants having carried away with them whatever might have been useful to the invaders by way of subsistence. Of some consolation was the fact that pistachio nuts were discovered growing plentifully, prompting Denon to record how they were 'the first relief that the soil of Egypt afforded to the soldiery – and of this fruit they never ceased to retain a grateful remembrance'.

Bonaparte departed Alexandria on 7 July, on horseback, with his military staff and the savants Berthollet and Monge. Before leaving he gave orders that a printing press be set up so that his Proclamation & Articles could be distributed to the people of Egypt in Arabic, French and Greek. No fewer than 4,000 copies of his first public proclamation were circulated in the villages and townships around Alexandria, urging the Egyptian people to accept the French as rightful occupiers of their country.

In anticipation of securing the cooperation of the Egyptian villagers, Bonaparte issued a further, more mundane, Order of the Day determining what he considered to be a fair rate of exchange for certain food supplies. Bonaparte wished the local people to know that the French army was prepared to pay for its needs. That was the principle. The reality was often very different. Soldiers on the rampage for something to eat are just as desperate as soldiers dying of thirst and are equally likely to revert to their basic instincts to secure whatever they need – Order of the Day or not.

Between 6 and 9 July all the French divisions reached Damanhûr, their interim stop before moving on to El Rahmaniya, from which they were to proceed to their ultimate destination – and prize – the city of Cairo. Almost twenty thousand men had braved near intolerable conditions and had survived terrible personal deprivations. The soldiers were given little time to rest however and were soon again on the march. On 9 July Bonaparte ordered the divisions to press on further east to El Rahmaniya situated close to the Nile.

Another savage trek through the harsh terrain and desert had to be endured. When the troops reached the Nile they raced unchecked to its banks where in their desperate bid to allay their thirst and find relief from the heat, they threw down their weapons and plunged into the river without waiting to undress. To their delight, they discovered watermelons growing in abundance and entire divisions of men gorged themselves on this welcome and unexpected feast. But watermelons, they soon discovered, carried their own hazards. Scores of men became afflicted by water-borne bacteria and succumbed to severe diarrhoea. To many soldiers Egypt, far from being 'a land flowing with milk and honey', had the semblance of a hell on earth.

Bonaparte was informed of the condition of his men and issued another Order of the Day: 'Officers will urge soldiers to eat very few watermelons unless they are cooked. Then they are healthy and nourishing.'

With his troops established at El Rahmaniya, Bonaparte was informed that Murad Bey was massing opposition forces of several thousand cavalry and troops with supporting gunboats, at Shubra Khit on the Nile, a location about 10 miles south of El Rahmaniya. Bonaparte reviewed his troops, urged upon them the strictest military discipline and reckoned the time had come to engage with the enemy.

When the French eventually confronted the Mameluke forces, the divisions adopted their well-rehearsed military strategy of forming defensive squares. These were ranks of armed troops, six or more lines deep, grouped in square formation with the support of artillery at their corners. Disposed like this, and with their capacity to fire and reload at speed, the French were practically invincible to charges by cavalry and foot soldiers. Nonetheless, when the Mamelukes appeared they were quickly perceived by the French as being formidable opponents. They had all been trained to fight from their youth. Moreover, they looked awesome and resplendent. Each combatant was heavily armed with sabre and pistols and was arrayed in the richest apparel.

When the attack commenced the French held their ground and repulsed a succession of charges 'with a veritable barrage of cannon balls, shells, grapeshot and small-arms fire'. Several of the artists and scientists were engaged in the conflict and had to play their part by helping to load and discharge guns.

On encountering the French barrage, the Mamelukes steadily retreated but not before the most savage fighting had taken place. Although shaken and wearied by the conflict, the French had gained valuable experience of Mameluke strategy. Significantly, they realised that the Mamelukes were not invincible despite their military prowess and superior numbers.

Although they had left the field of battle, the Mamelukes were by no means defeated. They had merely retreated to Cairo which they sought to defend. Bonaparte's divisions had several more days of gruelling marching to endure as they pursued their adversaries. Once more the troops had to haul and manhandle their equipment and heavy gun-carriages over the dried-out ruts of the irrigation channels. The pyramids of Giza came into view and were so startling and unfamiliar that the French soldiers initially mistook them for strangely shaped mountains.

On 20 July 1798, Bonaparte received intelligence that the Mameluke forces were regrouped defensively outside Cairo to protect the city from the French advance. The next day he uttered his celebrated encouragement: 'Soldiers, forty centuries look down upon you'. Denon, who was within earshot, gives a slightly different version: 'Push on and recollect that forty centuries watch over us'. Whatever Bonaparte's precise words, he was clearly possessed of a sense of history which he endeavoured to communicate to his immediate commanding officers. What subsequently ensued was a two-hour, hand-to-hand conflict known to military historians as the battle of the Pyramids. It was one of the most bloody and momentous battles in the history of eighteenth-century military warfare. The fateful events of 21 July 1798 have passed into legend.

In the Egyptian summer of 1798 two very different military regimes confronted one another. On the one hand were the Mamelukes, a fearless military caste trained to fight to the death. Only when the odds were impossibly against them would they desert the field of battle to serve the cause of Allah on a later occasion. They were skilled pre-eminently in the art of cavalry warfare. They represented the old order. Mounted astride their fabulous steeds, they were renowned for charging at the enemy with their Damascus-steel sabres flashing. They could remove the head of an infantryman as though it were a tulip being snipped from its stalk.

Opposing them were the French. Their military strategy was based on the musket, the fusillade and the unwavering discipline of the military square. They represented the new order. Both sides were courageous but however fearless the charges of sabre-wielding horsemen, they could never be a match for a hail of bullets and cannon-shot maintained with deadly efficiency from orderly rows of troops standing six or more columns deep. The conflict that ensued was either a great military victory or a bloodbath depending upon the point of view of the reader.

The battle of the Pyramids was fought on the Plain of Giza several miles distant from the pyramids themselves. The plain was like a patchwork quilt composed of the French, dressed in their practical uniforms, and the Mamelukes arrayed in their gorgeous costumes. The tactics of the Mamelukes were to charge the French with blood-curdling screams, scimitars flailing and eyes scanning the ranks of the troops to find a point of weakness. The response of the French was to form their squares, keep their nerve, take a steady aim and hold their fire until the last possible moment.

The battle of the Pyramids. Denon's most ambitious engraving, the original extends over two folio pages and is about 1 metre wide. Denon provides the following commentary: 'This tableau represents the action when the Mamelukes are departing [the field of battle]. They are charged by the divisions of Generals Desaix, Duga, Rampon and Reynier. Several Mamelukes are taken, many are abandoned. Heavy cannon fire! Chivalry! Instruments of war among the trees! The conflict continues to the vast horizon. Cairo and the pyramids are visible.' *(Denon, British Library)*

The field of battle was soon shrouded in a hazy veil of smoke from the French cannon. The smell of cordite was everywhere. The deep roar of cannon and the staccato snap of muskets merged with the sounds of men screaming as blood was shed and body parts were flung into the air. The charges and counter-charges of the Mamelukes were repulsed by the heavy fire from the files of French fusiliers. Carnage and slaughter were everywhere. In seeking to make their eventual escape, many Arabs were drowned in the Nile. At the close of the conflict Denon observed, with an understandable show of exuberance:

A handful of French, led by a hero, had just subdued a quarter of the globe. An empire had just changed its ruler. The pride of the Mamelukes had been completely humbled by the bayonets of our infantry. During this great and terrible scene, the result of which was to become so important, the dust and smoke almost obscured the lower part of the atmosphere.

The morning star, revolving over a spacious horizon, peacefully terminated its career – a sublime testimony of that immutable order in the calm stillness that renders it still more awful.

Denon's remarks require a few words of comment. The French force was in fact some twenty thousand men and can hardly be described as 'a handful'. Doubtless this is how they must have seemed, when tightly grouped in their military formations, on the Plain of Giza, dwarfed by the gigantic pyramids and surrounded by the relentless waves of Mameluke cavalry. More generally, amid the vastness of Egypt, the French expeditionary forces were little more than a handful of men when one considers the large armies at the disposal of the leader of the Mamelukes, Murad Bey. This leads to the qualification of the second, and more important, generalization. The pride of the Mamelukes had indeed been humbled but 'an empire had [not] changed its ruler'. When Murad Bey and a contingent of his forces escaped to Upper Egypt they posed a constant threat to the French army. For this reason Egypt was never completely subject to French domination.

We can digress here from the dramatic experiences of the French army and learn more about Denon's departure from Alexandria. He journeyed south, by way of the coastal route and Rosetta, in the company of General Menou who, it will be recalled, had been injured in the battle for Alexandria. Bonaparte asked Menou to go to Rosetta to 'regulate the government' – the local administration. General Menou, in response, requested Denon to accompany him. Denon readily agreed both by reason of personal friendship with the General and to share the company of 'an amiable and well-informed man'.

General Menou's party progressed south along a branch of the Nile until Rosetta, the object of their journey, came into sight. The branch of the Nile he and his companions journeyed down irrigates the western region of the Delta. This waterway, the Rosetta, discharges directly into the Mediterranean Sea and has given its name to the township of Rosetta. Situated on the so-called Bolbitic branch of the Nile, Rosetta is about 9 miles from the coast and about 30 miles east of Alexandria. The town was established in the ninth century by the Arabic conquerors of Egypt and became a flourishing centre of trade. At the period of the French conquest, Rosetta was still an important port from which merchandise was sent to other countries and shipped along the Nile to Cairo.

With General Menou safely ashore – he was still weak and recovering from the wounds he received at Alexandria – Denon was free to follow his artist's inclinations. His steps led him directly to Rosetta:

> Its ancient defensive wall implies it was once larger than it is at present. Its original compass is ascertained by the sandbanks by which it is covered from west to south. Walls and towers have been formed that have served as a nucleus for accumulated heaps of sand.
>
> The houses are in general better constructed than those of Alexandria but are nevertheless slight. Were they not favoured by the climate, which destroys nothing, not one of them would be left standing long at Rosetta. The storeys, that project one over the other, nearly touch and this renders the streets dismal and obscure. The houses situated on the bank of the Nile are not subject to this inconvenience. The greater part of them belong to foreign merchants.
>
> These houses, independently of having the advantage of a view of the river, have also the delightful prospect of the Delta and an island, of about a league in breadth, possessing all the beauties of a well-cultivated garden.

An Arab council. Many sheikhs have assembled to consider the opening of the canals in order to distribute the irrigation waters to the villages in their province. Each sheikh had to agree to bear a proportion of the cost. A magnificent sycamore provides shelter. Denon and his officer companions were allowed to witness the proceedings that were concluded with a splendid supper. *(Denon, University of Edinburgh)*

Denon and his fellow men of letters, free from military obligations, quickly adapted to life at Rosetta. It became their property and the venue for their 'daily promenades'. Some of the men were even motivated to turn a small coppice into a park where they 'amused themselves with shooting'. This was not wanton destruction of wildlife. They collected a number of hitherto unknown species – especially birds – that were of scientific interest to the zoologist members of the expedition.

Some days later, the sheikhs of the region were gathered together to receive Bonaparte's Proclamation & Articles of 2 July containing the high-flown words: 'Thrice happy shall be those who are with us'. According to Denon:

> They listened with respect and resignation to the manifesto. They recognised the paternal feelings of those by whom their punishment had been inflicted. They perceived very clearly we meant them no harm . . . [and] they consequently regarded us as conquerors who knew how to put bounds to our vengeance.

Denon is an eloquent and persuasive narrator. Whether the sheikhs reacted in quite such a subdued and gracious manner must be open to question. What he reported next, however, did take place. Steps were taken to bring friends and foes together. A feast was arranged in honour of the French. Egyptian hospitality, at its best, was not to be missed. No effort was spared to please the guests. Denon, always eager to participate in a good meal or similar expression of conviviality, gives the following account of the splendid meal laid on for the French officers and village elders:

A house of public entertainment that had almost invariably belonged to the head Mameluke – formerly the lord and master of the village – was furnished in a moment according to the fashion of the country with mats, carpets and cushions. A number of attendants, in the first place, brought in perfumed water, pipes and coffee. Half an hour afterwards, a carpet was spread and on the outer part three or four different kinds of bread and cakes were laid in heaps. The centre was covered with small dishes of fruits, sweetmeats and creams – the greater part of them pretty good and very highly perfumed. This was considered but a slight repast that was over in a few minutes.

In the course of two hours, the same carpet was covered afresh with large loaves; immense dishes of rice – either boiled in milk or in a rich gravy-soup; halves of sheep – badly roasted; large quarters of veal; boiled heads of different animals; and fifty or sixty other dishes all crowded together consisting of highly seasoned ragouts, vegetables, jellies, sweetmeats and honey in the comb.

There were neither chairs, plates, spoons, forks, drinking glasses, nor napkins. Each of the guests squatted on the ground, took up the rice in his fingers, tore the meat in pieces with his nails, dipped the bread in the ragouts and wiped his hands and his lips with a slice of bread. The water was served in a pot and he who did the honours of the table took the first draught. In the same way, he was the first to taste the different dishes, so as to prevent his guests from harbouring any suspicions of him, and to show them how strong an interest he took in their safety and how high a value he set on their persons. The napkins were not brought until after dinner when each of the guests washed his hands. He was then sprinkled over with rosewater and the pipes and coffee were produced.

When our repast was ended, our places were occupied by the natives of the second class who were very soon succeeded by the others. From a motive of religion a poor beggar was admitted. Next came the attendants and lastly all those who chose to partake until nothing was left.

If these repasts cannot boast the convenience of ours, and the elegance by which the appetite is satisfied, it is impossible not to be struck by their abundance, by the frank hospitality displayed and by the sobriety of the guests.

These agreeable moments when friend and enemy reconciled their differences over a bounteous meal proved short-lived. Terrible events were about to unfold. Bonaparte's sojourn in Egypt would be threatened and no less than the course of European history would be changed.

CHAPTER 5

Abukir Bay and the Battle of the Nile

Although the battle of the Pyramids was not decisive in securing Egypt for the French, it gave them superiority in the Delta region. The greatest prize was Cairo and the French wasted no time in taking possession of the capital. They met no resistance and two columns of soldiers marched into the town to the accompaniment of a military band. A few days later, on 24 July 1798, Bonaparte himself arrived and set up his headquarters in the house of one of the Mameluke chiefs at Ezbekiya Square. This location was one of Cairo's most salubrious, being on the east bank of the Nile north of Old Cairo. The residence was perfectly suited to the needs of a military headquarters boasting several spacious rooms and an enchanting pleasure garden where the officers and savants could sit and discuss their plans or promenade in the shade of its many fine trees. Cairo was placed under the governorship of General Dupuy, one of Bonaparte's most trusted senior officers.

Once settled into his headquarters, Bonaparte immersed himself in his administrative duties with typical zeal. His first action was to issue a Proclamation & Articles to the people of Cairo. The French had taken Cairo without recourse to military action. In fact the streets had been almost deserted when their soldiers marched into the town. The residents who had not fled kept themselves concealed indoors. These circumstances may account for the placatory tone of Bonaparte's Proclamation & Articles. Freely translated it reads:

22 July 1798

People of Cairo, I am pleased to be your leader. You have done well not to take sides against me. I come to destroy the regime of the Mamelukes [and] to protect the commerce and customs of your country. To all those who are fearful, to all those who are fled from their homes, [it is my wish that] you say your prayers today as normal – as I want you to continue to do. Fear nothing for your families, your houses, your property and, moreover, for the religion of the Prophet whom I respect.

Because it is essential that peace be restored, there will be a Council consisting of seven dignitaries who will meet at the Mosque of El-Azhar. Two will liaise with the Commander and four will have responsibility for maintaining public order by reporting to the police.

Following the occupation of Cairo, an uneasy peace descended upon the town as conquerors and vanquished eyed one another suspiciously and came to terms with their respective positions. Bonaparte, confined by work to his rooms, continued to busy himself with his Orders of the Day, Military Commands and, most significantly, his Report to the Directory in Paris, which he wrote on 24 July. What he has to say gives an insight into Bonaparte's first impressions of the country he had subdued. The following is a paraphrase of his memorandum.

He first acknowledges the sufferings his men had experienced on their protracted marches from Rosetta to El Rahmaniya, from El Rahmaniya to Alexandria and finally from Alexandria to Cairo: 'Despite fifteen days of marching, hardships of all kinds, the absolute deprivation of wine and of anything able to alleviate fatigue, we have no illness'. The reader may consider Bonaparte's assessment of the condition of his men as being rather generous, in view of how many of them had scorched skin, blistered lips, torn ankles – to say nothing of the dreaded diarrhoea!

Bonaparte then proceeds to give an account of the battle of the Pyramids. After setting the scene and outlining the conflict, he mentions the roles of his Generals Bon, Desaix and Reynier. General Rampon is singled out and commended for his courageous conduct. Nor does Bonaparte overlook the bravery of certain of his officers and makes mention of their promotion. Turning to the actual fighting, Bonaparte gives an estimate of two thousand elite Mameluke cavalry lost and refers to the thousands more wounded. He also adds a respectful comment concerning the bravery of the Mamelukes, particularly with regard to several of their leaders. Attired in their finery – even on the field of battle – they had charged against the French fusillades, with reckless abandon, only to fall prey to the hail of French bullets. Bonaparte then relates how his soldiers had found gold pieces sewn into their turbans to the value of 'as many as three, four and five-hundred Louis d'or'. As their spoils of war, soldiers had seized fine silks, daggers encrusted with jewels and richly worked sabres, their Damascene blades stained with blood.

Concerning Cairo, Bonaparte reflects how his army of 40,000 men, only half of whom had fought at the battle of the Pyramids, had taken the capital with a population of 300,000. Regarding the populace, Bonaparte's initial assessment of the Arabs was bleak. Here is a selection of his comments:

> It is difficult to find a land more fertile and a people more miserable, more ignorant and more brutalised. In the villages, they don't even have an understanding of a pair of scissors. Their houses are little more than mud. Their only furniture is a straw mat and two or three clay pots. They eat and subsist on hardly anything. We have been continually affronted by the nudity of the Arabs who are the worst thieves on earth and will assassinate the Turks, as well as the French, for anything that they may thus lay their hands on.

In considering these views, we should bear in mind they were Bonaparte's initial impressions, doubtless influenced by the pejorative remarks of his officers who had more day-to-day contact with the common people than did the busy Commander-in-Chief. It so happens that as the French, particularly the artists and men of letters, circulated among the people of Egypt, they acquired a deeper sense of respect for the classes of ordinary people, especially the craftsmen whose work, as we shall see, they came to admire.

Turning to the wider proposition of Egypt as a future colony of France – one of the fundamental purposes of the Egyptian Campaign – Bonaparte comments: 'There is very little money [gold and silver] in this country but sufficient to pay the army. There is a lot of corn, rice, vegetables and cattle. The Republic can [here] have no more than a colony that supports itself from the most fertile soil.'

During the following week, Bonaparte settled into a daily routine of issuing more Orders of the Day. Nothing escaped his vigilance. His first concern was for the welfare of the sick and wounded soldiers and he sent out instructions for hospitals to be established at Bulaq, Old Cairo and Giza. Bulaq was an obvious choice of location for a military hospital since, although it was a separate township from Cairo, being on the Nile it served as the capital's port. The sick and wounded could thus be ferried there in some comfort to save them the hardship of being bumped overland.

In the late eighteenth century, Bulaq had a considerable trade in cotton, linen, henna (for dying cloth), rice and natron – the latter being a form of soda that was extracted from the nearby salt lakes. At the time of the French occupation, Old Cairo retained its identity as a community on the island of El-Rôda – now within modern-day Cairo. Many of the fine residences of the Mamelukes were situated in Old Cairo and were ideal locations for the infirm to convalesce, with their high-walled gardens and avenues lined with flowering trees and shrubs. Giza was another small township opposite Old Cairo. It was here that the Mameluke leader Murad Bey had one of his several residences. The Plain of the Pyramids occupies the eastern extremity of Old Cairo. This district therefore favoured the location of a hospital for the treatment of those injured at the battle of the Pyramids.

After concerning himself with the wellbeing of his men, Bonaparte turned his mind to matters of state. He issued orders for the protection of the women of the beys and Mamelukes who were still resident in Cairo. However he did not let them off too lightly. Mindful of their wealth, he imposed taxes on them, the level of the tax being determined according to the value of their property and the extent of their furniture and possessions. At the same time he drafted a list of questions for the Divan, or governors of Cairo, requiring them to address a variety of matters concerning civil and criminal law, the administration and maintenance of justice, the imposition of taxes and the system of punishment to be enforced upon defaulters. He allowed just five days for posters detailing these matters to be printed and circulated.

While Bonaparte was occupied with the administration of Cairo, momentous events were taking place elsewhere. They would threaten the security of the French in Egypt and would result in their eventually having to abandon the country altogether.

Admiral Nelson was still in search of the French fleet. In growing desperation of finding his quarry, he berthed at Syracuse in south-eastern Sicily where he obtained fresh water and supplies for his ships. He then had a stroke of good fortune. A few days after reaching Sicily, a merchant ship was seized and Nelson learned from her captain that Napoleon's flotilla had been sighted off the coast of Crete, sailing on a south-easterly course. Nelson wasted no time in readying his ships. By 1 August the English fleet had sailed eastwards, bound once more for the Port of Alexandria. This time they found the

The battle of the Nile. Evening, 1 August 1798, and the English fleet are harassing the French men-of-war. Within a few hours and despite being wounded in the head, Nelson wrote his famous dispatch: 'Almighty God has blessed his Majesty's arms in the late battle by a great victory.' *(Thomas Luny, National Maritime Museum)*

harbour filled with French transport vessels under the protection of the heavy guns and batteries that Bonaparte had ordered to be put in place.

Shortly afterwards, Nelson received news that his reconnaissance vessel the *Zealous* had sighted the French fleet moored at Abukir Bay. The French armada consisted of thirteen heavily armed ships and four frigates under the command of Admiral Francis Paul de Brueys. On approaching, it became apparent to Nelson and his captains that the French fleet had not moored within Abukir Bay itself but was riding at anchor about 2 miles from the shore. Admiral Brueys had secured his ships in open water, aware that a shoal extended for about a mile from the shore.

Disposed in their battle order, from west to east, the French squadron consisted of *Le Guerrier, Le Conquérant, Le Spartiate, L'Aquilon, Le Peuple Souverain, Le Franklin, L'Orient, Le Tonnant, L'Heureux, Le Timoléon, Le Mercure, Le Guillaume Tell* and *Le Généreux*. Behind this line of ships were the frigates *La Diane, La Justice, L'Artemise* and *La Sérieuse*. Altogether the French had 1,190 guns at their disposal: nine ships had 74 guns, three had 80 guns and the mighty *L'Orient* had no fewer than 120 guns. The four frigates contributed the fire-power of a further 164 guns.

A lesser commander than Horatio Nelson would have regarded the French line of ships as impregnable. Nelson, his star rising to its apogee, was no ordinary commander. He was not to be deterred. He had at his command fourteen ships of the line which, in their battle formation, were *Culloden, Theseus, Alexander, Vanguard, Minotaur, Leander, Swiftsure,*

Audacious, *Defence*, *Zealous*, *Orion*, *Goliath*, *Majestic* and *Bellerophon*. All of Nelson's ships were so-called '74s', giving a combined fire-power to the English of 1,012 guns – somewhat short, therefore, of the combined fire-power of the French. Nelson had considered what he would do if he were to engage with the French fleet at anchor. Finding this to be the case his mind was clear. His ships would bear down on the French, at full sail, and would circumvent their defences.

As the sun was setting, Captain Thomas Foley, in the *Goliath*, led the English assault and found a sufficient depth of water to make an attack on *Le Guerrier*. He was followed by Captain Samuel Hood in the *Zealous*, by Captain David Gould in the *Audacious*, and by Sir James Saumarez in the *Orion*.

The hapless *Le Guerrier*, after taking repeated broadsides, was the first of the French ships to be reduced to a shattered wreck. Nelson conducted the English operations in the *Vanguard*, from the seaward side, and was the first to fire on the French from that quarter.

What ensued in the following hours has passed into naval legend. Of the French fleet, *Le Généreux* and Rear Admiral Villeneuve's flagship *Le Guillaume Tell* were among the few ships to escape capture or destruction. The French tally of men lost and injured is put at about 5,000 against English losses of 218 with 700 wounded. At the height of the battle, Nelson himself was wounded in the head. When he was carried below deck for treatment he is said to have insisted on taking his place in the surgeon's queue, covering his head so that his men could not catch sight of him and become dispirited. This show of gallantry was surpassed by the courage of his adversary Admiral Brueys. While commanding the French response to the English onslaught from the deck of *L'Orient*, his legs were shot from under him. Undeterred – and inconceivably – he had the stumps of his bleeding limbs bound with tourniquets and continued to issue orders to the desperate men about him while he was supported in a barrel of bran. He only ceased to command when he finally fell, shot to pieces, on his own quarter deck. Not long after, *L'Orient* was blown sky-high in an explosion that could be heard many miles away at Alexandria. Brueys went down with all but 70 of his crew of 1,010 men.

For some time Denon and his companions were uncertain as to the outcome of the battle. With daybreak, the extent of the French defeat became apparent:

> We found our situation was altered. Separated from our mother country we were become the inhabitants of a distant colony where we would be obliged to depend on our own resources for subsistence.
>
> We learned the English fleet had surrounded our line, which was not moored sufficiently near the land to be protected by our batteries. The enemy, formed in a double line, had attacked our ships one after the other and had by this manoeuvre . . . rendered the one-half of the fleet witness to the destruction of the other half.
>
> We learned lastly that . . . the destruction of our fleet . . . had restored to the enemy the empire of the Mediterranean.

Bonaparte had lost his fleet and his army of invasion was now isolated in Egypt. With the destruction of *L'Orient*, Bonaparte's treasure chest had gone to the bottom of the sea and with it the priceless possessions captured from the Knights of Malta – millions in gold, silver and precious stones. Perhaps the keenest loss would be felt in due course by

Destruction of *L'Orient*. Bonaparte's flagship went down with the loss of a thousand men in an explosion that could be heard at Cairo. The plight of the French 'drew tears down the victors' cheeks'. In commemoration, the Nile Medal was struck and the composer Haydn consecrated a mass to Nelson. Felicia Hemans captured the popular imagination with her verse: 'The boy stood on the burning deck, whence all but he had fled'. *(Mather Brown, National Maritime Museum)*

the artist, scientist and engineer members of the expedition who had thus been deprived of the greater part of their field equipment and scientific instruments – the finest that eighteenth-century technology could provide.

The disaster could have been even worse for the French. Bonaparte's army, having been brought ashore in longboats, was intact. The French were also able to defend the coastal approaches to Egypt with their land-based batteries armed with cannon.

Putting his personal sorrows behind him, Denon made a reconnaissance of the Nile and its estuary. He was fascinated by the power of the river and the manner in which it deposited great quantities of rich alluvial silt. The next passage in his *Journal* reveals the discerning eye of a modern-day ecologist:

> The plants that are produced in the first place, on the new land, are three or four kinds of seaweeds around which the sand throws itself up in heaps. From its surface they spring up afresh and their subsequent decay furnishes a manure that favours the vegetation of reeds. These reeds give a greater elevation and solidity to the soil. The date palm now appears and, by its shade, prevents the sudden evaporation of the moisture and renders the soil fruitful and productive.

Following the loss of the French fleet, a detachment of soldiers was sent to strengthen the coastal defences at Rosetta. Eager to explore the region, Denon joined the party. At Raschid, near to the township of Rosetta, he came upon the ruins of a fortress, which he noticed had been constructed from fragments of old buildings and ancient temples. The gun embrasures were hewn from the beautiful freestone quarried in Upper Egypt, some of which bore traces of hieroglyphics.

As he explored the chambers below the fortress, Denon made a remarkable discovery. He came across a magazine filled with rusting arms and armour. These included helmets, crossbows, arrows and swords fashioned in the style of those used at the time of the crusades. The hoard may have lain there for centuries. In fact, Damietta fell to the crusaders in 1219 and Lower Egypt was momentarily threatened until the invading forces overreached themselves. In a bid to take Cairo they became literally bogged down with the flooding of the Nile – which took them by surprise. They had to retreat to Acre and the threat to Egypt passed.

Denon's rummaging through the heaps of military treasure was brought to an abrupt end. He disturbed a great number of bats 'as large as pigeons' and made a hasty departure from the subterranean caverns.

Looking about him he was impressed by the fertility of the countryside. He saw numerous herds of sheep and goat, the sight of which enthused him with the idea of Egypt becoming a colony of France:

> We shall see a new colony spring up with cities ready built and with skilful workmen accustomed to toiling and inured to the climate. With their aid, and by the help of the canals which are already traced out, they will, in a few years time, create new provinces the future abundance of which cannot be doubted since it will depend on modern industry alone to restore to them their ancient splendour.

Denon's excursion in the Delta with the army was protracted for military reasons. General Menou was instructed to form a detachment and to proceed along the shore.

Hearing this, Denon seized the opportunity to accompany him. He was eager to explore more of the northern coast of Egypt than he had been able to scan through his telescope when he had approached Alexandria in the frigate *La Junon*.

To undertake the journey a caravan was formed. This excited the attention of the local inhabitants, a number of whom joined the procession. The caravan left Rosetta at dusk to benefit from the cooler air. As the caravan spread over the sleek surface of the sandy hillocks surrounding Rosetta, it produced a most striking and picturesque effect. The groups of soldiers, the lines of merchants in their different costumes, sixty laden camels, an equal number of Arab guides, horses, asses, foot travellers and a few instruments of military music, all contributed to give the scene a romantic appearance.

As the detachment progressed, Denon, who was eavesdropping, records how the soldiers could talk of one thing only. A rumour had spread among them that Murad Bey had a fabulous white camel draped in gauzy silk covered with gold and diamonds. This was an exaggeration but it was enough to fuel the men's desires and enable them to forget, for the time being, the hardships of marching in the desert. On departing Rosetta, the troops passed first through groves of palm trees on the outskirts of the town. These gave way to hillocks and sand dunes until the detachment eventually entered a vast desert, the horizontal line of which was broken by just a few small brick monuments standing in eerie isolation. These were markers whose purpose was to prevent travellers from losing their way in the wide expanse of open terrain. Without the benefit of these, the slightest error of navigation could be fatal in the harsh and unforgiving landscape.

As the convoy proceeded, the fatigues of the journey took their toll. The idle talk among the troops about Murad Bey and his richly draped camel gradually subsided. The men marched in the silence of the desert under a starlit sky. Once out on the plain they encountered encrustations of salt. These covered the surface of their route and offered some relief by providing a more secure foothold than the eternal shifting sand. With the onset of darkness the troops had to exercise caution not to fall behind. The shadows concealed predators in the guise of marauding Arabs who were on the lookout for stragglers.

Denon and his party reached the shore at midnight. Nothing could have prepared them for what they discovered. As the rising moon shed its ghostly light, the scene that met their horrified gaze was like a phantom. Evidence of the catastrophe that had befallen the French fleet was scattered everywhere and, in the moving words of Coleridge, 'the many men so beautiful they all dead lie'. It was a harrowing scene that disposed Denon to write one of the most affecting passages in his *Journal*:

> The shore, to the extent of four leagues, was covered with wrecks that enabled us to form an estimate of the loss we had sustained at the Battle of Abukir. To procure a few nails, or a few iron hoops, the wandering Arabs were busy on the beach burning the masts, gun carriages and boats that had been constructed, at such vast an expense, in our ports. Even their wrecks were a treasure in a country where so few of these objects were to be found.
>
> The robbers fled at our approach. Nothing was left but the bodies of the wretched victims, drifted on to the sand, by which they were half covered and exhibiting a spectacle as sublime as it was terrifying.

The sight of these distressing objects plunged my soul by degrees into a deep melancholy. I endeavoured to shun these nightmarish spectres but in vain. All those that I came across attracted my attention by their various attitudes and made different impressions on my mind. But a few months before, young, replete with health, courage and hope they had, by a noble effort, torn themselves away from the embraces of their weeping mothers, sisters and wives and from the feeble struggles of their tender infants. I said to myself, all those by whom they were cherished – and who yielding to their ardour had allowed them to depart – are still offering prayers for their success and for their safe return. Waiting for news of their triumphs, they are preparing feasts for them and are counting the moments as they pass – while the objects of their expectation lie on a distant beach, parched by the burning sand with their skulls already bleached.

With the rising of the sun, yet more of the horrors of the wrecked ships were revealed and the unfolding scene further subdued 'the gloomy complexion' of Denon's thoughts. But the caravan was moving on and he had to shake off his despondency and keep up with the troops. They reached the edge of a salt-water lake separating the desert plain from the coastal peninsula at the extremity of which Abukir is situated. The deep and extensive lake had once formed part of the Canopic branch of the Nile but, at some period in its history, its banks had given way and the sea had encroached. The party crossed the mouth of the lake, today named Lake Idku, and arrived at the outskirts of Abukir.

Denon was becoming used to the sight of impoverished dwellings and mud-brick hovels and what he discovered confirmed his worst expectations. All he could find were some forty to fifty houses in a ruinous state intersecting the peninsula. He moved on until he reached the remains of the fortress of Abukir, located at the extremity of the headland. This had little architectural merit although Denon found four large stones of dark green porphyry that had been removed from an ancient monument. He made use of the ramparts to survey the scene and to draw a panoramic view of the peninsula stretched out before him.

The following day, eager to discover fresh architectural antiquities, he accompanied a detachment of troops along the coast. After a search his diligence was rewarded when he came upon a pier constructed centuries earlier out of colossal fragments. This was his first encounter with Egyptian monumental remains and he was clearly stirred by his discovery:

> I felt an inexpressible pleasure on perceiving, in the first instance, a fragment of a hand belonging to a statue [estimated to be] thirty-six feet in height. The granite workmanship, and style of this fragment left no doubt in my mind but that it belonged to the earliest period of the Egyptians.
>
> It is easy to recognise in this fragment the figure of Isis holding a Nileometer. It might readily be removed from the spot where it is placed but this would greatly diminish its value.

Isis, to whom Denon refers, was the embodiment of Egyptian motherhood and was the wife of Osiris – the most important of the Egyptian deities who ruled the underworld and the afterlife. Isis may have originally been worshipped in the Delta region but her most revered sanctuary was in Upper Egypt on the island of Philae near modern-day Aswan. The Nileometer, which he also mentions, was a form of deep well by means of which a record was taken of the level of the Nile as it rose during the period of the inundation. It was important to know this in order to be able to establish when the dykes, which held back the floodwaters, could be breached so as to enable them to irrigate the land. Egyptian Nileometers were elegant pieces of masonry engineering. They consisted of a deep circular shaft containing a spiral staircase that wound about a central column, or newel post, that was calibrated in cubits – the ancient linear measurement equal to the distance from the elbow to the fingertips. One of the best preserved Nileometers is to be seen today on the island of Elephantine.

Progressing along the shore, Denon came upon more fragments of the colossal statue and the remains of a sphinx, the head and forelegs of which were encrusted with shells and seaweed deposited by the action of the waves that had encroached upon the monument's original location. Denon thought he could detect in the workmanship the hand of a Greek sculptor. The sphinx was hewn from white marble 'which had a transparency not to be met with in this substance outside Egypt'.

Proceeding inland in the direction of Alexandria, Denon discovered more Greek remains in the form of several large Corinthian capitals. These were well executed in marble but were too decayed for him to take accurate records. Further on he found more fragments, this time in the form of rose-coloured granite columns. Here, everything was wrought with care and indicated the ruins of a large temple executed in the Doric style.

Denon realised he had found the Graeco-Egyptian remains of Canopus, known to the Greeks as Kanopos. In the Hellenistic era, a temple to the god Sarapis had stood there and had been a place of pilgrimage. In Roman times the region became a pleasure resort for the people of Alexandria. This ushered in a period notorious for its dissoluteness, which may have contributed to the demise of the township in the fourth century AD. The term 'canopic jar' is associated with Canopus. Canopic jars were stone or earthenware vessels that were used in the ceremony of embalming, acting as receptacles for the major organs that were removed from the body of the deceased.

Denon made his way to Abukir satisfied that he had noted all there was to see of the remaining antiquities. At Abukir he learned that military dispatches were to be sent by another detachment of soldiers to Cairo for the Commander-in-Chief. He seized the chance to return with them, remarking: 'The opportunity of quitting so dismal a spot gave me an inconceivable pleasure'. The sight of so many wrecks and corpses washed up along the shore had preyed heavily on his mind.

The journey back to Cairo meant marching by the coast to Rosetta. They were soon reacquainted with the horrors of death which they had previously encountered:

> The night was so dark we had to grope our way at times wading through the sea and at others in the midst of thickets by which we were torn. We stumbled now and then among the wrecks that were scattered on the beach. At three in the morning we reached Rosetta where I reposed myself voluptuously, not on my bed, for I had not seen one since my departure from France, but on a clean mat in a cool chamber.

When the detachment reached Cairo, the senior officer presented Bonaparte with the military dispatches with which he had been entrusted. They told of the crushing

Bonaparte reviewing his cavalry on the Qubbeh plain to the north-east of Cairo on the border of the eastern desert, 2 December 1798. It was here that the French army, under the command of General Kléber, defeated a Turkish force of 40,000 men. A few weeks later Kléber was assassinated by a religious fanatic. His penalty was to have his right hand burned off before being impaled on a rod of iron and left to die. *(Dutertre, National Library of Scotland)*

naval defeat at Abukir Bay, together with a chilling inventory of the grievous loss of men – no less than one admiral, six captains, 1,700 seamen dead and many more captured or wounded. Bonaparte is said to have borne this news resolutely with no outward show of feeling. When he had assimilated the information, he reported it to the Directory in Paris, outlining the circumstances of the encounter with the English and the appalling outcome.

A few days later he wrote a gracious letter of condolence to Madame de Brueys sparing her the horrific details of her courageous husband's death:

> Your husband has been killed by a cannon shot while in combat on board ship. He died without suffering and his death was most peaceful – that most envied by the military.
>
> I feel your grief deeply. The moment when we are separated from the object of our affections is terrible. It isolates us from the world. It makes our being convulse with agony. The faculties of the spirit are extinguished. They do not retain their relationship with the world – the nightmare changes everything. In this situation we feel that if we had no reason to live it would be better to die. But, when such thoughts pass, we hug our children close to our heart, [shed] tears, [express] tender feelings that rekindle our nature and we live for our children. Yes, Madame, you will cry with them, you will raise them in infancy and cultivate their youth. You

The interior of the house of Hasan Kâchef occupied by members of the Commission of the Sciences and Arts of the Institute of Egypt. The President of the Institute, the mathematical genius Gaspard Monge, welcomes Bonaparte as Vice President to the inaugural meeting, 22 August 1798. *(Dutertre, Author's Collection)*

will speak to them of their father, of your sadness, of the loss they have experienced [and] of that [also] to the Republic.

When your soul is reunited once more with the world, through your filial and maternal love, [please] value as something the friendship and keen interest that I shall always take in the wife of my friend. Persuade yourself that [your husband] is one of those small number of men who are worthy of hope and grief because they feel with warmth the heartache of the soul.

Bonaparte's letter is remarkable for its expression of feeling for Admiral Francis Paul, Count de Brueys and its expression of compassion for Madame de Brueys. They are worthy sentiments with which to close the account of the tragic, and fateful, events that took place a few miles from the north shore of Egypt in August 1798.

Although the English were the victors following the battle of the Nile, they were also weakened. Nelson's ships had taken a considerable pounding and others were weighed down with the French sailors they had rescued. This was not the moment for Nelson to attempt further conquests. He consolidated his position at Abukir Bay by taking possession of the few French ships that had not been sunk or made their escape. On 19 August 1798, Nelson dispatched Captain Saumarez to Gibraltar with the remnants of the French fleet. He then relocated himself with his ships *Alexander*, *Culloden* and *Vanguard* to Naples. The *Goliath*, *Swiftsure* and *Zealous*, together with three frigates, were left to patrol the Egyptian coast, thereby isolating Bonaparte and his army from France.

CHAPTER 6

The People of Rosetta

When Denon reached Rosetta, he decided to remain there for a few days in the company of General Menou. It was a wise decision since he was then able to relax and enjoy the pleasures of life. The first such opportunity presented itself on the occasion of the anniversary of the birth of Mohammed, the most solemn in the Arabic Hegira. General Menou was surprised to find no preparations afoot to celebrate this festival; doubtless the recent hostilities between the French and the Arabs had put such considerations out of mind. However, when the General asked if such a ceremony could be put in hand his guests were eager to oblige and, within a quarter of an hour, a festival was proclaimed. The town was illuminated and 'hymns of piety blended with those of rejoicing and gratitude'. A splendid meal was provided followed by music:

> After supper we were invited to retire to the quarter of the first Civil Magistrate, in front of whose house we found all the preparations [were in hand] for a Turkish festival [to commemorate the anniversary of the birth [of Mohammed]. The street [served as] the assembly room and was lengthened, or contracted, according to the number of guests. The distinguished personages occupied an alcove covered with carpeting. Fires, combined with a number of small lamps and large tapers, formed a whimsical illumination. On one side was a band of martial music consisting of short squeaking oboes, small kettledrums and large Albanian drums. On the other were stationed violins and singers and, in the middle, Greek dancers. Attendants provided sweetmeats, coffee, syrups, rose-water and pipes. In this way the festival was furnished.
>
> As soon as we were seated the martial music commenced. A kind of leader of the band played alternately two different airs that the other musicians repeated in chorus. Whether it was owing to the calmness of the atmosphere, or a wish of introducing too many flourishes into it, it so happened the second measure was a true cacophony – a discordance of harsh sounds as disagreeable to sensitive ears as it was enchanting to those of the Arabs.

When the musical part of the entertainment was over, dancing followed. Dancing was frequently associated with music-making, especially in the vibrant life of Cairo. Dancing girls could be seen everywhere and were appreciated by all classes of society for their 'artifices and charms'. The dancer, her hands ornamented with castanets, made all manner of amorous gestures. Sometimes they sat on the ground and executed the same movements with a suppleness and facility that both enticed and astonished. The girls who performed in the houses of the Mamelukes were particularly beguiling: 'The robe is split such as to reveal the throat. The hair is curled in tresses and decorated with ribbons

Two dancing girls. The French savants were attracted by the grace and charm of young Egyptian women but record how the modest demeanour of dancers, of the lowest class, could become lewd and suggestive. These women have posed déshabillé for the artist with their trunk of stage garments and instruments. *(Dutertre, Author's Collection)*

and the head is coiffured with a turban. The eyelashes and eyebrows are darkened with mascara. The fingers and the toes are painted red with henna.'

Some dancing girls were less sophisticated and their performances were suggestive and 'most licentious'. Male dancers were also to be seen and the artistes – if that is how they can be described – who were hired to perform for General Menou and Denon appear to have belonged to this category. Their lewd behaviour did not impress the French guests:

The dance that followed was of the same kind as the singing. It was not the expression of joy or gaiety but was of an extravagant pleasure that made hasty strides towards lasciviousness. This was the more disgusting since the performers, all of them of the male sex, presented in the most indecent way scenes that discretion has reserved for the two sexes in the silence and mystery of the night.

The finest studies in Denon's portfolio were his portraits of the people he encountered on his travels. Produced with alacrity, they captured the likeness and physiognomy of the subjects admirably. Left: A pasha who had been taken prisoner. He was leader of a band of Turkish troops who opposed the French.

Denon found much to admire in the energy and vitality of Egyptian musicians but the shrillness of their wind instruments was too strident for his European ears. On one occasion he went so far as to condemn the band to which he was obliged to listen as being no more than a 'tin-kettle orchestra'. However, as he journeyed with the soldiers he observed how important music was in the social life of the Egyptians. In the streets male balladeers could be heard singing popular melodies in their strong tenor and baritone voices. Dancing girls – to the delight of the French soldiers – could be seen swaying to the accompaniment of their tambourines. In the houses of the noblemen, musicians gathered to participate in the celebrations associated with special social and religious events.

Following the celebrations to commemorate the anniversary of the birth of Mohammed, Denon had time on his hands. This allowed him to pursue his vocation and go out armed with his sketchbook. People fascinated him and his engravings contain many delightful studies of the individuals whom he encountered, either by chance or in

II

Upper, from the right: A young Arab prince whom Denon met on his journey to Quseir. With him is his uncle. They dined together in the desert, prompting Denon to remark: 'They were both very interesting, their manner was soft and polite and their character tranquil'. The man with a lance was an escort.
Lower: A Mameluke with three boy attendants. He became a favourite of the French and was known even to Bonaparte. (Denon, British Library)

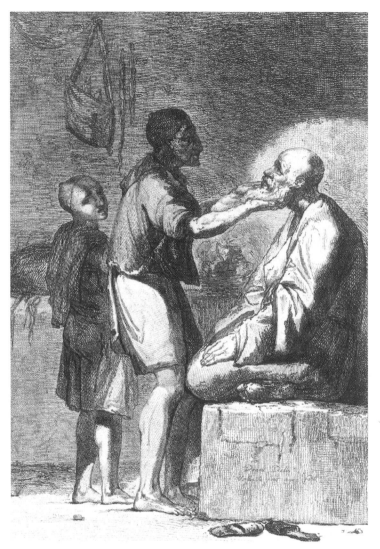

An Egyptian barber in his shop. They performed their work dextrously and with 'solemn gravity and calm patience', shaving the head and trimming the beard of their customer according to his physiognomy and social standing. Like barbers everywhere, they discussed the news and shared the gossip. They sold hair-removing ointment derived from quicklime and arsenic which 'made the hair fall very promptly'!

the course of his more formal social engagements. He took particular pleasure in the study of the local people. He had the keen, practised eye of an artist and it was second nature to him to observe people as though they were subjects in his studio, being sized up for a portrait.

In the late eighteenth century, Rosetta was a multicultural town thronging with people of different races and an ideal place for an artist to explore. Denon lost no time in walking the streets, sketchbook in hand, to absorb the scenes of everyday life all about him. He sketched some individuals because they were distinguished by their social standing; others came to his attention because they were important representatives of religious orders or sects; merchants and traders from foreign countries fascinated him; and – in the tradition of a true artist – he sketched some people because their distinctive features captured his interest.

A village elder beating a drum. To elevate his social status he is wearing elaborate garments. Denon dismissed him as a fool. *(Denon, British Library)*

Rosetta was the perfect location for a portrait artist. The people of different nations had not intermarried and had retained their individual ethnic and racial character. Denon was quick to seize on these:

It struck me that this city, a station of intermediate commerce, must necessarily have collected together persons belonging to all the nations of Egypt and has preserved them more apart, and in a better characterised state, than in a great city, such as Cairo, where the relaxation of morals has crossed them and caused them to degenerate. I fancied I could distinguish, in the Copts, the ancient Egyptian stock – a type of swarthy Nubian such as we see represented in old sculptures with flat forehead, eyes half-closed and raised up at the angles, high cheekbones, a broad and flat nose – very short, a large flattened mouth – placed at a considerable distance from the nose, thick lips, little beard, a shapeless body, crooked legs – without any expression in the contour and long flat toes.

The next group of people at Rosetta to be studied by Denon were the Arabs:

After the Copts come the Arabs, the most numerous of the inhabitants of modern Egypt. Without possessing influence in proportion to their numbers, they seem to be placed there to

Costumes of the people of Egypt.
Top, from the left: A young Mameluke, his hands concealed by long velvet sleeves. His turban could unwind to form a shawl. In his belt are a sabre and dagger and a copy of the Koran is in his shoulder bag. An elegant *almée* (dancer) attired in a robe of fine cloth with a shift of gauze. Her girdle served as a shawl. A Mameluke dressed for battle. In the background two men practise their skills with staffs.
Above, from the left: A merchant holding his pipe. His turban is wool and likewise his loose surtout. Over his shoulder is a length of calico in which to wrap his purchases. A lady shrouded in her everyday garments – typically black or blue in colour. Her veil conceals all but her eyes. Some women sported a talismanic ring to drive away evil spirits or bad luck. A peasant from Upper Egypt carries a handful of lucerne (alfalfa), probably his only subsistence for the day. *(Denon, British Library)*

people the country, to cultivate the land, to tend the flocks or to be in the degraded state of the animals. They are, however, lively and have a penetrating physiognomy. Their eyes, which are sunk in and overarched, are replete with vivacity and character. All their proportions are angular. Their beard is short and hanging in filaments. Their lips are thin and open displaying fine teeth. Their arms are fleshy and in other respects they are more active than some and more muscular than well shaped.

Denon's racial inventory continues with the Turks:

> The beauties of the Turks are that they are more dignified and their shape is more delicate. Their thick eyelids allow but little expression to the eyes. The nose is thick, the mouth and lips handsome, the beard long and bushy, the complexion is less swarthy and the neck plum. In all the gestures and motions of the body they are dull and heavy. They possess a beauty that cannot be defined or a reason given why it should be considered as such.

Denon then describes the Jews in terms that testify to the long years this race has suffered from prejudice and persecution:

> Next come the Jews who are in Egypt what they are everywhere – hated without being dreaded, despised and persecuted incessantly. Without ever being expelled, plundering constantly without being very rich and rendering themselves useful to all the world at the same time that their only incentive is self-interest.
>
> I do not know whether it is due to their being nearer to their own country that their physical character is better preserved here than elsewhere – it struck me, however, very forcibly. Those among them who are ugly resemble our Jews while the handsome ones, more particularly those who are young, bear a strong resemblance in point of character to the head that painting has handed down to us of Jesus Christ.

The last group of people Denon mentions in his survey of the different races and peoples of Rosetta is that which was known as the Barâbras. This was a race who lived in the southern border region of Egypt near the Cataracts – formerly Nubia, now Sudan. They were a placid and genial people renowned for being trustworthy and reliable. It was known that a master could leave his house and all his possessions in the care of one of these men with absolute confidence. For this reason they were widely employed as servants. Rather perversely they were not to be hurried. They worked at their own pace and to the stranger unfamiliar with their nature they could appear lazy and indolent. Denon says of them:

> The Barâbras are people from the upper countries – inhabitants of Nubia and the frontiers of Abyssinia. Their characteristic traits are very numerous and are strongly delineated. In these fervid climates nature has, in an economical mood, denied them every superfluity. They have neither flesh nor fat but simply nerves, muscles and tendons. [They have] greater elasticity than vigour. They perform by activity and address what others effect by strength. It would seem as if the barrenness of their soil had exhausted the small portion of substance that nature has bestowed on them. Their skin is shining and jet-black, exactly similar to that of antique bronzes. They have not the smallest resemblance to the Negroes of the western parts of Africa.
>
> They are most commonly employed to guard the magazines and timber yards. They are clad in a piece of white woollen cloth, earn but little and subsist on almost nothing. They are faithful to their masters to whom they are strongly attached.

Denon concludes his survey of the people of Rosetta with remarks concerning Egyptian women. Those of the lower classes worked very hard. This can be inferred from the various portraits of working women drawn by Denon and his artist companions. Women of the subordinate classes carried heavy jugs of water on their heads, often having to walk a considerable distance to the nearest well or cistern. This daily activity was but

Costumes of the people of Egypt.
Above: Leader of a caravan train draped in a simple cloak of wool; below: a *santon* or holy man of whom Denon remarks: 'They are pitied when they live and revered when they die'; right: a woman of high social standing with her attendant. She is wearing indoor clothing without her veil. *(Denon, British Library)*

one of their tasks. Others included the endless responsibilities of cooking, looking after children and spinning and weaving. The lowliest task performed by Egyptian women was collecting camel dung for fuel. Since wood was a valuable commodity in Egypt it was not available for use as fuel. An alternative source was animal droppings that were gathered from the streets and byres by women and girls. They collected the sun-dried cakes in bowl-shaped baskets called *couffes* which, when full, they carried on their heads to a source of water. The cakes were then moistened and mixed with fragments of straw – a revolting undertaking – after which they were exposed to the sun to dry. Camel dung was preferred; this gave a good heat with little smoke.

Egyptian peasant women went about dressed in a full-length robe that was open at the front to the midriff. This garment was usually made from cotton dyed blue. An accessory garment was a pair of cotton trousers. *De rigueur* was a veil – more like a shroud – called a *turhah* that fulfilled the requirements of modesty and religious conviction.

Costumes and portraits. The French
artists observed all classes of people as
they explored Egypt. They recorded
their costumes and facial expressions
with near photographic precision.
Left: A handsome boy from Alexandria.
Below: A stern-featured Abyssinian
bishop. (*Dutertre, National Library of
Scotland*)

Right: A lady of social standing who has lowered her veil.
Below: An *agha* from Cairo – a high-ranking official wearing his elaborate garments. (*Dutertre, National Library of Scotland*)

Left: A sheikh from Cairo – typical of the village leaders with whom the French had to negotiate.
Below: The dragoman of Murad Bey – a translator fluent in several languages.
(Dutertre, National Library of Scotland)

Egyptian women of social standing were a world apart from their humbler counterparts. They lived in magnificent houses, wore garments made from the finest materials, anointed themselves with exotic perfumes and were waited upon by an entourage of servants. Within the screened and shaded apartments set aside for them in the great town houses of their masters, women of distinction and noble birth could pass their leisure hours reclining on soft cushions, managing their lives and conversing with their companions.

Of the women passing by in the streets at Rosetta, Denon remarks:

The women of the lower classes take greater pains to conceal the nose and mouth than any other part. They manifest, from time to time, not attractions but fine slender limbs, the shape of which display more activity than grace. As soon as their breasts have attained their full growth they begin to fall and their gravitation is such it would be difficult to say how low some of them reach.

The complexion of the women is neither black nor white but a dusk-brown. They dye their eyebrows and eyelids with a black colour . . . but without producing any great effect. I have not, however, seen any women carry with more elegance a child, a vase, or a basket of fruit or walk with greater ease and serenity.

Their long drapery would by no means be unbecoming were it not that a veil, in the shape of a ship's pennant, casts a gloom over the whole of their dress so as to make it resemble the dismal costume of a nun of the order of penitents.

Denon's high standing among the French invaders gave him access to the homes of rich merchants who were anxious to offer him their hospitality as they adapted to life under French rule. This circumstance gave the artist further opportunities to observe their womenfolk and their manners. One such visit resulted in a delightful and amusing incident:

One of the inhabitants, who was under some obligations to me, by way of testifying his gratitude invited me to his house. On account of my advanced age [Denon was fifty-one years old], and of my being a foreigner, he thought he might allow his wife to be at the breakfast party and thus contribute more to my entertainment. As he was engaged in mercantile pursuits, he spoke a little Italian and acted as interpreter between myself and the lady whose beauty was accompanied by a soft tinge of melancholy.

She was extremely fair and her hands were uncommonly delicate and attractive. On admiring them she held them out to me. We had very little to say to each other and, to make up for this silence, I kissed her hands which, as she was perplexed to know what she should afterwards do to interest me, she did not let them go. On my side, I dared not release them as I could not envisage how this scene would have terminated if refreshments had not been brought to relieve us from our embarrassment. These were handed to her and she presented them to me in a very particular manner and with some degree of grace.

I fancied I could perceive that her negligent and pensive air was merely the affectation of a great lady who persuaded herself that, by assuming it, she should become superior to all the magnificence by which she was surrounded and covered.

Another of Denon's female acquaintances provided him with a further insight into the manners and conventions of women of social standing at Rosetta. This time what he

The beautiful wife of a merchant seated at her window. Denon was captivated by this lady and took breakfast with her. She had pretty hands which Denon was allowed to clasp – under the protective gaze of her husband. *(Denon, University of Edinburgh)*

witnessed had a tragic aspect and concerned a woman friend of the merchant's wife to whom reference has just been made. She was beautiful, was married to a Franc – of whom she was fond – and was of 'engaging manners'. She spoke some Italian and was therefore in a position to share her confidences with Denon. From his rooms, which were near to where she and her husband lived, he watched their domestic entanglements and the lady's assignations. Although she was devoted to her husband she was not so constant in her relationship as to forgo conferring part of her affections elsewhere. As a consequence:

> The jealousy that ensued, on [the husband's] side, was the occasion of perpetual strife. She was all submission and never failed to renounce the object of his suspicions. On the following day, however, there was a fresh complaint. She again wept and repented and, notwithstanding, her husband was never without some motive for scolding her.
>
> The house in which this couple lived was opposite to mine and, as the street was narrow, I became very naturally the lady's confidant and the witness of her chagrin. The plague broke out in the city [probably typhoid which was endemic] and my neighbour was so very

An amorous lady. She sits languidly by her window with her veil drawn aside. Her fan of feathers and slippers are nearby. Within a few days of Denon making this sketch she had died of the plague, contracted from one of her many lovers. *(Denon, University of Edinburgh)*

communicative that she could not fail either to give or take it. Accordingly, she caught it from her lover, bestowed it very faithfully on her husband and they all three died.

I regretted her death. Her singular good nature and ingenuousness in the midst of her irregularities, and the sincerity of the regret she manifested, had interested me and, more particularly, being a mere confidant I could have no dispute with her either as a husband or as a lover.

Fortunately for Denon, as he intimates in the passage just quoted, he was not so close to the lady as to contract any illness from her himself. Rosetta, however, was most terribly ravaged by the plague. Once more Denon was lucky. He had occasion to quit the town to explore the Delta region of Egypt, to which our narrative now turns.

CHAPTER 7

The Delta

In early September 1798, Generals Marmont and Menou received orders to make a military reconnaissance of the Delta region of the Nile, east of Rosetta, where the French army had yet to establish its presence. This provided an exciting opportunity for a number of civilian members of the French contingent to accompany the army into this, then relatively little known, region of Egypt. Their incentive to do so was the prospect of discovering architectural and archaeological antiquities. These civilians were selected from Bonaparte's Commission of the Sciences and Arts and included the geologist Dolomieu, the musician Villoteau, the painter-draughtsman Joly – who was to meet with tragedy – and a member of the medical staff who, by reason of his linguistic skills, was able to act as an interpreter. On hearing about the intended expedition, Denon's response was characteristically enthusiastic: 'We at length set out for the Delta, the excursion to which I had so long and so eagerly looked forward, to tread ground that had never been explored by any European and, indeed, but imperfectly by any other persons.'

In Pharaonic times, the Delta region of the Nile was irrigated by five tributaries that included three major water-courses known as the Canopic, Sebennytic and Pelusiac. By the Islamic period, these had been largely exhausted by a combination of canal-building and topographical changes in the nature of the terrain caused by the encroachment of wind-blown sand. At the time of the French occupation of Egypt, the Delta was irrigated by only two branches of the Nile, the Damietta to the east and the Rosetta to the west.

On the afternoon of 10 September, about a dozen men of letters, including Denon, set out on their exploration of the Delta with a detachment of 200 soldiers. They crossed the Rosetta branch of the Nile in boats specially arranged to transport the officers' horses. Unfortunately, when the men prepared to mount, it was discovered the horses were ill-tempered and proceeded to give their riders a good deal of trouble by biting and kicking. To make matters worse, some horses were without a bridle or saddle and, consequently, several officers had to make do with asses. At first they considered the prospect of riding on the back of an ass to be too humiliating, but they relented when they realised the alternative was to trek through the desert alongside the foot soldiers. When all the problems of horsemanship and transport were overcome the motley assortment of officers and the company of foot soldiers duly departed.

The expedition made its way eastwards and passed through a seemingly endless succession of villages and small townships. These included Madie, Elyeusena, Abugueridi, Melahue, Abuserat, Ralaici, Bereda, Ekbet, Estaone, Elbat, Elfezri, Suffrano, El-negars and

Madie-di-Berimbal. These locations have long since crumbled into dust or have been effaced by the encroaching desert or supplanted by modern-day settlements. At the time of the French excursion into the Delta, however, they were thriving communities whose vigour and vitality prompted Denon to comment: 'The different villages through which we passed conveyed an indication of the population, within [an expanse of] four leagues of territory, and of the fertility of the soil that nourishes so many inhabitants and contains on its surface so many habitations.' In addition to providing for the needs of the local people, the land had also to supply the tithes and levies imposed by the titular head of the region – the chief Mameluke – for his benefit and that of his entourage. Failure to comply with his edicts would usually result in swift and terrible retribution.

By midnight the travellers reached Madie-di-Berimbal. It was by then pitch dark and the guides, who were unfamiliar with the terrain, led the party on a false trail. This resulted in the transport camels stumbling into the irrigation channels that criss-crossed the region. Denon recorded: 'Our baggage and provisions were drenched, all thoughts of our arrival had been given up and, after having procured a supper, we reposed ourselves as well as we could at two o'clock in the morning. The following day, after having dried our clothes, we set out and reached Metubis. After two hours we met with as many villages as on the former occasion.'

On reaching Metubis, General Menou was instructed to make enquiries concerning the hostile conduct of certain sheikhs in the vicinity. As a consequence, the patrol was halted, giving Denon the chance to slip away on his own to explore and search for antiquities. He was hopeful of making discoveries since Metubis was built on the ruins of the ancient township of Metelis, renowned – if not notorious – for the 'licentiousness of its manners'. On this occasion Denon was disappointed: 'Our researches after antiquities were ineffectual. All the granite we could find was employed for grinding corn and appeared to have been brought there from some other place to be applied to that use.'

Because of its durability, and resistance to wear, granite was the stone preferred by Egyptian millers for use as millstones. Regrettably for posterity, they found a ready supply of this material at the sites of ancient monuments. Lengths of granite columns, typically about 1 metre in diameter, made ideal millstones for grinding corn. These mills also served the ignominious purpose of creating lime for the fields by the crushing of limestone fragments that were hacked from surviving temple ornaments and sculptures. It is believed entire structures may have disappeared through this process.

After exploring several sites, over a distance of 'a league and a half', Denon gave up his enterprise. It was getting late and a curiosity of another kind attracted his attention. Denon learned that several officers in the party had requested the sheikhs at Metubis to permit them to see the female dancers give one of their set-piece performances. These girls were known as the almée and they adopted a style of dancing similar in movement and gesture to that assumed by the female temple dancers of India. At first the sheikhs raised difficulties at the prospect of the dancers being 'polluted by the inspection of infidels'. This reaction led Denon to suppose that the dancing girls must be chaste and that it would be profane for their performance to be viewed by Christian eyes. As he was to discover, he need not have concerned himself on this point.

Dancing girls perform for a sheikh. A favourite beauty reclines languorously in the lap of the sheikh. One of
her companions begins her dance to the accompaniment of pipes and tambour – a small earthenware drum.
The young woman at the far right tinkles a small pair of castanets. The scene is chaste and quintessentially
Eastern. Denon observed how dancers of a lower order 'could become lascivious and express . . . the giddy
transports of the passions'. *(Denon, British Library)*

The reluctance of the sheikhs to allow the French to see the dancers was finally
overcome when it was made known to them that General Menou himself wished to see the
performance. Perhaps they allowed their decision to be influenced by the realization that
he had the power and authority to have their town laid to waste should they displease him.
Be that as it may, 'the presence of a General together with that of two hundred soldiers . . .
soon removed every obstacle' and the girls were duly summoned to perform:

> The almée arrived and we could not perceive that they participated, in the slightest degree, in
> the political considerations and religion of the sheikhs. They made some difficulty, however –
> and that with a tolerable share of grace – in granting us what we should have considered as the
> smallest of their favours – that of uncovering the eyes and mouth.
>
> In a little time their forms were completely displayed through coloured gauze, fastened by a
> sash that they tightened from time to time negligently and with an air of levity, by no means
> disagreeable, and somewhat *à la française*.
>
> They had brought with them two instruments, a pipe and tabor, and a kind of drum made
> from an earthen pot on which the musician beat with his hands. They were seven in number.
> Two of them began dancing while the others sang with an accompaniment of castanets in the
> shape of cymbals of the size of a crown piece. The movement they displayed in striking them
> against each other gave infinite grace to their fingers and wrists. At the commencement the
> dance was voluptuous. It soon became lascivious and expressed, in the grossest and most
> indecent way, the giddy transports of the passions.

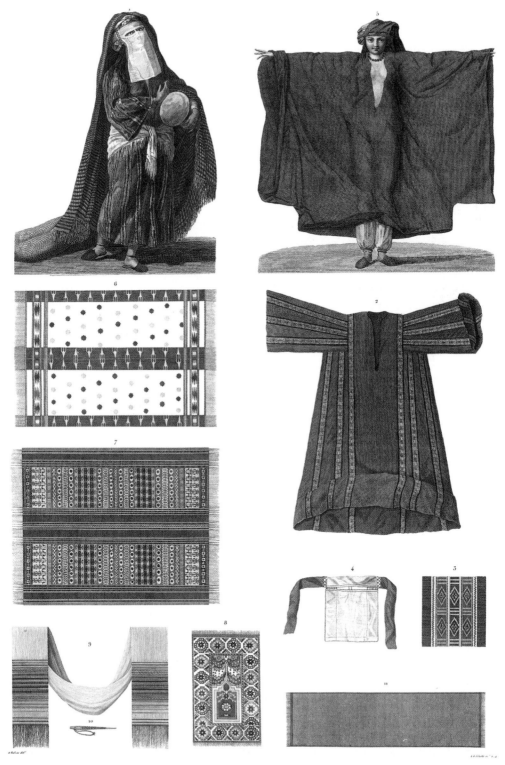

Female entertainers with examples of their garments. Upper: A singer beating rhythmically on her drum with her veil chastely in place. With arms outstretched, a young woman shows a day dress worn by the poorer classes – blue was a popular colour. Middle: An ornate dress with embroidered silk fabrics. Lower: Decorative sashes and a woman's veil that Denon likened 'to a ship's pennant'. *(Balzac and Dutertre, University of Edinburgh)*

> The disgust that this spectacle excited was increased by one of the musicians of whom I have just spoken. At the moment when the dancers gave the greatest freedom to their wanton gestures and emotions, with the stupid air of a clown in a pantomime, [he] interrupted with a loud burst of laughter the scene of intoxication that was to close the dance.

When the performance was concluded, Denon took a close look at the dancers and observed how they 'swallowed large glasses of brandy as if it had been lemonade'. He also noted the extent to which, although they were all young and handsome, their countenances were showing signs of becoming haggard and jaded, with the exception of two whose beauty 'bore a striking resemblance to that of the Paris *belles*'. Indeed, when the dancers finally removed the veils concealing their faces, the audience of Frenchmen 'all joined in a general exclamation on disclosing their features'.

The dancing over, the party of French officers and soldiers left the entertainment, prompting Denon to give expression to one of his philosophical reflections:

> So truly is grace a pure gift of nature that Josephina and Hanka who had received no other education than that which is bestowed on the most infamous professions in the most dissolute of cities, when the dance was ended, possessed all the delicacy of manners of the women whom they resembled, and the soft endearing voluptuousness that they, no doubt, reserve for those on whom they lavish their secret favours.
>
> I could have wished, I must confess, that Josephina had not resembled the others in her style of dancing. Despite the licentious life of these females, they are introduced into the harems to instruct the young persons of their sex in all that may render them agreeable to their future husbands. They give them lessons in dancing, singing, gracefulness and, in general, in all voluptuous attainments . . . They are admitted to the festivals that the grandees give to those of their own rank and when from time to time a husband wishes to entertain his harem in a particular manner, they are also sent for.

The following day Denon renewed his search for antiquities. He went to a location known as Koam-El-Hhamar which was the colloquial Arabic term for the 'red mountain', a name derived no doubt from the circumstance that the mountain was, in effect, a great mound of red bricks. These were the ruins of some ancient structures. On investigating, Denon and his companions could not determine any definite archaeological characteristics other than that the remains may have belonged to the dwellings and buildings of an ancient city. All traces of former monuments and edifices had disappeared other than the brick ruins themselves. Such was the havoc beneath his feet that Denon wondered if the ruins were those of a modern-day settlement that had incurred the wrath of the Mamelukes and had suffered the penalty of being razed to the ground.

Despite his disappointment at their failure to find any interesting remains among the mountain of red bricks, the geologist Dolomieu persuaded Denon to look further afield. The incentive to do so was to locate the site of the former township of Metelis. The French believed that in ancient times Metelis may have been the so-called 'nome' of the Delta region. In the Ptolemaic period Egypt had been subdivided into more than forty nomes or provinces. Each nome had its own capital and some were designated by step-pyramids. The nomes extended from the Delta region in the north to the cataract region

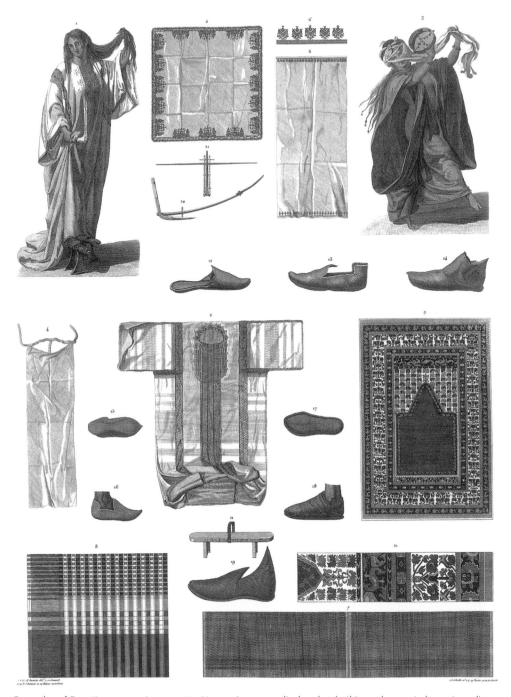

Examples of Egyptian women's garments. Upper: A woman displays her bathing robe – note her extraordinary 'platform' shoes. An animated dancer beats her tambourine. Centre: Details of the bathing robe and examples of indoor shoes. Below: Ornate woven fabrics and a further example of a raised-up shoe. *(Balzac, Dutertre, Févre and Jomard, University of Edinburgh)*

in the south. Contemporary research has established that the Delta region was subdivided into as many as twenty nomes, each with its own distinctive sign incorporating symbols derived from representations of animals, birds and stylised images.

Their search for antiquities took the party in an easterly direction along the shores of Lake Burullus where, to their further disappointment, the countryside presented little more than 'an uncultivated morass'. They decided to head south where they subsequently reached Fuwa, which afforded a welcome resting place. This was a prosperous town known to traders for its various markets. It also exhibited a picturesque aspect with its elegant mosques nestling amid clusters of mud-brick dwellings.

The following day their route took them north-west whither they proceeded with the intention of examining several more ruins, similar to the 'mountain of red bricks' they had previously inspected. They were no more fortunate than on the preceding day. All they found were mounds of rubbish that, as Denon remarks, 'is the only name that can be bestowed on a mass of shapeless fragments of pottery and heaps of broken bricks not one of which was to be found in an entire state'.

Although the small party of adventurers explored even further afield, they encountered nothing more than a few artificial watercourses created for irrigation. They returned to their base dissatisfied with the result of their researches and, furthermore, without having collected any information that could aid them in any future enterprise.

In making their futile excursions in search of antiquities, the party had left the main company of soldiers with which it was now imperative to be reunited for reasons of safety. Accordingly, in the company of a few local and friendly guides, they headed directly for a village by the name of Desuk which was to be their rendezvous. On the way they had the satisfaction of marching by the township of Gabrith. This was fortified with imposing walls and towers similar to the defensive works they had seen protecting larger settlements along the banks of the Nile in the vicinity of Fuwa.

The excursions of the French explorers were not entirely without benefit. Apart from a few solitary travellers, Denon and his party were the first Europeans to travel extensively in the Delta region for centuries, perhaps even since the time of the crusader-invaders. They observed and recorded the terrain through which they passed. As they progressed further inland the countryside assumed a more inhospitable aspect:

> Here the territory was not so well cultivated and the soil, being more elevated and more difficult to irrigate by means of the watering machines, waits for the inundation [in order] to be sown with corn and maize, ground in which no other crops succeed. In the portion of land of this nature, as soon as the harvest is got in the ground – abandoned to the piercing rays of the sun and without one reviving drop of moisture to allay its thirst – it cracks and bears the form and semblance of a desert.

As Denon and the company of soldiers journeyed further south, they encountered the township of Sulmie. It bore extensive traces of the conflict wreaked by the main French army as it had progressed, some weeks previously, on its way to conquer Cairo. The local people gathered to watch the French detachment march by but showed no enmity or resentment in their countenances. They even provided a guide 'with much generosity and good grace'. He was required to conduct the party safely to the next major town, Mehhal-El-Malek, and the Canal of Sfa'idy. This canal was important for the progress of the French army since it was sufficiently wide to allow for the passage of boats from the Nile to Lake Burullus.

In the late eighteenth century a sizeable township had existed in this region by the name of Desuk which was renowned for its large mosque. According to contemporary accounts: 'It is resorted to twice a year by all the nations of the east in which two-hundred thousand souls pay their devotions.' What was unusual about these ceremonies was that women were allowed to participate openly in the proceedings – 'the enjoyment of a liberty by which they are said to profit to the fullest extent imaginable'.

To the pleasant surprise of Denon and his fellow travellers, they were told a fine residence had been prepared for General Menou and they also were allowed to occupy it. This accommodation included a handsome court with a gallery. Once settled in, these facilities provided Denon with the opportunity to observe the principal guests who came to visit the General to pledge their allegiance and offer tokens of friendship. Amid these convivial scenes, Denon took several portraits of the visitors who then sat down with their host to a hearty meal.

The next day was spent visiting the local villages that were now under the protection and authority of the French. Denon was once more encouraged in the belief that antiquities were to be seen, this time as they approached the locality of a settlement called Sanhur-El-Medin. Once more, however, on inspecting the mounds to which their guides directed them, they encountered nothing but a heap of shapeless ruins. They examined fragments of flint and granite stones but these appeared to be of relatively recent origin. Having discovered nothing of historical importance, they returned dissatisfied to Desuk where they spent the night.

The following day's march took them northwards towards the interior of the Delta. Passing by Sanhur-El-Medin, the party encountered several irrigation canals that were abundantly supplied with fresh, clear water which they supposed had its source at Lake Burullus. Beyond these canals the entire country appeared to be covered with water, even though the terrain was elevated several feet above the ground over which they had just marched. Fortunately for the patrol, the irrigation water was directed to, and maintained in, the canals by high mud-dykes. In the wet season these dykes served as roads of communication between the different villages that appeared to rise like islands above the surrounding water.

The savants' enthusiasm for antiquities was stirred again when they were told that ancient remains were to be seen at a more distant locality called Schaabas-Ammers. Venturing this far into the Delta region, however, incurred risks. It entailed the small party of adventurers leaving behind the security of their detachment of soldiers and, furthermore, entering territory known to be frequented by bands of marauding Arabs. Undeterred, and impelled onwards by their sense of curiosity and adventure, Denon and a few companions decided to proceed along a narrow serpentine dyke that divided two areas of inundation. Tragic events ensued:

The *shaduf* was used to raise water along the banks of the Nile. Men worked a series of balanced panniers made from palm leaves lined with leather, chanting in unison to maintain their rhythm. The water fed an irrigation system to the adjacent fields and plantations. The French were amazed to see the Egyptian labourers perform such hard work in searing temperatures. *(Cécile, Author's Collection)*

We had advanced a league beyond our detachment. A guide on horseback, two guides on foot, a young man from Rosetta, the two Generals Marmont and Menou, a physician who served as our interpreter and a draughtsman and myself formed the foremost party of our company . . . . While we were observing the advantages and picturesque situation of Kafr-Schaabras . . . we saw the physician riding to us at full gallop crying out: 'They are waiting for us with muskets and are crying to us "Erga" [Halt]'. Our guides wished to parley with them but they only answered us by discharging their weapons which, though they were very near us, fortunately

Vegetable gardens near Cairo. Individual plots were watered from irrigation channels supplied by a nearby pond created by the flood waters of the Nile. The rich silt supported the cultivation of abundant fruit and vegetables. A mother, with her children, takes produce home. *(Conté, National Library of Scotland)*

did us no injury. We made another attempt to parley but a second volley warned us not to expose the legs of our horses to the enemy's gunshot since [our horses] were our only resource.

As we were returning, we perceived another troop of armed men who were coming up by a road covered with water and who threatened to cut off our only retreat. At this moment, the draughtsman [Joly] was seized with such a degree of terror as to be unable to think and act for himself and fell from his horse. In vain we tried to remount him, to take him behind one of us or to persuade him to seize hold of the tail of one of our horses. His last hour had arrived. Without being able to make use of any chance of escape, he remained on the spot crying out through terror until his head became the prey of the merciless enemy.

Denon and the other members of the party were fortunate to make their escape and all returned safely to Kafr-Ammers.

Although the Delta region of Egypt had not yielded the hoped-for treasures of antiquity, upon which Denon and his fellow savants had set their heart, the next stage of their travels would more than reward their curiosity and scholarly inclinations.

CHAPTER 8

Cairo and the Pyramids

Denon and his fellow savants had been disappointed at their failure to find architectural antiquities or artefacts during their excursion into the Delta region. On returning to Rosetta with their military escort, their hopes in this direction were rekindled. Waiting for them was an order from the Commander-in-Chief requiring them to go to Cairo to participate in the activities of the Institute of Egypt. As Bonaparte's adviser on artistic matters, Denon was particularly enthused. This journey held out the prospect of travelling further south into the interior of Egypt. He embarked down the Nile the next day with his comrades, recording in his *Journal*:

> In quitting the province of Rosetta, we left behind us the richest and most cheerful part of the Delta. In ascending the river, after passing Rahmanieh [30 miles south of Rosetta], the sands of the desert sometimes approach the water's edge on the left bank. [Beyond] the country becomes naked, the trees are thinly scattered and the horizon is marked by a uniform line that is almost impossible to represent by the pencil.

Despite his frustrations with the flat nature of the landscape, which is typical of the region neighbouring Rosetta, as the journey progressed Denon found opportunities to illustrate the countryside unfolding before him. He also sketched a view of the village of Demichelat where he made the following observation concerning the Egyptian style of architecture: 'The reader will find here that the pyramidal form of the ancient Egyptian style of architecture, the regularity of the plan and the simplicity of the capitals are sometimes preserved – even in the slight modern edifices – and give an air of historical gravity to the villages in Egypt that is not to be found elsewhere.'

Towards evening on the same day, Denon had reason to give expression to more lofty thoughts. Coming into view were the Great Pyramids of Giza, the very embodiment of the spirit of ancient Egypt:

> At more than ten leagues from Cairo, we discovered the points of the pyramids piercing the horizon. Soon after we saw Mount Katam and opposite to it the chain of hills that separates Egypt from Libya. They form a barrier to the banks of the Nile against the destructive scourge of the beneficent river. The encroachment of sand [here] often overwhelms the country, changes its fertility to barrenness, drives the labourer from his house – whose walls it covers up – and leaves no other mark of vegetable life than the tops of a few palm trees that add still more to the dreary aspect of destruction.

I felt delighted at seeing these mountains and [the prospect] of visiting structures of which both the date and object of construction are lost in the night of past ages. My mind was full of emotion on contemplating these vast scenes. I regretted the approach of night. It spread a veil over this picture that was so striking to the imagination.

At dawn the next day, Denon 'saluted the pyramids with his eyes' and took several views of them. He wished to be able to draw them with the fine transparent hue they derive from the volume of air in which they are enveloped, a peculiarity of the great pyramids which they owe to their immense elevation. The vast distance at which they are distinguishable renders them almost transparent and the blue tint of the sky causes their angles to appear sharpened and well defined, even though they have been rounded by the decay of years.

At nine o'clock in the evening, the discharge of a cannon announced to Denon and his fellow voyagers that they were approaching Cairo. The cannon shot was to signify the feast of the New Year whose festivities were already in hand. From his boat, which was illuminated by the red glow of sunset, Denon could see numerous minarets clustered at the foot of Mount Katam. Bordering the banks of the Nile the pleasure gardens of the Mamelukes came into sight, scenting the air with heavy perfume from their rich plantations. The party navigated by Old Cairo, the location of centuries of history and tradition. Finally they came to moor at Bulaq, the eighteenth-century port of Cairo. The gardens, the steady flow of the Nile and its gentle murmuring, the numerous buildings bathed in the effulgence of the dying sun all contributed impressions of verdure, freshness and magnificence.

The next day Denon visited the French headquarters where General Bonaparte and his chiefs-of-staff were in residence. Upon arrival, he learned that the Commander-in-Chief was preparing to set out for the pyramids surmounting the Giza Plateau. Ready to accompany him and to give protection to the party when making its researches were 200 men. This news, though welcome to Denon, put him in a quandary:

> I now lamented that I had not known of this expedition a few hours sooner. I considered it fruitless to set out on such a journey without being provided with what was required to observe these subjects with advantage. Besides, I was so fatigued with my former journey that I wanted to rest my limbs. I determined to delay this expedition until the astronomers should go [there] to make their observations in these celebrated places.

Denon had learned of Bonaparte's intention to visit the pyramids in the course of informal conversations with him and his senior officers across the dinner table. The General had remarked: 'It is impossible to visit the pyramids without an [armed] escort and one cannot often spare a detachment of two hundred men for such a purpose.' Denon realised that if he did not seize this chance to go with Bonaparte another opportunity might not arise. With his characteristic eloquence and sense of the importance of the occasion, he comments: 'The ascendancy that some minds have over others at once overcame all my reasoning. It was this ascendancy that now determined me to go with the party to the pyramids.'

The party made the excursion to the celebrated monuments the following day, so affording Denon time to rest and complete his preparations. He returned to his quarters, which were located in Old Cairo, then a self-contained township separate from the capital. Lying to the south of the city, located on the island of El-Rôda, it enjoyed the benefits of being watered by the Nile. The rich moist soil, created from centuries of silt deposits, favoured the cultivation of the plants and trees that grew in profusion there. This location was a favourite of the Mamelukes, a number of whom had chosen El-Rôda to establish their residences and pleasure gardens, the very same gardens that had enchanted Denon when he had gazed from his boat on first approaching Cairo. The opportunity to experience them at close quarters now presented itself.

It was full night when he and his companions arrived. The party struck out and, after wandering for some time, by good fortune found themselves before a splendid residence. On entering they discovered, as though enchanted, 'a hall furnished with velvet cushions and scented with the perfume of an orange grove that the gentle air wafted to us'. Fortuitously, the adventurers had stumbled upon the pleasure house and garden of none other than Murad Bey – the most resolute and implacable of Bonaparte's opponents. Murad Bey lived sumptuously, as befitting one of the supreme rulers of Egypt, and the splendour of his country house at Giza reflected his exalted status. When the French forces entered Cairo, Murad Bey had fled with his army into the desert leaving his property to be occupied by the French. Denon wasted no time in exploring the house and its garden.

> The oriental luxuries have their charms and fill the senses with voluptuous pleasure. We do not find here those long alleys that are the pride of French gardens, nor the serpentine walks of the English – where health and appetite are the reward of the exercise required to survey them. In the east, where indolent repose forms one of the chief luxuries, the tents or kiosks are pitched under the thick branches of a cluster of sycamores and open at pleasure upon a fragrant undergrowth of orange and jasmine.
>
> To all this is added the voluptuous pleasure of enjoyments that are still imperfectly known to us [in the West] but which we may easily imagine. Such [pleasures], for instance, as to be attended by young slaves who combine elegance of form with gentle and caressing manners. To be indolently stretched on vast downy carpets strewn with cushions in the company of some favourite beauty breathing perfumes and intoxicated with desires. To receive sherbet from the hands of a young damsel whose languishing eyes express the contentment of willing obedience – not the constraint of servitude.

After savouring the perfumed ambience of the pleasure garden of Murad Bey, Denon spent a restful night. The following day he made himself ready for the exciting prospect of visiting the Great Pyramids. While his preparations for the visit were not as complete as he would have wished, he was nevertheless determined to seize the opportunity to inspect 'the most powerful symbols of Egyptian iconography – and perhaps of all antiquity – standing majestically on the rocky plateau of Giza'.

The French designated the Pyramid of Cheops the 'First' pyramid because of its immediate proximity to Cairo. They designated the Pyramid of Chephren the 'Second' pyramid. The Pyramid of Mycerinus, the most distant from Cairo, they referred to as the 'Third' pyramid. Justly numbered among the Seven Wonders of the World, they had been visited by numerous travellers but the French artists and engineers were the first to

The rocky plateau of Giza surmounted by its three great pyramids. In the centre is the Pyramid of Chephren with part of its limestone casing still intact. To the right is the south-east corner of the Great Pyramid of Cheops showing the huge blocks of limestone that form its inner core. The French engineers surveyed the height of each course to an accuracy of a few millimetres. In the distance is the Pyramid of Mycerinus together with one of its attendant pyramids. *(Dutertre, Author's Collection)*

make a systematic topographical survey of the pyramid site. This was remarkable for its extent and accuracy.

The officer who commanded the escort was one of Denon's friends and he entered him in the list of the excursion party, which was about three hundred in number. After waiting for the group to assemble they set out. They first sailed through the nearby fields, along the irrigation canals, after which they trekked through the desert in the full heat of the sun. By noon they were half a league from the pyramids. As they approached them Denon took several views from different positions.

We found ourselves in the desert sands and climbed to the level on which these monuments rest. In approaching these stupendous structures their sloping and angular forms disguise their

Entrance to the Great Pyramid of Cheops. The French engineer Rigo helped Denon to measure and copy each of the enormous stones 'faithfully'. The angled blocks serve as an arch to distribute the pressure from above. Sand encumbered many of the inner galleries, which could only be explored on hands and knees. On hearing this, Bonaparte declined to go any further. *(Denon, British Library)*

real height and lessen it to the eye. In addition, as everything is only great or small by comparison, and as these masses of stone eclipse in magnitude every surrounding object – and are yet themselves much inferior to a mountain (the only thing with which our imagination can compare them) – one is surprised to find the first impression, given by viewing them at a distance, is so much diminished on a nearer approach. However, on attempting to measure any one of these gigantic works of art by some known scale, it resumes its immensity to the mind. By way of illustration, as I approached the opening a hundred persons, who were standing under it, appeared so small I could hardly take them for men.

The time available to Denon to survey the pyramids was all too short:

We had two hours only to devote to the pyramids and I had employed an hour and a half in visiting the interior of the only one that was accessible. I had extended all my attention to retain what I had seen. I had taken drawings and measurements as well as I was able with a single foot ruler. In short, I had filled my head and I hoped to bring away many observations worthy of remark but, on recalling them to memory the next morning, I found I had a volume of queries still to make. I returned from my journey harassed and agitated and found my curiosity more stimulated than satisfied by my visit to the pyramids.

Given its close proximity to the Pyramids of Giza, the Sphinx was the next monument on the itinerary for Denon and the band of French officers and soldiers. To the poet the Sphinx is 'The most famous of all the mystery-laden monuments of Old Egypt and has remained immutable through forgotten centuries – the austere guardian alike of the illimitable desert and the lost ages of the world'. It is located on the great causeway leading to the Pyramid of Chephren and was sculpted from the living rock of the limestone plateau. Early travellers mistook the layers of strata visible about the neck of the monument for courses of building stones and thereby conjectured it had been constructed, like the pyramids, layer by layer. The head is a human representation, perhaps of the pharaoh Khafre (Chephren) and the body is that of a crouching lion, a symbol of regal power. On the occasion of Denon's visit to the Sphinx time was once more limited:

I had time only to view the Sphinx that deserves to be drawn with more scrupulous attention than has ever yet been bestowed upon it. Though its proportions are colossal, the outline is pure and graceful. The expression of the head is mild, gracious and tranquil. The character is African but the mouth, whose lips are thick, has a softness and delicacy of execution truly admirable – it seems flesh-like and real. Art must have been at a high pitch when this monument was executed. If the head wants what is called *style* – that is to say the straight and bold lines that give expression to the [sculptured] figures that the Greeks have imparted to their deities – sufficient justice has been rendered to the fine simplicity and character of nature that is displayed in this figure.

In the time remaining to him at the Giza Plateau, Denon cast a final glance at the monuments at the base of the pyramids: 'I just had time to snatch a glance at the tombs, or small temples, decorated with bas-reliefs and statues and of niches in the rock . . . but so many objects worthy of investigation remained it would have required many such visits, as the present, to have undertaken even a sketch of them.'

The Great Sphinx at Giza. Engineers and artists are busy making their survey and convey a sense of its great proportions. The Sphinx was already considerably eroded at the time of the French expedition, but traces of red paint were still visible on the striped bands of its ceremonial headdress. Sentinel-like, it remains 'the austere guardian of the illimitable desert and of the lost ages of forgotten centuries'. *(Denon, British Library)*

At the time Denon explored the Giza pyramid complex, wind-blown sand shrouded much of the site concealing from view all but the Great Pyramids and their smaller satellite pyramids. The Sphinx itself was half buried in sand that was not cleared away until 1818 when another French survey of the site was undertaken. Denon and his colleagues could discern the forms of other structures beneath the sand, but time allowed only for limited archaeological excavations – for which the soldiers proved to be a useful source of labour. The French artists could only guess at what other monuments might lie hidden. Subsequent researches have revealed much that was unknown in the late eighteenth century.

The small tombs to which Denon refers were the mastabas arrayed at the southern perimeter of the base of the Pyramid of Chephren. Mastabas were small, flat-roofed tombs used to commemorate the burial of lesser royal personages and for the private burial of high-ranking officials and close members of their families. The principal features of a mastaba were a vertical burial shaft that led to a burial chamber housing the sarcophagus that contained the deceased's mortal remains. Decorative wall carvings bore testimony to the identity of the deceased and his achievements in life. Small statues of the departed were also entombed and could be viewed through niches in the masonry walls by members of the deceased's family coming to mourn.

View of the head of the Great Sphinx with the Pyramid of Chephren in the background. The Sphinx is shrouded in wind-blown sand which was not cleared away until 1818. The face may be a likeness of Chephren without his ceremonial beard. The Sphinx symbolised the strength and protective power of Egypt's ruler. The king's royal status is symbolised by the *nemes* or headcloth. The French Commission reported: 'It is easy to recognise in this colossal head – unfortunately very mutilated – a sculpture of great character and that which remains of the eyes and mouth are not devoid of a certain grace'. *(Dutertre, Author's Collection)*

The next entry in Denon's account of his travels is concerned with his impressions of Cairo. He had now resided in the town for almost a month, busying himself with walking the streets, taking in the sights and sounds, noting his impressions in his *Journal* and making sketches of the more interesting subjects that caught his eye.

The Silk Vendors' Bazaar. Products were sold from various districts of Cairo which gave them a strong identity and character. Each market was regulated by an Agha who exercised strict authority – the savant Jomard witnessed a trader receiving 150 lashes for unfair dealing. The bazaars were confined to streets and passages that were closed at night and guarded by watchmen. Shopkeepers sat crossed legged or smoked their pipes as they waited for a customer. Coffee was served during a transaction, involving protracted bargaining when voices could be raised 'as though in a quarrel'. *(Roberts, British Library)*

The visitor wandering the streets of Cairo at the close of the eighteenth century soon gained the impression of a multicultural city whose streets bustled with a rich diversity of people of many different races going about their daily affairs. The marketplaces and bazaars were thronged with shoppers and traders transacting their business. Concerning these, Denon remarks: 'I did indeed see a numerous population', an observation borne out by research undertaken by members of Bonaparte's Commission of the Sciences and Arts. For the year 1798, they estimated the population of Cairo to number about a quarter of a million people. Muslims and Arabs accounted for the majority (210,000). Others included: Nubians, Ethiopians, Africans and Negroes (12,000); Mamelukes (10,000); Turks (10,000); Greeks and Syrians (10,000); Jews and Armenians (10,000); and a minority of Franks and Europeans (1,000). According to the census that the French undertook, adult men accounted for 114,000 of the population and women and children 195,000. Cairo was therefore more crowded than many contemporary European towns.

In the late eighteenth century Cairo retained much of the physical form and appearance it had exhibited in medieval times. Not surprisingly, Denon looked in vain for the grandeur of the European cities to which he was accustomed. He complained that he saw 'a vast extent of buildings but not a single handsome street'. Instead, he found a maze of narrow alleyways in which rubbish accumulated, where animals were herded and where the poorest inhabitants lived in mud-brick hovels.

The town had a number of large open spaces but these made little, if any, concession to civic dignity and showed no adherence to the principles of formal planning and civic design. Nevertheless, Cairo's public spaces played an important part in the trade and commerce of the town and provided the setting for numerous vibrant markets and bazaars. These places each had a distinctive character and usually bore the name descriptive of the trade and commerce transacted at each particular location. Within each district workmen practised the same trade and were united by the bonds and affiliations of their particular craft. As Denon moved about Cairo's streets he had opportunities to observe workmen practising their skills. Concerning these he remarks:

> That class of society who are obliged to work for their livelihood . . . have been long taught to expect no other reward from industry than a bare subsistence and thus have no motive to depart from their ordinary routine and to exercise their invention. They particularly dislike every occupation that keeps them standing. The joiner, blacksmith, carpenter and farrier all work sitting – even the mason raises a minaret without standing to his work. Like savage nations, they do everything almost with a single tool so that one is surprised at the dexterity with which they manage it. Their invariable method of proceeding [is] almost a kind of instinct – like the insect whose workmanship we admire while we know it has not the power of applying the same skill to different purposes.

As the French men of letters learned more about Egyptian workmen, they acquired a better understanding of their skills. They admired the manual workers' facility for copying an article imported from another country – 'in a manner to confound which is the copy and which is the original'. They also recognised that Egyptian workmen chose to work seated not, as Denon implies, for reasons of indolence but because this allowed them 'to use their feet with dexterity – almost as an additional pair of hands'. In the

The Coppersmiths' Bazaar situated in the Nahhâsyn district of Cairo. Typical items sold included plates, jugs, pans, bowls and decorative articles. Coppersmiths also traded lanterns and kettles in all shapes and sizes. Old and broken items could be traded in and were then repaired and sold on. The striped awnings shelter a schoolroom. Children could be heard each day, from the street below, chanting verses from the Koran. *(Roberts, British Library)*

course of time the French relied upon Egyptian workmen for their skills and trustworthiness. Denon recounts how: 'Artisans, when not under the restraint of their master, came to offer their services to the workmen among our soldiers. [They] assisted them in their operations and, sure of wages adequate to their industry, endeavoured assiduously to give us satisfaction by patient and active service.'

Nowhere was the cultural richness and diversity of Egypt more evident to Denon and his fellow artist-illustrators than on the streets of Cairo. Here, the astonishing variety of dress and costume was a constant source of delight and intrigue to the onlooker. People passing by, or transacting their business, could be seen arrayed in garments indicative of their racial types and ethnic and cultural origins. Moreover, clothing and decorative apparel gave an indication of a person's military and ceremonial responsibilities as well as providing a pointer to an individual's status and social standing. The Mamelukes were richly attired, as befitting their status as governors, in three-quarter length coats worn over full skirt-like trousers. The warrior class of beys wore splendid robes and turbans worthy of their high position in Cairo's society. Their garments were fashioned from rich fabrics sporting such features as a full collar and elaborate sleeves. Being military men weapons formed part of their sartorial attire. They attached their elaborately decorated swords and daggers – items that were highly prized – to brightly coloured belts and sashes.

The costume of Turkish men and their demeanour caught Denon's attention:

Their dress is a kind of close petticoat that confines the legs. Their large gloves stretch nearly eight inches [20 centimetres] over the fingers' ends and their turbans prevent the head from stooping. [They have] the custom of always holding a pipe in their hands and of intoxicating themselves with its smoke. All these circumstances conspire to destroy activity and imagination so that they meditate without an object and pass every day in the same tasteless manner – even their whole existence – without seeking any new object to relieve its dull monotony.

The great houses of Cairo's wealthy subjects afforded every convenience and luxury. Some of these were veritable fortified palaces set behind high protective walls with strong defensive doors. Their forbidding exteriors, however, belied their ornate and shaded interiors:

They are adorned with handsome marble baths, voluptuous vapour stoves and with mosaic saloons in the middle of which are basins and fountains of water. [They have] large divans, furnished with tufted carpets, and raised beds covered with rich stuffs [that are] surrounded with magnificent cushions. These generally fill three sides of each room. The windows, when there are any, never open and the daylight they admit is darkened by coloured glass and close lattice-work. The light comes principally in through a dome in the centre of the ceiling. The Muslims, who make but little use of the light, take little pains to procure it in their houses and in general all their customs seem to invite repose.

In contrast to the wealthy, the social and domestic conditions of Cairo's poor were pitiable. The lowliest among those in Egypt's capital lived at a level little above subsistence. This was most evident in the conditions of their dwellings, if such a description can be used for what were little more than mud-brick hovels. The French were appalled at what they discovered:

A street scene by the Zuwailah Gate. This gate with its towering minarets gave access to the centre of Cairo. Public executions took place here and headless bodies were left on the ground as a warning to others. To the right is the Al-Muayyad mosque encumbered with rough sheds and awnings. These were used by traders in perfume, oil and scent. Others sold fine Damascus blades and richly inlaid firearms. More modest shopkeepers sold boots, shoes and long pipes. Denon became a regular sight to passers-by as he travelled the streets of Cairo on the back of a donkey. (Roberts, British Library)

One would believe [their habitations] are more suited to accommodating animals because they are [little more than] niches . . . constructed from earth, mixed with stones, and wide open [to the elements]. An entire family lives in these holes . . . the misery and dirtiness of these people make one recoil with disgust.

It is almost the same circumstance in the hovels found in neighbouring districts. On entering one of these houses I was seized by a pervasive odour and was surprised by the horrible filthiness to be found there. The walls were all blackened throughout from the flame used for lighting. There were various animals living pell-mell with the inhabitants. They allow the filth of these animals to accumulate – it is a major cause rendering many of these houses of Cairo uninhabitable and to be abandoned without the residents making efforts to clean and repair them.

Denon visited several homes of the poor and observed how the owners of the dwellings paid little attention to their maintenance:

The inhabitants of this country build as little as possible and repair still less. If a wall threatens to come down they prop it up. If, notwithstanding, it falls in, it only makes for fewer rooms in the house and they quietly arrange their carpets by the side of the ruins. If, at last, the house falls altogether they either abandon the spot or, if they are obliged to clear it out, they carry away the rubbish for as little a distance as possible. [As a consequence] in almost every town of Egypt, and especially in Cairo, the eye of the traveller is constantly arrested by heaps – or rather mountains – of rubbish scattered about.

The French made a scientific survey of Cairo's housing. In the closing years of the eighteenth century this was a pioneering study. They estimated the number of houses in Cairo to be about twenty-six thousand. Given that the population was a little more than a quarter of a million, this suggests an occupancy of about ten persons per household. Overcrowding was rife in the poorest homes, obliging people, as remarked, to coexist with their livestock. Circumstances were worst in the commercial quarters where the prospect of work attracted large numbers of men from outlying districts.

As a consequence of the conditions of Cairo's poor, infant mortality was particularly high, the loss of children accounting for about half the annual deaths recorded by the French physicians. The scourge that took its toll on men, women and children alike was the plague. According to French medical records:

About every four or five years the plague escalates in Cairo in a violent manner. The history of Egypt presents examples of appalling plagues and epidemics that exceed belief. We ourselves, in 1801, suffered one that was typical. [On this occasion] there died in Cairo about 10,000 individuals in a month – the multitude of deaths did not allow us to observe the funeral rites.

Smallpox was the cause of frequent plagues and could decimate the population in one month by as much as the deaths typically occurring in a whole year. Looking for reasons to account for such frequent and widespread occurrences of contagious diseases, the French realised overcrowding and bad housing alone were not responsible. They deplored the practice that prevailed in Cairo of burying the dead within the town itself. No fewer than three burial grounds were close to residential areas – in addition to the large necropolises by the city gates. The problem was that these were low-lying areas that

A bazaar leading to the Maristan. The street is typically thronged with people making it difficult – and hazardous – to move about. French soldiers had javelins hurled at them from the windows of the upper floors. The minaret identifies the Maristan of Cairo – a place of healing and care for the insane. Patients were calmed with music 'rich in harmony' and storytellers were employed to assist with their rehabilitation. Violent inmates were chained by the neck to the wall. *(Roberts, British Library)*

became flooded at the time of the annual inundation of the Nile, thereby increasing the likelihood of water-borne infections.

Despite Denon's genuine concern for the conditions of Cairo's poor, the study of the capital's architectural monuments was more congenial to his artistic temperament. An edifice that captured his attention, even though it was in part constructed from the remains of older buildings, was the so-called Palace of Joseph. This was a magnificent structure that tradition held was the mosque, or divan, of the ruler Salâh El-Din Yusaf (Joseph). It was here that the beys assembled and it was often the scene of angry debates and bloody strife. The surviving architectural features that attracted Denon's admiration were a series of majestic arches supported upon lofty granite columns. There were thirty-two of these, each supported upon a broad sandstone base. The workmanship was of a high order. Denon noted in his *Journal*: 'The curved outline of the capitals approaches [in style] the Corinthian . . . the granite is red and very beautiful. I admired the mass of the columns, the polish of the material and the time and effort required to transport them to such an elevation.'

The ruins of the Palace of Joseph were sited within the precincts of the so-called Citadel of Cairo. This was an elevated stronghold surrounded by a series of massive defensive walls and bastions. Access to the Citadel was by means of a number of great defensive gates, one of which bore the stirring name the Gate of the Mountain. The mountain in question was part of the Mukattam Hills that formed a dramatic backdrop to the Citadel, the magnificent fortress-architecture of which derived from the period of the Crusader Knights and may well have had an influence on the design of European castles and defensive works.

The Citadel itself was more than a stronghold. It was a small township complete with living-quarters, mosques and a remarkable series of cisterns to provide a supply of water – particularly in times of siege. These were known as the Wells of Joseph. Denon had time only to pay a brief visit to these but his engineer-colleagues made a thorough survey of them. There were no fewer than fourteen wells, each one of which had been hewn from the living rock with primitive hand tools wielded by, among others, 'an incredible number of crusader prisoners'.

The so-called Well of Sibyl Kykhyey is reputed to have been able to supply as many as ten thousand people with water for most of the year. This well was sunk in two shafts. The upper shaft descended to a depth of 50 metres and the lower shaft descended a further 40 metres. A stone dropped into the well, in the time-honoured fashion, took almost five seconds to reach water level. The water was raised in large clay pots attached to an endless rope. This was hauled up the lower shaft of the well by a strong horse that had to descend half-way down the well, to reach the mechanism it was required to turn. Access for the animal was by means of a spiral ramp that wound around the well-shaft and was itself a remarkable feat of mining engineering. Two powerful buffaloes hauled the water up the remaining shaft of the well. Because of its great depth, water from this well was about 5°C cooler than water drawn from shallower wells in the Nile Valley.

Cairo's burial grounds next attracted Denon's attention, not least for the remarkable diversity and ornateness of their funerary monuments. Despite the inherently sombre

Great entrance to the Mosque of Sultan Hassan. The French considered this mosque to be 'one of the most beautiful monuments of Cairo and of all the empire'. Jomard made several drawings of its interior – having to flee for his life on one occasion chased, as an 'infidel', by an angry mob. Bronze, aromatic wood and richly coloured texts contributed to its magnificent decoration. Externally, the great entrance rises more than 100 feet above street level, its inner faces being intricately carved. *(Roberts, British Library)*

nature of these necropolises, he found much within their precincts to delight his artist's eye and engage his attention:

> In quitting the rubbish of Cairo the stranger is astonished to see another town. It is all built of white marble where edifices, raised on columns and terminated by domes, or by painted, carved and gilded palanquins, form a cheerful and inviting picture. Trees alone are wanting to render this funereal retreat a delightful spot. It would seem as if the Turks, who banish gaiety from their houses when alive, wish to bury it with them in the tomb.

Cairo had two principal burial grounds that were known as the 'cities of the dead'. This was an appropriate description since these necropolises were almost the size of small townships. One burial ground was sited to the east of the Citadel and the other to the south; both contained monuments and funerary ornaments celebrating the memory of Cairo's deceased rulers. The largest tombs were remarkable for their elaborate construction and the use of ornate materials that included marble, fine limestone and surface decoration worked in gold and brilliant colours – the use of the latter 'was prodigious'. Large enclosures were reserved for wealthy families and were secured by walls and ornate metal gates. What is perhaps most remarkable about Cairo's burial grounds, aside from the decorative splendour of their monuments, is that they were venues for social gatherings:

> Between the hundreds of tombs are avenues, almost like streets, where people can stroll and sit on the stone benches provided for them. The custom is to visit the family tomb each Friday at daybreak. There, mourners can pray, plant flowers and scatter aromatic leaves. Women and children go with the men. The crowd of visitors is immense. It is a spectacle at once religious [and] touching.

While Denon was completing a drawing in one of Cairo's 'sanctuaries of death', he became aware of a disturbance. He heard loud cries that he initially supposed to be the sounds of worshippers – it was the custom at Cairo to hire female mourners to offer their lamentations for the deceased. However, on the occasion in question, Denon turned to find the women running away in fear of their lives indicating, as they fled, that Denon should cease work and follow them. He thought the mourners were filled with apprehension at the imagined signs of an outbreak of some pestilence or plague. At this thought he too was gripped with fear but looking about him – and seeing no obvious indications of anything being untoward – he overcame his anxieties and resumed his drawing. Directly afterwards, however, he saw several men 'flying off'. At this he thought it prudent that he too should leave, particularly since he was a considerable distance from the security of the French military posts.

Having left the burial ground, Denon found signs of agitation in the streets and threatening looks upon the faces of the inhabitants. Arriving safely back at his quarters he learned there had been an affray in the town and that the French governor had been assassinated. It appeared the peaceful alliance between the French and the population of Cairo – that had held for several weeks – was now being threatened by dissidents. Denon's apprehensions were confirmed when he heard sounds of gunfire. He and his companions became anxious both for their personal safety and for the security of the

Institute of Egypt which came under attack. He realised he would have to set aside his artist's materials to take up arms with the military to help put down the insurrection.

Denon joined a group of soldiers and men of letters who took up defensive positions in houses close to the French quarters. Heavy fighting ensued, the Institute was overrun and much valuable scientific equipment was pillaged. It was an anxious moment for Denon and his companions. With nightfall the hostilities ceased since, as Denon remarks, 'the Turks do not like to fight after dark and make it a point of conscience not to kill their enemies when the sun is gone down'. The next morning the conflict resumed, obliging Bonaparte to send detachments of men with heavy guns to clear the streets and public buildings of rebels: 'General Dumas . . . made a great carnage of the rebels, on entering the town, and cut off the head of a seditious chief who was haranguing the people. French military superiority gained the upper hand and the rest of the night passed quietly. The next day we were at liberty.'

The incident described here was the most serious to have occurred at Cairo since the French occupation. The trial of strength between the French forces and their adversaries was, however, decisive. Cairo surrendered and was finally under the control and authority of the French. Even so, the city remained a hazardous place for any Frenchman to enter unaccompanied since, as Denon comments, 'The desire for revenge in our enemies was not extinguished . . . as I could read the next day in the attitude and countenance of the malcontents.'

The ringleaders were rounded up and 'punished' – which probably means they were shot as this was the usual way the French army dealt with dissidents. As a gesture of reconciliation the mosques, where so much fighting had taken place, were restored to the people.

A short time after these events a tragic incident took place that confirmed Cairo remained a dangerous city of occupation. Denon's *Journal* records:

> General Dupuis, an excellent captain who for two years had braved the dangers that beset the path of glory in the brilliant Campaign of Italy, was assassinated at this time by a cowardly blow while reconnoitring. A knife, fastened to the end of a stick, was thrown from a window and cut the artery of his arm. He expired in a few moments. His death cast a melancholy cloud over the victory of 23 October.

When calm was finally restored throughout Cairo, Denon reflected on the incidents that had taken place and their consequences. Amid the animosity towards the French he experienced mitigating acts of kindliness and forbearance towards himself and his fellow countrymen:

> Although [many of] the populace, the ringleaders and some of the prominent people of Cairo had showed themselves fanatical and cruel in this revolt, the middle class – which in all countries is the most accessible to reason and virtue – was perfectly humane and generous to us despite the wide difference of manners, religion and language. While murder was devoutly preached from the galleries of the minarets, and while the streets were filled with death and carnage, all those in whose houses any Frenchmen were lodged were eager to save them by concealment and to supply and anticipate all their wants.

An elderly woman in the quarter in which we lodged gave us to understand that as our [adjoining] wall was weak we had only to throw it down and seek shelter in her quarters. [Similarly] a neighbour, without being asked, sent us provisions at the expense of his own store – when no food was to be purchased in the town and everything announced approaching famine. He even removed everything from before our house that could render it conspicuous to the enemy, and went to smoke at our door – as if it was his own – in order to deceive any that might attack us.

Many other such anecdotes could be given of considerate attitudes that demonstrate the feelings of human nature at times in which it seemed to be entirely abandoned.

Following the bloody uprising at Cairo, Bonaparte endeavoured to maintain a policy of peaceful coexistence with the peoples of Egypt, but means were frequently adopted that were far from placatory. As the military campaign progressed, 'heads fell by the score' in yet more bloody conflicts. Entire communities were sacked and burned and Bedouin tribes had their flocks and cattle seized to meet the needs of the army. But Denon was fortunate. He had survived the military encounters and was ready to commence the next stage of his travels in search of the ancient monuments and antiquities of Egypt.

CHAPTER 9

On the Plain of Saqqara

The weeks immediately following the insurrection at Cairo ushered in a period of relative calm. This was welcome to Denon and his artist companions insofar as it enabled them to venture further afield into the neighbouring regions of Cairo in search of antiquities. The Plain of Saqqara awakened the curiosity of the French explorers and it soon became the object of their research.

Saqqara lies less than 20 kilometres south of Cairo and the pyramid group at Giza. It was the site of the principal necropolis of the ancient capital of Memphis and, like Giza, is renowned for its great pyramid structures. In antiquity, successive generations buried their dead at Saqqara and such was the extent of their building operations and excavations that the site became a veritable labyrinth of tombs, catacombs and subterranean galleries. The associated burial chambers had been plundered by tomb robbers centuries before the French arrived in Egypt – as was apparent from the numerous shafts and excavations they had left as evidence of their marauding depredations. Despite the tombs having been violated in this manner, archaeological remains were still to be found at Saqqara, as the French men of letters discovered when they commenced their own exploration of the site. First among their finds was a great hoard of mummified remains of the ibis.

In the iconography of ancient Egypt the ibis was a sacred bird whose distinctive physical features – pure white body, black neck and long curved bill – lent themselves to beautiful and expressive visual imagery and three-dimensional representation. The ibis was so revered that great numbers of these birds were preserved by mummification. The remains of the bird were frequently preserved in intricately woven, conical-shaped baskets or clay pots. In life, the ibis was to be found in many households and, in death, was venerated in much the same way that present-day families cherish the memory of their departed dogs and cats. Denon had the good fortune to be present when an excavation of the remains of many ibis was in progress:

> The vaults of Saqqara had just been opened and more than five hundred mummies of the ibis had been found. There is a considerable variety in the degree of care bestowed in embalming these birds. Nothing but the earthen pot, in which the whole is contained, is common to all. We may suppose that the ibis, as it destroys all reptiles, was in great veneration in a country in which these noxious creatures abound at a certain time of the year.

Denon and Citizen Geoffroi, a fellow savant with an interest in ornithology, were privileged to be given two specimens of the ibis, and immediately set about investigating them in the laboratory at the Institute of Egypt where the necessary means for research were available. Denon, pencil in hand, made illustrations of the skeletal finds for his *Journal*.

The ibis is now a relatively rare visitor to Egypt but in ancient times, according to the Greek historian Herodotus, 'the ibis abounded everywhere'. It was particularly common in the marshes of Upper Egypt. As these were progressively drained, the birds retreated to the lower provinces in search of food. By the late eighteenth century, their numbers had decreased considerably although Denon and his fellow travellers report seeing specimens on the shores of Lake Manzala close by present-day Port Said.

Snakes were the next subject to engage Denon's interest. They abounded in the hot marshlands bordering the Nile and filled the French travellers with the mixture of fear, fascination, loathing and respect commonly reserved for this particular reptile. Snakes, or 'serpents' as Denon usually refers to them in his *Journal*, were also venerated in the culture of ancient Egypt and were typically regarded as a source of evil and danger. However, the serpent, in the form of a cobra, was also perceived as the embodiment of protection and in this guise it frequently appeared in the ceremonial headdress of the pharaoh – as is to be seen, for example, featured on the celebrated golden mask of Tutankhamun.

At the time when Denon and his companions were making their discoveries of ancient Egyptian remains, snakes continued to occupy a prominent place in the popular imagination 'especially with regard to sorcery'. This remark is best explained with reference to a chance incident in which Denon found himself involved with his Commander-in-Chief.

The pair were out strolling one day when they were introduced to a group of snake charmers known as the Sect of Psylli. The two Frenchmen 'put many questions to them relative to the mystery of their sect'. They were interested, in particular, in how the snake charmers exercised the power of command over their reptiles. Denon and Bonaparte received answers 'with more assurance than intelligence' which made them all the more determined to see whether proof could be established in these matters. They decided to set the snake charmers a challenge to elicit evidence of their powers: 'Can you tell us,' asked the Commander, 'whether there are any serpents in the palace [where we have our lodgings], and, if there are, can you make them come out of their hiding places?' Denon continues:

> The snake charmers searched all the rooms and sometime later declared there was in fact a snake in the house. They then renewed their search to establish where it was hidden and [subsequently] made some convulsions in passing before a jar placed in a corner of one of the rooms. It was here they declared the serpent was – where indeed we actually found one. This [we considered] was a trick! We looked at each other and acknowledged they were very adroit!

Curious to find our more about the snake charmers, Denon made enquiries of the chief of the sect who was also the headman, or keeper, of the *okel* where the snake charmers lived. An okel was a form of hostel where unmarried men of a particular trade or profession could find accommodation for the night. For a poor street-trader, this

'Bread ovens are the first prerequisite of the army' proclaimed Bonaparte. Arabic ovens were fired with palm leaves and date stones which sent clouds of smoke billowing into the air.

usually meant little more than sleeping rough on the floor in the crowded room of a mud-brick shelter. But even lowly street traders had rites of initiation into their particular calling, as Denon learned.

The headman told Denon that he too could become initiated into the brotherhood of snake charmers through the ceremony of 'blowing into his spirit'. Denon remained enthusiastic – until he discovered exactly what 'blowing into his spirit' entailed: 'The headman . . . proposed to initiate me which I accepted. But when I learned, in the ceremony of initiation, that the grand-master spits into the mouth of the neophyte this circumstance cooled my ardour. I found that I could not prevail on myself to go through this trial!'

Still curious about the rites of initiation, Denon paid a sum of money to the headman, who agreed to allow him to witness their proceedings. Several snake charmers gathered together in preparation for the ceremony. With them they brought their serpents, which they let loose from a large leather sack in which they were kept; they then proceeded to make them raise their bodies by hissing in imitation of them. Denon noticed that it was exposure to the light that principally induced the reptiles' anger since, as soon as they were returned into the sack, 'their passion ceased and they no longer endeavoured to bite'. He also observed that 'when angry the neck was dilated for six inches below the head to the size of one's hand'.

Denon grew bold and ventured to handle the snakes himself. He had noticed how the snake charmers could manage the serpents perfectly well without fear of their fangs. This was achieved by taunting the snake with one hand, while restraining it firmly on the back of the head with the other. He comments: 'I did the same with one of the serpents with equal success – though much to the indignation of the performers themselves'. They clearly did not take kindly to being upstaged by this European in their midst!

The snake charmers were but a few of the many entertainers and itinerant vendors who thronged the streets of Egypt's principal towns vying for the attention of passers-by – and their money. Cairo, in particular, was a magnet for them and prompted the following observations from the men of letters as they recorded their impressions of the capital's vibrant street life:

Cairo's public places are filled with a throng of idle persons and individuals who are charlatans and tricksters occupied in amusing the crowds – as one sees in European towns. In the middle of the square, boutiques are set up on the boulders [scattered about the square] from which are sold tobacco, sugar cane, scrap and discarded objects. In this same place musicians assemble in the form of a circle and play instruments. One sees conjurers, who are very agile, playing with goblets and who have no less dexterity than our own. Other men entertain with dressed monkeys and play with scorpions and serpents with a familiarity that, at first encounter, astonishes.

The charlatans have great facility in training monkeys and several sorts of creatures. Among others they train goats and put saddles on them and place monkeys on 'horseback' and teach the goat to make leaps and bounds. They teach other animals to feign death. They have large animals, that the ancients called the dog-faced baboon, that are so well behaved and understanding they go from man to man holding out their hand making signs to put money there.

As Denon made more frequent forays around the neighbourhood of Cairo, he came to recognise the important part that camels played in Egyptian society. He noted: 'Camels do all the office of carts at Cairo. They bring there all the provisions and carry away the filth.' Camels were also used to transport water from the Nile. The water was contained in two great leather skins, slung one on each side of the animal, from which it was poured into drinking fountains or, on the required payment being made, into the vessels of passers-by in need of refreshment.

In due course the French men of letters and the more senior army officers acquired the skills of mounting a camel and of adapting themselves to its rolling gait – often with comical results. Camels were used only for making expeditions through the desert. When in town the principal means of conveyance was the humble ass, hence the donkey boy was

a common sight in all the major towns. This was particularly the case in Cairo where a veritable taxi service was available to the French as they journeyed from one part of the town to the other. It must have been a comical sight to see distinguished army officers – their feet almost trailing along the ground – careering along the streets at great speed mounted on the back of one of these small beasts!

Denon made frequent use of asses and donkeys and has the following to say about them:

> The saddle-horses and asses are chiefly devoted to transporting passengers from place to place and they are seen in every street saddled, bridled and always ready to start. The ass, which in Europe and the northern countries is heavy and dull, appears [to be] in its natural climate in Egypt. Here it enjoys all its powers in full perfection. It is healthy, active and cheerful – the mildest and safest animal to mount that one can possibly have. His natural pace is an amble or

Although much decayed, this ancient sycamore was venerated by the local people who considered it possessed magical powers. They attached fallen teeth and hair to it in the hope it would rejuvenate new growth. Bonaparte's soldiers caused pandemonium when they started to cut it down for firewood. *(Denon, British Library)*

A grove of sycamores on the island of El Rôda bordering the Nile. This was adopted as the pleasure garden of the Institute of Egypt. In the foreground are cultivated gardens from where produce is being loaded on to a camel. *(Denon, British Library)*

a gallop and, without fatiguing his rider, he carries him rapidly over the large plains that lie between different parts of this straggling city.

This mode of conveyance was so agreeable to me that I spent almost the whole day on the back of asses. I became known to all the people who let them out for hire and they were so used to my habits as to carry for me my drawing portfolio and chair. [They] served all day as my valets and, by double wages, I could get them to attend me mounted as I was and thus I passed from place to place, as rapidly as on the best horses, and could continue my employments a much longer time.

As Denon toured Cairo on the back of his donkey, his resourcefulness came to the attention of the members of the Institute of Egypt and he was commissioned to make drawings of subjects of interest in the vicinity. He required little encouragement. Such an undertaking was congenial to his active nature and creative disposition. His first venture led him to Old Cairo:

> It is at Old Cairo where cargoes are loaded and dispatched for Upper Egypt and where duties are levied on barques that traffic the river laden with corn, barley, beans, dates, sugar and animals. All this activity makes this part highly frequented and very commercial. Sailing ships [dhows] stop here regularly in great numbers. In general, the view of Old Cairo is pretty, animated and picturesque.

Continuing his services as illustrator for the Commission, Denon next visited the township of Bulaq. During the French occupation of Cairo, Bulaq was a separate township serving the capital as its inland port. Bulaq was the centre of a considerable trade in such goods as cotton, linen, henna, sugar and rice. Natron was also traded and was extracted from the soda lakes located to the north-west of the town.

Merchandise of all kinds reached Cairo's marketplaces by means of caravans. Caravans from North Africa sold exotic imported goods such as ostrich feathers, elephants' tusks, rhinoceros horn (used for the hilts of expensive daggers), musk, ebony and budgerigars. The caravan trade also reached Cairo from the interior of Africa and the Barbary Coast. On one occasion, Denon noticed an Arabian caravan arriving from Sinai bringing charcoal, gum and almonds. It consisted of no fewer than 500 camels.

The fact that this particular caravan had journeyed from Sinai fired Denon's imagination. It turned his attention from merchandise to what he enjoyed most of all – travel in search of adventure. The prospect of journeying across the desert to the north-east region of Egypt formed in his mind. He remarks: 'I was tempted to take the ancient journey of the Israelites'. He resolved to travel to the granite mountains where tradition holds God revealed Himself to Moses and gave him the Ten Commandments. Bonaparte consented and allowed Denon twelve days to make the expedition.

An armed escort was offered for the protection of the artist and his companions. One thing only was required, namely, a guide to escort the party across the inhospitable terrain. This should have been a formality but Denon had not reckoned on the hostility felt towards his fellow countrymen in the remoter regions of Egypt. When he asked an Arab chief who knew the region if he would act as a guide he received an outright refusal. Denon relates: 'He told me that for all the gold in the world he would not take charge of me and that it would be risking his life and that of every individual in the caravan. Two powerful tribes [in the region] had vowed vengeance against the French.' This information restrained even Denon's enthusiasm. Some other adventure had to be found.

As he was coming to terms with his disappointment, he received news that Bonaparte was sending a detachment of soldiers south under the command of General Belliard. This journey offered Denon the prospect of inspecting the ancient necropolis of Memphis at Saqqara. Bonaparte agreed to Denon's request to travel with the military. He issued the requisite papers and within a few hours Denon was on his way.

It took the troops a day and a night to make the journey by river to Saqqara. The wind had been slack and their progress was slow. The next day Denon set his sights on the extensive pyramid and temple complex for which Saqqara is famed:

We were still a league short of Saqqara [but] I took a view of the pyramids as far as I could distinguish them – which at this distance seemed to occupy a space of two leagues. Despite [being] so far from the river, I could distinguish that the nearest, which is of middling size, is composed of stages rising one above the other. After this come into view other small pyramids almost destroyed. Half a league further is one whose base seems as wide as those of Giza but of less elevation and little decayed. Further still is the largest of all those of Saqqara whose form is irregular.

Denon's estimation of the site at Saqqara as being 'two leagues' was a reasonable one. In modern-day terms the pyramid and temple complex is known to extend for some six kilometres. His pyramid 'composed of stages' was the so-called Step Pyramid of the Third Dynasty ruler Djsoer. This was conceived by the architect and man of learning Imhotep, to whom belongs the honour of constructing the first pyramid and, thus, the first large stone building. Imhotep's vast complex is contained within a perimeter wall no less than 1,600 metres in extent.

At the time of Denon's visit, the lesser features at the site would doubtless have presented only a confused array of indistinct mounds. Subsequent archaeological research has established the presence of no fewer than fifteen royal pyramids and numerous associated tombs for persons of noble standing and their families.

By evening, Denon and the troops had arrived at a small township known as Saoyeh. Everyone in the party had to accept improvised accommodation including the leader of the detachment General Belliard. Fortunately for Denon he got on well with Belliard; indeed, he enjoyed cordial relations with all the French senior commanding officers – perhaps the personal friendship he enjoyed with Bonaparte had a bearing on the respect he received from the military. His gregarious nature also made him a popular figure.

An indication of the close ties Denon maintained with General Belliard is evidenced by the following anecdote:

General Belliard obligingly offered to share his dwelling with me. This was so small that our beds fitted the whole room such that we were obliged to turn them out, when we wanted to set up our table and then to remove the table when we had need of our beds. This union proved as happy as it was close since we did not quit each other's society during the whole campaign.

The second night both our kitchen and our table were overthrown but, [being] as phlegmatic as Muslims, we did not think of quitting the place and, besides, irrespective of this accident, our dwelling was the best and most respectable in appearance of the whole village.

Denon noted down his observations of the dwellings in which he and the troops were billeted. He was particularly intrigued by their construction and the local people's use of mud-brick as a building material.

In this part of Egypt all the buildings are made of mud and chopped straw that are dried in the sun. The stairs, window-openings, hearths, utensils – and even furniture – are all of the same simple material.

If it were possible that the invariable order of the climate that nature has here fixed should be for a moment changed – and that unusual winds should arrest and dissolve in rain some of the groups of clouds that the north wind perpetually draws over their heads in summer – the

Pyramids from the Old and Middle Kingdoms south of Cairo between El-Fayum and Dahshur. Denon was only able to view these through his telescope but the French engineers made accurate surveys of them. Top: The brick pyramid of Amenemmes III at Hawara north of the ancient Canal of Joseph. Above: The brick pyramid of Sesostris II neighbouring the village of El-Lahun. The pyramid is much collapsed, especially at the top which three engineers have ascended – a fourth contemplates the last part of the ascent.

towns and villages would be softened down and liquefied in a few hours. Thanks to the climate, a house built of this frail material will generally last the life of the builder.

On completing his study of Egyptian building construction, Denon learned that the military needed to secure additional provisions before further progress could be made. The French decided to adopt a tactic of intimidation upon the local people as practised by the Mamelukes, whose custom it was to levy a form of land tax, called the *miri*, on the villages and townships that fell within their particular domain. In the case of communities that showed reluctance to pay, the Mamelukes sent an armed contingent to collect the required revenues by force. The Turks would parade their armed men before the recalcitrant community, flashing their sabres under the gaze of the terrified onlookers. This was usually sufficient to secure the required payment.

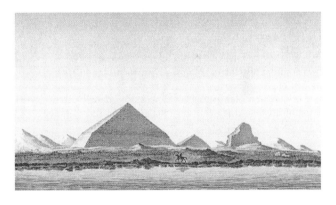

Top right: The Stepped Pyramid of Sneferu at Meidum. Two great towers of dressed stone rise above a mound of debris which has now been cleared. Middle right, below and right: Three views of the Bent Pyramid of Sneferu at Dahshur. Building commenced at too steep an angle which imposed stresses on the masonry – with the threat of collapse. The structure was continued at a shallower incline giving it a bent appearance. *(Jomard, Author's Collection)*

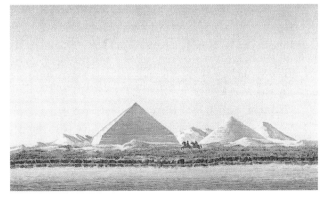

It was no surprise to Denon, therefore, looking out from his small room the following morning, to see a column of 300 French soldiers marching off in the direction of the local village – their weapons clearly visible. Some time later came evidence that the tactic of intimidation had worked – the troops returned leading an impressive herd of buffalo and a supply of horses. With these General Belliard's detachment could now continue its reconnaissance of the area.

When Denon had earlier scoured the horizon through his telescope, noting the locations of the various pyramids, his gaze had been drawn to the great tower-like structure of the Pyramid of Meidum. It was towards this that he and the troops now made their way:

> The first journey brought me near the Pyramid of Meidum that I had already seen at a distance. I was now no more than half a league from it but was separated by the Canal of Joseph, and another smaller one, and we were not provided with a boat. However, with the assistance of an excellent glass, and as clear fine weather as possible, I was able to make my observations upon it almost as well as if I touched it.
>
> It is built on a platform made by one of the secondary hills of the Libyan chain. The form of the pyramid is five large retreating steps or stages. The calcareous stone of which it is composed is more or less friable. The base and lowest stage are more worn than any of the others and, in the middle of the second stage, several courses have undergone the same decay.
>
> On passing the village of Meidum . . . I had an opportunity of observing three sides of this pyramid. It appears an opening has been attempted at the second stage on the north side. The rubbish, covered with drifted sand, rises as high as this opening and covers all but the angles of the first stage. The ruin begins at the third stage, of which about a third part remains. The entire height of all that is left of this pyramid is about two hundred feet.

As the French convoy departed Meidum, Denon was able to study the nature of the country through which they were travelling:

> All the land we passed was abundantly fertile [and] sown with wheat, sainfoin, barley, beans, lentils and *doura* or sago which is a kind of millet that is cultivated almost universally in Upper Egypt. While the grain of this plant is still milky, the peasants roast it like maize and chew the green stalk like sugar cane. The leaves are food for cattle and the *medulla*, or pith, when dry serves for tinder. The cane supplies the place of wood for firing and heating the ovens. The flour is made of the grain itself and cakes are made of the flour – but none of these parts are wholesome.

The expedition progressed to Meimund, described by Denon as 'a very rich village with ten thousand inhabitants'. Like others of its kind, it was surrounded with dunghills and heaps of rubbish which, in so flat a landscape, formed hills that could be discerned from a considerable distance. Curiously, these provided a form of social meeting place for the elders of the village:

> Every evening each of these eminences is seen covered with people who recline upon them and breathe their noisome vapours, smoking their pipes and observing if all is quiet in the fields. These heaps of dung and rubbish produce many inconveniences. They obscure the houses, infect the air and fill the eyes of the people with an acrid dust, mixed with minute straws, that is one of the numerous causes of the diseases of the eye to which the people of Egypt are so much exposed.

From Meimund the party proceeded to El-Eaffer, 'a pretty village in an excellent country'. Gum arabic was collected here that the local people obtained by making an incision into the stem of a species of mimosa which the French botanists called *nilotica* or Egyptian thorn. This was also valued for the perfume given off by its 'fragrant golden buds'. El-Eaffer provided the party with more horses and the officers with an excellent breakfast. Outside the village a dozen or so Arabs were met with at an encampment. This scene provided Denon with fresh material for his *Journal*:

> I was afforded a view of the Chief's tent that was composed of nine poles supporting an indifferent woollen cloth. Beneath this were all the articles of his household furniture consisting of a mat, a carpet – of the same stuff as the tent – two sacks, one of wheat for the man and another of barley for his mare, a hand-mill to grind corn, a chicken pen, a jar for his hens to lay in, pots, coffeepots and cups. The women were hideous and likewise the children.

From El-Eaffer the party moved on to another settlement called Benniali. Here they were refused all hospitality until a show of military intimidation, and a meeting with the local sheikhs, produced a supply of fresh horses and tribute money. Immediately thereafter an unfortunate incident occurred that was the cause of further agitation. Having been on the march for several hours the soldiers had decided it was time to eat. Their preparations for this seemingly innocent activity were the cause of the tense atmosphere that prevailed. Denon relates: 'We heard an outcry [from the local people] that we thought proceeded from some terrible catastrophe – but it was only occasioned by our soldiers cutting down the withered branches of a decayed tree to make a fire to boil their soup.' What the soldiers did not realise was that the tree they had chosen to cut down was venerated by the local people, by whom it was believed to be endowed with special powers.

Denon went to inspect the tree and was struck by the extent of its decay. Only one of its branches bore any leaves and the others, which were dry and broken off, were carefully preserved at the very spot where they had fallen. He made other discoveries. He found locks of hair and teeth attached by nails. On making enquiries about these he was told the hair had been left by women 'in order to fix the roving affection of their husbands'. The teeth had belonged to adults who, believing the tree had miraculous properties, left them in the hope of being granted a second set. Having heard these explanations, Denon had a better appreciation of the reaction of the local people, furious at the sight of their precious tree being chopped up for firewood.

Soon after this incident General Belliard returned to Cairo. His reconnaissance of the region was completed and Denon's sketchbook was filled with images of antiquities. Denon was now at liberty to extend his exploration to the Fayum region.

CHAPTER 10

In the Province of Fayum

The Fayum province of Egypt is an extensive fertile region lying about 60 kilometres to the south-west of Cairo. Its fertility derives from the freshwater Lake Moeris (Birket Qârun) which is connected by an irrigation network to the River Nile. These circumstances so favoured the region in ancient times that Egypt's capital was relocated there during the period of the Middle Kingdom (2055–1650 BC).

Denon commenced his exploration of the Fayum district by making researches at Beni Suef and the surrounding locality. In the late eighteenth century Beni Suef was already an important centre of population. Moreover, sited on a bend in the River Nile where centuries of rich alluvial silt had accumulated, it was at the heart of one of the most cultivable regions of Egypt. Dhows moored at Beni Suef to disembark their plentiful cargoes from the surrounding countryside. The township itself, however, was undistinguished. It consisted of a walled enclosure containing a number of mosques, with their attendant minarets, nestled amid groups of modest mud-brick houses.

Denon remained at Beni Suef for some time but found 'little inviting to the artist'. This did not deter him from making excursions into the surrounding countryside. He was not able to visit the Greek-named site of Herakleopolis Magna, significant for its Pharaonic temples, but he did venture into the desert to glean what he could of the remains of several villages he found there. He compiled the following rather bleak account:

> The mouth of this valley [extending beyond Beni Suef] exhibits little but a dreary plain, the only part of which is a narrow slip of land on the bank of the river. Some vestiges of villages, overwhelmed by sand, may be discovered and present the afflicting sight of the devastation produced by the continual encroachment of the desert.
>
> Nothing is so melancholy to the feelings as to march over these ruined villages and to tread under foot the roofs of the houses and the tops of the minarets – and to think that there were once here cultivated fields, flourishing trees and the habitations of man.
>
> Everything has disappeared, silence is within and around every wall and the deserted villages are like the dead – whose skeletons strike terror.

Turning his attention from the arid regions, Denon directed his curiosity to the measures taken in previous ages to contain the River Nile in order to control the flood waters created by the annual inundation. Signs of defensive works and embankments were still evident and were kept in a good state of repair by the local people to ensure the correct irrigation of the land and also to avert the ever-present threat of flooding:

Denon at work as the sun is about to set. He remarks: 'I have represented myself in the costume essential for long marches – with my equipment. I had little time for the care of my person. [He was often made fun of by the soldiers for his dishevelled appearance.] I was constantly occupied with my *Journal* and drawings. I never left sight of my portfolio; I carried it everywhere and at night it served as my pillow'. *(Denon, British Library)*

The elevation of the Nile and the raising of its banks have made it an artificial canal. The Fayum [region] would be under water if the Caliph Joseph had not raised up new dykes upon the old ones and dug a parallel canal below Beni Suef to restore to the river part of the water that pours every year into this vast basin.

If it were not for the causeways that stop the inundation, the great swells would soon convert the whole province into a large lake. This threatened to happen twenty-five years ago by an extraordinary inundation in which the river ran over the banks at [the township of] Hilaon. It was feared the province would remain under water or that the stream would resume [the course of] an ancient channel which it was evident it had occupied in remote ages. To remedy this inconvenience, a graduated dyke has been raised near Hilaon where there is a sluice erected.

As soon as the inundation has reached the proper height to water the province without drowning it, [the sluice] divides the mass of water, takes the quantity necessary to irrigate the Fayum and turns off the remainder by forcing it back into the river through other canals of a deeper cut.

Despite his appreciation of the efforts made by the Egyptians to regulate the flow of the annual inundation, Denon considered their hydrological and water-engineering principles could be improved. During their relatively short occupation of Egypt, the French engineers made extensive topographical surveys of the River Nile and other watercourses in order to gain a better understanding of the irrigation of the Nile Valley. For example, in the province of El-Minya, at a location north of the temple site of Beni Hasan, no fewer than 28 sectional profiles were surveyed, including the constructional details of bridges and embankments. At Asyût, about 140 kilometres south of the Fayum district, the topography of the Nile Valley was also surveyed in a series of traverses, and traces were taken of the ancient canal at Abu El-Khyr. And in the north, by Alexandria, further land-surveys were made and a series of measurements taken of the depth of the bed of Lake Maryût.

An opportunity now arose for Denon to join a detachment of soldiers with instructions to reconnoitre the countryside and levy provisions from any villages found in the locality of Beni Suef. This was a congenial undertaking since it entailed making a further excursion through Egypt's fertile region. Denon considered this a veritable Garden of Eden:

> In Egypt, when nature is charming, it is so in spite of all that men can add to it. Nature here produces spontaneously groves of palm under which flourish the orange tree, sycamore, opuntia, banyan, acacia and pomegranate. These trees form groups of the finest mixture of foliage and verdure. When these delightful thickets are surrounded – as far as the eye can reach – with fields covered with ripe *doura*, with mature sugar canes, with fields of wheat, flax and trefoil [they] spread a downy carpet over the land as the inundation retires.
>
> In the months of our European winter, which [in Egypt] promises the abundance of [our] summer, we may well agree with the traveller [who considers] nature has organised this country in a most astonishing manner. It only requires woody hills, with brooks flowing down their declivities, and a government that would make the people industrious – and prevent the incursion of the Bedouin – to render it the best and most beautiful country on the face of the earth.

Crossing this fertile region where, Denon remarks, 'the eye discovers twenty villages at once', the excursion party arrived at the township of Dindyra where they stopped for the night. Denon found an opportunity here to satisy his wish to survey the antiquities. In particular, the pyramid of El-Lahun had captured his admiring gaze. To him it seemed 'like a fortress raised to command the province':

> The Pyramid of El-Lahun, the most shattered of all the pyramids that I have seen, is also that which is built with the least magnificence. It is constructed of masses of calcareous stones that serve as points of support to heaps of unbaked bricks. Perishable as this kind of building is, and perhaps more ancient than the pyramids of Memphis, it still holds together. So favourable is the climate of Egypt to these monuments that [they] endure for ages here but would fall to pieces under the rigour of a single European winter.

Research has established the brick pyramid of El-Lahun to be that of Senusret II. As Denon observed, the core of the pyramid is constructed from mud-bricks that have been secured by four great limestone retaining walls, sections of which still remain. Excavation has revealed that the builders took advantage of the natural terrain by siting the core of the structure around and upon an outcrop of rock. The shattered appearance of the pyramid, remarked upon by Denon, can be attributed to the removal, in previous ages, of its polished limestone outer casing. This did not deter the French engineers from taking measurements of the weathered profile. They estimated the surviving base to measure 60 metres with an elevation of about 20 metres.

His survey of the pyramid site at El-Lahon completed, Denon travelled back to Beni Suef with the detachment of soldiers. His journey was not without incident:

> There are some unlucky moments when everything one does is followed by danger or accident. As I returned from the journey to Beni Suef, the General [responsible for the detachment of soldiers] instructed me to carry an order to the head of the column. A soldier who was

marching out of his rank turned suddenly to the left, as I was passing to the right, and presented his bayonet against me. Before I could avoid it I was unhorsed by the blow and, at the same time, was thrown down. 'There is one savant less' said he while [I was] falling – for, with them, everyone who was not a soldier was a savant. However, some piastres [coins] that I had in my pocket received the point of the bayonet and I escaped with only a torn coat.

On 10 December, General Desaix returned from Cairo to Beni Suef bringing with him some twelve hundred cavalry, six pieces of artillery and between two and three hundred infantry. These resources increased the overall strength of his division to some three thousand infantry and eight pieces of light artillery, enabling the General to carry out Bonaparte's most recent command. This was to pursue the Mameluke leader Murad Bey and endeavour to engage him on the field of battle. It was known the wily Murad had retreated south, into Upper Egypt, which was therefore the direction General Desaix and his troops planned to march. The enterprise entailed making a great journey, almost the length of Egypt, to the cataract region.

The prospect of accompanying General Desaix and his company of men filled Denon with a sense of patriotism and, more particularly, the anticipation that he would fulfil his desired objective. He realised that, as the company progressed into Upper Egypt, he had every prospect of observing and recording the ancient temple sites. He could hardly contain his excitement:

> I [anticipated] marching cheerfully with the pleasing hope of arriving first at Syene and of realizing all my projects and seeing the object of my journey fulfilled. In fact, the most interesting part of my travels was now beginning. I was going to break into, as it were, a new country. [I would] be the first to see without prejudice, and to make researches in, a part of the earth hitherto covered with the veil of mystery and for two thousand years shut out from the curiosity of Europeans.

His spirits elevated, Denon quitted Beni Suef on 17 December amid Desaix's great company of soldiers: 'The spectacle was very fine. I regretted being too busy to be able to make a sketch of it. Our column extended a league in length and everything breathed joy and hope.'

Denon's romantic anticipations of adventure were quickly supplanted by the harsh realities of the situation in which he found himself. The first day's march was singularly unrewarding since the route taken by the convoy passed through countryside that was bleak and inhospitable. It also bore signs of devastation. It was apparent that several villages had been abandoned by their owners. Taxed to the point of extortion, they had deserted their homes and were compelled to live the nomadic life of marauding brigands. Denon explains the circumstances of these unfortunate people:

> At the close of day we were saddened by the view of uncultivated land and a deserted village. How many melancholy ideas are combined in the silence of night, the neglect of culture and the ruins of the habitations of man.
>
> Tyranny begins this disastrous waste; despair and crime finish it. This is how it happens in Egypt. When the master of a village has exacted from it all that it can provide – and the misery of the inhabitants is further reduced to extremity by fresh demands – the villagers, in

despair, oppose force with force. They are then treated as open rebels and each party has recourse to arms.

An hour before sunset, on the first day of marching, the party reached El-Berankah where the infantry and officers made camp. Rising early to take advantage of the cool morning weather, they made their way to the next large village, called Bebeh, which Denon describes as being 'nothing remarkable except that it possesses the wrist of St George – a relic that should recommend it to every pious son of chivalry'.

As it progressed, the retinue was delayed by several accidents. Manoeuvring the heavy gun carriages and fieldpieces across the desert plains proved troublesome, especially where irrigation channels and dried-up watercourses were encountered. However, the time required for the artillery to be brought up gave the main party a moment of respite. The infantry sought such shade as they could find out in the open and replenished their water bottles. In the meantime an incident occurred which although of small consequence touched Denon, who noted the circumstances in his *Journal*. Denon's anecdote can be introduced with the following generalizations.

One of the hazards of the military was to be pursued – with remarkable stealth – by opportunists, knaves, thieves and robbers. They would creep up on the unsuspecting columns of soldiers, especially under the cloak of darkness, and take away literally anything that was movable. Their artifice and cunning were boundless. Officers would wake to find their horses had been spirited away – with only their tethers left behind as evidence of their existence – and foot soldiers would discover, to their dismay, that their boots were missing. The incident Denon recorded suggests these opportunists, if that is how they may be described, acquired their skills at an early age:

A criminal came before General Desaix. Those who brought him said: 'He is a thief. He has stolen some guns from the volunteers and has been taken in the act.' We were surprised to see the robber [to be] a boy twelve years old, beautiful as an angel with a large sabre-wound in his arm that he looked at without emotion. He presented himself to the General, whom he perceived to be his judge, with an air of confidence and simplicity. So great is the charm of native grace that not a person could preserve his anger.

He was asked who bid him steal these guns? 'Nobody.' What had induced him to do it? 'I do not know. It was the great God'. Had he parents? 'Only a mother, very poor and blind.' The General told him if he confessed who sent him, he should be released; if not, he should be punished as he deserved. 'I have already told you nobody sent me; it was God alone that put it into my head.' Then, laying his cap at the feet of the General he said: 'There is my head, you can cut it off'!

'Poor little wretch,' said the General. 'Let him go.' [The boy] saw his sentence was passed. He looked at the General then at the soldier who was leading him off and, guessing the meaning of what he could not understand, he parted with a smile of confidence.

An unusual event followed this moving scene. In the midst of the desert it started to rain. This induced memories of home in the minds of Denon and his fellow travellers. Denon remarks: 'It gave us for a moment a sensation that recalled Europe to our minds and the first soft showers of spring.' Some minutes later these pleasant evocations were disturbed. The party learned that Mamelukes were waiting to ambush them with an

Interrogation of a boy thief. General Desaix, seated beneath a palm tree, questions a twelve-year-old boy accused of stealing – Denon, hand on chin, listens to the proceedings. In the foreground Jean Rapp, aide de camp to Desaix, turns to Officer Douzelot to pass some remark. The boy is about to place his cap on the ground with the invitation to Desaix to cut off his head! 'Let him go,' responds Desaix, impressed by the boy's courage. *(Denon, British Library)*

army of local people 'about two leagues off'. Everyone was immediately put on the alert expecting to do battle that evening or, at the latest, the next day.

On approaching the village of Fechneh the French came upon the Mamelukes who initially allowed the party to approach to within 'half a cannon shot'. They then resorted to their evasive tactics of retreating out of harm's way.

The French later discovered the main Mameluke forces were encamped at the township of Saste Elsayeneh, about a league further off, but were prevented from engaging them since their own artillery was still in the rear. The problem was caused by the difficulty of manoeuvring the heavy guns over yet more irrigation channels that criss-crossed their path. As a consequence, Saste Elsayeneh was not reached until late evening, by which time the Mamelukes, hearing of the approach of the French, had made yet another tactical retreat.

The French themselves departed from Saste Elsayeneh at daybreak on 19 December. As they progressed they left behind the fertile regions and headed further west towards the desert. In ancient times a great canal called the Bahr Yûsef had been cut at this location running along the western bank of the River Nile. Its headwater was located about 60 kilometres south of El-Minya from where it ran parallel to the Nile, with which it was united about 40 kilometres south of Cairo. At the time of the French survey of this region, Denon noted that stretches of the watercourse had fallen into neglect:

> In this [region] I did not find the straight canal as it is marked on all the charts. Only an actual survey of the levels can give knowledge of the system and regulation of the irrigations and of the works [that can] be attributed respectively to art [engineering] and to nature in this interesting part of Egypt.
>
> Towards evening we forded the canal of Bahr Yûsef which, at this place, appears to be only the receptacle of the flood waters because it is the lowest part of the valley and in no part [is it] the work of human industry.
>
> All these questions will be determined by a grand operation to be performed in time of peace, from which the best way may be suggested of recovering the advantages of this mysterious canal now lost or sunk to neglect.

Denon's remark – 'will be determined by a grand operation' – is worthy of comment. Denon was anticipating a time when Egypt would be colonised by France, a state of affairs that would enable the French engineers to survey the Nile Valley, restore the ancient waterways and improve the system of irrigation with modern technological advances. None of this was destined to take place, however, since the French were subsequently obliged to surrender Egypt to the British. During Denon's travels, these events lay in the future and he was free to speculate about the nature of Egypt's waterways and her system of irrigation. He reflected further on the subject:

> From a simple inspection of the different levels, I believe this part of Egypt has become lower than the elevated banks of the Nile and that, after the general inundation, the drainage of the water collects at this spot.
>
> In Upper Egypt I have seen the effect of the filtration that occurs there. The waters, having neither canals nor valleys through which they can be carried off after the inundation, the entire mass penetrates the whole depth of the vegetable soil. At the bottom of this it encounters a bed

of clay that it cannot penetrate. It returns [therefore] to the river by small streamlets when the fall of the flood has sunk it below the surface of this bed of clay.

Not having encountered the enemy, Denon and the division of soldiers with which he was travelling continued their journey south, advancing all the time nearer to the desert region. Two buzzards flew overhead prompting the ever-alert artist to comment: 'They were smaller than those of Europe as is the case with every animal common to the two continents.' The party progressed to the edge of the plain that forms a border between the desert and the cultivated region with the mountains 'still two leagues off'. They halted for the night near the village of Benachie 'in a fine wood of palm trees'.

The following day another pursuit of the Mamelukes ensued. At daybreak, the party departed 'in the constant hope of reaching the enemy'. To achieve this the rearguard, with its heavy artillery, had marched through the night. The Mamelukes, unencumbered by heavy guns, had the open desert before them providing endless opportunities to skirmish with the French and, as Denon comments, 'to defy our eagerness'. In spite of this hazard, the party made progress until the hardships of the march and the rigours of the climate began to take their toll, especially on the men and horses drawing the heavy artillery pieces. It was therefore decided to make a brief halt at the township of Behnesa. This circumstance was congenial to Denon since Behnesa had been built upon the site of the Graeco-Roman city of Oxyrhynchus. A sojourn here offered the prospect of discovering antiquities.

Today, Oxyrhynchus is best known to scholars for the many papyri that have been discovered bearing texts written in Arabic, Demotic-Egyptian, Greek, Hebrew and Latin. These tell of a once-thriving metropolis set within a walled enclosure, whose gates led to arcaded streets adorned with public buildings, a temple, theatre, hippodrome, gymnasium and public baths. Little wonder that Denon was eager to undertake researches at this site. His hopes, though, were not entirely fulfilled:

Behnesa was built on the ruins of the ancient Oxyrhynchus, the capital of the thirty-third Nome or province of Egypt. [Contemporary reckoning equates this to the nineteenth province.] Nothing, however, remains of this city but some fragments of stone pillars and marble columns. In the mosque, a single column [is] left standing – along with its capital – and part of the entablature. These show it is the fragment of a portico of the Composite Order.

It was not without some danger that I arrived here alone, half an hour before the Division. It would have been attended with still greater risk for me to have remained behind. I therefore had time only to take a general view, on horseback, of this desolate country and to sketch the single standing column – the only remains of its former magnificence. This solitary monument brings a melancholy sensation to the mind. Oxyrhynchus, once a metropolis surrounded by a fertile plain, has disappeared beneath the sand.

The waters of the irrigation canal, and the fertile nature of the countryside that it sustained, provided Denon with some compensation for his disappointment at not finding the classical antiquities in a more complete state:

This fine canal seemed to our sight to offer its verdant banks so as to console us for the prospect of the desert that lay before our eyes. The desert presents such a gloomy idea to all who have once beheld it. Its barrenness oppresses the mind by the immensity of distance. Its appearance, where level, is only a dreary waste and, where broken by hills, shows only another feature of decay and decrepitude. The silence of inanimate nature reigns throughout undisturbed.

The next day the order was given to depart and the great phalanx of men, with their horses and equipment, set forth. They followed the course of the canal that, at its widest, appeared to Denon 'to resemble our river La Marne'. Shortly after setting out, an almighty explosion rent the air, disposing the French to fear that they were either under attack or that it signalled the commencement of hostilities. Nothing more was heard, however, and the division progressed without further alarm. It was later discovered that the powder arsenal of the Mamelukes had caught fire, rending the air with its sound. This appeared to have created consternation and disarray in the camp of the enemy since the French, shortly afterwards, discovered a flock of about eight hundred sheep wandering on the plain. They had evidently taken advantage of the confusion and had made their escape. Their reprieve was short-lived; Denon remarks that 'in the evening they consoled our troops for the fatigues of the day'.

The next village the French encountered was that of Elsack. From its desolate state it appeared to have been pillaged by the Mamelukes. Denon comments: 'We arrived . . . too late to save this village. In a quarter of an hour there remained nothing at all in the houses, literally nothing. The Arab inhabitants had fled into the fields. We invited them back [whereupon] they answered coldly: "Why should we return to our houses?" We had nothing to reply to this laconic answer.' The party continued its journey south and encountered a watercourse which Denon refers to as Lake Bathan. That night they slept at a large village called Tata that was inhabited by Copts. For their sleeping quarters Denon and Desaix were fortunate enough to commandeer the residence of an Arab chief who had fled to join the forces of Murad Bey. Denon relates: 'He had left at our disposal mattresses on which we reposed a delicious night for we could rarely be lodged so commodiously.' On the following day, 22 December, the party crossed whole fields of peas and barley that were in flower – testimony to the fertility of the region – and by noon they had arrived at El-Minya.

Denon describes El-Minya as 'a large and handsome town in which there had formerly been a temple of Anubis'. In Egyptian iconography, Anubis was deified in the form of a seated black dog, or a dog endowed with the head of a man. His power was connected to the rituals of embalming and mummification and later came to be associated with the cult of Osiris. El-Minya is sited on the west bank of the Nile about 220 kilometres south of Cairo where, as already noted, the flood plain makes the land very fertile.

During Denon's travels in the region, El-Minya was the capital of the Muhafaza province and was the meeting point for various caravan routes. Time did not allow Denon to make extensive explorations of the township but he did chance upon a number of elegant columns adorning a large mosque, that had been hewn from granite and were well cut with fine mouldings. Unknown to Denon, lying some 20 kilometres to the north of El-Minya was the necropolis of Beni Hasan where numerous small tombs are sited on the east bank of the Nile. These were the resting places of the governors of the province and other persons of distinction.

In the late eighteenth century, El-Minya possessed many of the features of a Nile-bank town including a waterfront for the loading and unloading of goods, a walled enclosure, mosques, public buildings and several large houses for the ruling classes. The sight of these prompted Denon to comment: 'El-Minya was the most handsome town we had yet seen. It had good streets, substantial houses and was very well situated with the Nile flowing through a large and cheerful channel.'

From El-Minya, Desaix's party headed further south until they reached El-Casar where the country was richer and more abundant than any so far encountered. Denon enthused: 'The villages are so numerous and contiguous to each other that, from the middle of the plain, I reckoned [there to be] twenty four around me. They are planted with trees so thickly interwoven that they put me in mind of the descriptions travellers have given of the islands in the Pacific Ocean.'

The next morning the party continued their journey south and by midday reached a point on the Nile between the Roman city of Antinoopolis, situated on the east bank, and Hermopolis Magna – modern-day El-Ashmûnein – sited on the west bank. Antinoopolis had been founded by the Roman emperor Hadrian (Publius Hadrianus) in AD 130. By his decree the township was established in accordance with Roman precepts of town planning and civic design.

With only limited time available to him, Denon decided not to journey to Antinoopolis. A number of his artist companions did undertake the journey and found architectural remains there that gave breathtaking indications of the former splendour of the township. They discovered long streets that bore signs of having been lined with elegant columns and arcades with a central avenue more than 1,300 metres in extent. The principal streets terminated in city gates and one was adorned with a triumphal arch. In addition, there were the remains of public buildings, including great baths, a theatre and a circus – or hippodrome – where charioteers had raced. Yet again, and tragically for posterity, over the centuries the fine limestone casings and decorations to these structures had been removed, and had been ground to powder in the mills to provide lime for the local farmers to spread on their fields.

Denon resolved to direct his attention to Hermopolis Magna. This was the site of an ancient township that had served as the capital of the fifteenth province of Upper Egypt. It was also where the deity Thoth had been worshipped. In Greek mythology, Thoth was identified with Hermes who possessed universal accomplishments in science, the arts and oratory. Hermopolis Magna had flourished in Graeco-Roman times and was renowned for a majestic temple, in honour of Thoth, fronted by a magnificent portico. Denon provides the following account:

I was enchanted with delight at thus seeing the first fruit of my labours. For, excepting the pyramids, this was the first monument that gave me an idea of the ancient Egyptian [style of] architecture. [These were] the first stones I had seen that had preserved their original construction, without being altered or deformed by the works of modern times, and had remained untouched for four thousand years. [They] gave me an idea of the immense range and high perfection to which the arts had arrived in this country.

A peasant, who might be drawn out from his cottage and placed before such a building as this, would believe that there must exist a wide difference between himself and the beings who were able to construct it. And, without having any idea of architecture, he would say: 'This is the work of a god. A man could not dare inhabit it.'

Once Denon had completed his sketches of the portico of Hermopolis, his party continued their journey half a league further south from El-Ashmûnein to Mallawi where they spent the night. Denon found Mallawi larger and more beautiful than El-Minya, having regular streets and a well-built bazaar. The military also found a large house, belonging to one of the Mamelukes, which they promptly set about fortifying as a defensive position.

The French party had arrived late and Denon lost no time in going up and down the town in search of sleeping quarters. He had to accept lodgings on the outskirts but was lucky to find a handsome and commodious house. Being fatigued by the day's travels, he was relieved at the prospect of enjoying Egyptian hospitality. In this instance, however, it left much to be desired:

The owner was sitting at his ease before his door and beckoned me into a chamber where I found General Belliard who had already taken advantage of his hospitality. I was hardly asleep

Ruins of the Temple of Hermopolis Magna. The shafts of the columns of the portico are in the style of bundles of reeds with papyrus capitals. They supported a cornice made from five massive blocks of stone each 22 feet long. These bore decorations – executed in brilliant colour – celebrating one of its builders, Alexander the Great. Nothing now remains of this splendid monument – its limestone was crushed for fertiliser. *(Denon, University of Edinburgh)*

when I was awakened by an intolerable restlessness that I took to be the beginning of an inflammatory fever. After remaining a long time in this state of agitation, I found my companion as ill as myself. We both started up and left the room and, looking at each other by moonlight, [we saw] our whole skin was red, inflamed and our features hardly distinguishable. On further examination we found ourselves covered with vermin of every kind.

The houses in Upper Egypt are nothing but vast pigeon lofts in which the owner reserves to himself only a room or two for his convenience. There he lodges, along with poultry of all kinds, and all the vermin that they engender between them – which it is part of his daily employment to hunt. At night, the toughness of his skin defies their bites and thus our host, who intended to do us a civility, could not conceive the reason of our quitting him so abruptly.

We got rid as well as we could of the most troublesome of the pests, vowing faithfully never again to accept such hospitality.

Denon and the army journeyed on until they reached the neighbouring township of Beni Sanet. On the next day, 26 December, the party was once more on the march, this time heading for Asyût. The company followed the course of the Nile giving Denon further opportunities to observe the great river and the irrigation systems put in place by the local people. A large bridge caught his attention since such structures were an uncommon sight. He also saw a lock and a system of floodgates concerning which he remarks: 'These Arabian works were doubtless made on ancient models and are as useful as thay are well contrived.' More generally, Denon considered the irrigation waters were better managed in Upper Egypt and were ordered 'with more intelligence and affected with simpler means than in the lower provinces'.

Denon, in the company of General Desaix and the French army, had now marched more than 250 kilometres south of their original point of departure in the Fayum region. They were in the very heart of Egypt. For Denon this held out the exciting prospect of undertaking further searches for antiquities.

CHAPTER 11

Under the Shadow of the Libyan Mountains

Denon and the French army had made good progress in their march south and were now in the vicinity of Asyût, about mid-way between Cairo and Aswan. However, this meant the lines of communication of the military were severely extended and it was therefore necessary for the French to establish a secure garrison in the region. The township of Asyût was a natural choice.

In Pharaonic times, Asyût was the capital of the thirteenth province of Upper Egypt and was also the site of the ancient settlement of Lycopolis. During the French occupation, the town had lost much of its former grandeur and was encumbered with the remains of houses that the local people made little effort to clear away or repair. The shortcomings of the town were compensated for by the fertility of the region and the prosperity this conferred on the inhabitants in terms of trade and commerce. Asyût was also connected to a number of important caravan routes by means of which the produce of the locality was transported to other regions. Denon gives the following brief account of the township:

> Asyût is a large well-populated town built, to all appearances, on the site of Lycopolis or the 'city of the wolf'. [Denon is here making reference to the jackal-god Wepwawet to which a temple had once been erected.] No antiquities are found in this town but the Libyan Chain, at the foot of which it stands, exhibits here such a vast number of tombs that without doubt this town occupies the territory of some very ancient and flourishing city.
>
> We arrived here an hour after noon and employed the remainder of the day in procuring food for the army, in exercising the sick and in taking possession of barques and provisions that the Mamelukes had not been able to carry away with them.

Once settled in the town the French came upon a large market – evidence of the considerable amount of produce that was bought and sold – and were impressed by the sight of several fine houses. These, although largely constructed from mud-brick, had decorative quoins (corners) and string courses (horizontal decorative bands) worked from kiln-fired bricks. More importantly – and to the dismay of the art historians in the party – some of the grander houses had doorways and thresholds ornamented with columns of porphyry and granite that had been indiscriminately removed from ancient temple structures.

French troops enter Asyût, ancient Lycopolis, by the West Gate. Two horses haul a cannon followed by an armed patrol that has been in pursuit of Mamelukes. A house has been fortified to serve as a garrison. Local people look on – one man preventing his wife and child from getting too close! The distant mountains were the location of tombs and quarries that were explored by the French artists. *(Dutertre, Author's Collection)*

The principal commerce of Asyût was in linen, cloth, pottery and carbonate of soda, the latter being extracted from the neighbouring dried lakes of natron. There was also a thriving trade in vegetable oil. Cultivation, as remarked, was well developed in the province and especially in the immediate environs of the town bordering the Nile. Growing in profusion were wheat, barley, linseed and beans of various kinds. Also harvested was an abundance of poppies from which opium was derived and exported by caravan.

On the outskirts of the town the French were delighted by the prospect of several fine gardens planted with apricots, pomegranates, oranges, lemons and palm trees that were weighed down with succulent dates. These gardens were highly prized and could be rented 'for a considerable price'. Close by, groves of fine sycamores offered welcome shade and a place for the French officers to promenade and think of home.

Between Asyût and the mountains were the imposing houses of the Mamelukes. It was in one of these that the French established their military quarters and a suitable residence for General Desaix. Because of their elevated location these houses had a commanding view of the town. The French took advantage of this by having crenellations built on

their flat roofs to allow the houses to serve as defensive works in the event of an uprising. The roof of the most elevated of the houses was equipped with a small cannon.

The common soldiers billeted under their tents and mat shelters which they erected on the plain just outside the city walls. It was safer for them here since, despite their military prowess, they were only tolerated by the local inhabitants with surly impatience bordering on insolence. Several of the savants in the party shared the quarters of the soldiers so as to be nearer to the rock-cut tombs they were eager to visit. Denon was the first to explore them:

> Out of the rocks are excavated a vast number of tombs of different dimensions and decorated with more or less magnificence. All the inner entrances of these tombs are covered with hieroglyphics. Months would be required to read them, even if one knew the language, and it would take years to copy them.
>
> At different periods or annual festivals, or when some new inhabitant was added to the tombs, funeral rites were doubtless performed in which the pomp of ceremony might vie with

Ruins of the temple of Antaeopolis, 40 kilometres south of Asyût. The decorative palm-leaf capitals of the Hypostyle Hall were still standing when the French made their survey. The entablature is decorated with Egyptian ornamentation and Greek inscriptions. Two artists discuss the ruins in the company of a local man who carries their equipment – and a weapon for their protection. The temple was swept away by a great inundation of the Nile in 1821. *(Cécile, Author's Collection)*

the magnificence of the place. [The latter] is the more probable since the richness of decoration in the interior part forms a most striking contrast with the outer walls – which are only the rough native rock.

I found one of these caves with a single chamber in which were an innumerable quantity of graves cut in the rock in regular order. They had been ransacked to procure the mummies. I found several fragments of their contents such as linen, hands, feet and scattered bones.

In previous centuries, these rock-cut tombs had been the abode of self-professed holy men who had lived a life of austere self-denial. Small niches, stucco paintings and inscriptions could still be seen in the remains of their gloomy cells:

Some of these quarries have been the abode of pious hermits. In these rocks, among these vast retreats, [they] united the austere aspect of an inhabitant of the desert with the gentle majesty of one who partakes of the bounties bestowed by a river that dispenses to its banks plenty and fertility.

In these regions, the unchanging and august splendour of the sky forcibly impels one to constant but chastened admiration. The dawn of day is not enlivened by the cries of joy or the

Entrance to the Tomb of Hepzefa II, a former governor of Asyût. This conveys the forbidding nature of the rock face which the Egyptians excavated – to labyrinthine depths using only simple tools. Two French artists record the scene. One stands within the entrance studying the bas-reliefs, the other, portfolio beneath his arm, gazes at the large-scale carving of Hepzefa who carries his staff of office. A local man brings a supply of drinking water. The French Commission found traces of coloration and fine carving, all of which have now disappeared. *(Cécile, University of Edinburgh)*

bounding of animals. The song of no bird proclaims the return of morn. Even the lark, which in our climate enlivens and animates our countryside, in these burning regions only calls to his mate but never chants his happiness.

The grotto of the coenobite seems to have been placed here by the order and choice of the Deity himself and every animated being partakes with him in his grave and silent meditation.

Denon did not return to Asyût until late in the evening. His curiosity concerning the rock-cut tombs induced him to stay to examine them longer than he had intended. Being informed that General Desaix was about to commence his march south in pursuit once more of Murad Bey, he just had time to catch a few hours sleep before setting out at daybreak with the army. They were accompanied by Arab guides whose knowledge of the region meant they could alert the French officers to places of potential ambush.

Interior of a rock-cut tomb at El-Kab. The ghostly forms, in the recess, represent Paheri, a high-ranking temple official, with his mother and wife. The artist Cécile records the scene. He cuts a fine figure with his shock of curly hair, flowing pantaloons and, nearby, a splendid top hat! Close at hand is his scimitar, a reminder of the risks the French savants took when undertaking their researches. A guide smokes as he keeps watch. *(Cécile, Author's Collection)*

The convoy followed the sinuosities of the canal of Abu-Assi (the modern-day canal of Ibrâhimîya) that was so wide the French considered it to be virtually an arm of the Nile. During the whole day's march, the fertile plain bordering the Nile maintained an extent of 'more than a league' and was cultivated 'with more care and skill than any part we had yet seen'. On the journey, several well-marked tracks were discovered that Denon thought could easily be improved and turned into highways, which he thought 'would be excellent and completely durable in a country like this where neither rain nor frost are ever seen'.

Not only was their route along a well-formed track but every few miles they encountered 'a small monument of hospitality' in the form of a well at which both men and horses could quench their thirst. Denon paused at the largest of these to make a sketch of what he describes as 'these small philanthropic establishments'. He considered them to be 'as agreeable as useful' adding, 'they characterise the natural charity of the Arabs'.

Towards the middle of the day, the party approached the desert. Denon, seated on horseback with notebook in hand, recorded the following observations:

> I found three new subjects:
>
> One was the *doum*-palm tree. It differs from the date palm in having from eight to fifteen stems, instead of only a single one, and its ligneous fruit is attached by clusters to the extremity of the principal branches – from which proceed numerous tufts that form the foliage of the tree. The fruit is of a triangular form and of the size of an egg. The first, or outer coat, is spongy. The taste is sweetish like honey, resembling the flavour of spiced bread. Under this coat is a hard bark, filamentous like the cocoanut that it resembles more than any other fruit – but it wants the fine, hard ligneous shell of the cocoanut. Its gelatinous part is tasteless. It becomes very hard upon drying and beads are made of it – strung upon chaplets – that take a good dye and polish.
>
> I also saw a charming little bird which, by its shape and habitation, should be arranged in the class of the *fly-catchers*. It seized and devoured these insects with an admirable address. Thanks to the indolence of the Turks, all birds are tame in their country because, although the Turks love nothing, they disturb nothing. The colour of the bird I have just mentioned is a clear and lively green. The head and feathers beneath the wings are golden, the beak is long, black and pointed. The size of this bird is about the same as the small titmouse.
>
> A little further off I saw in the desert some swallows of a clear grey colour – like that of the sand over which they were flying. These never emigrate or, at least, only go into similar climates as we never see any of them in Europe of this colour.

Thirteen hours of gruelling march ensued, by which time the party had reached a village by the name of Gamerissien:

> Unfortunately for this village . . . the cries of the women soon convinced us that our soldiers, profiting by the darkness of the night, under pretence of seeking provisions and notwithstanding their weariness, were enjoying by violence the gratifications that the place offered them. The inhabitants – pillaged, dishonoured and goaded to desperation – fell upon the patrols whom we sent to defend them. These attacked the furious natives, in their own defence, for want of being able to explain their [peaceful] intention or to make themselves understood.

Oh war! Thou art brilliant in history but frightful when viewed with all thy attendant horrors, naked and undisguised.

By evening, the party skirted the edge of the desert that was bordered by a succession of villages. Denon remarks on how cold the nights could be, requiring camp fires to be lit. The heat of day, though, was sufficient to remind him they were approaching the tropic. Once more the abundance of the land became apparent: 'The barley was now ripe, the wheat was in ear and the melons – planted in the open field – were already in full flower.'

The night was spent camped in a wood near a village called Norcette and the next day the party crossed the desert. They passed by a monastery which the Mamelukes had set on fire the previous evening and which was still burning so as to prevent any of the French party from entering. In making their escape, the monks had left the gates wide open and through these the servants of the brotherhood could be seen attempting to salvage what was not destroyed. Denon came upon a few brothers, clothed in rags, 'who had scarcely recovered from the fright and agony they had experienced'.

While halting at this place Denon made a drawing of the monastery. He considered it was typical of other such establishments which he saw on the edge of the desert. Despite their inhospitable location, they enjoyed a commanding view of the rich country all about them, watered by the Canal of Abu-Assi. These monasteries were fourth-century constructions.

That evening the party camped at a village bordering the Nile called Bonasse Bura. The next day they returned along the Nile. Denon and General Desaix 'very imprudently got half a league ahead of the army'. Denon, turning to General Desaix, saw the risk to which they had exposed themselves and jested: 'How ridiculous it would be, to have it recorded in the annals of history, if the General had lost his head in an encounter with half a dozen Mamelukes, and that he, Denon, would be inconsolable to leave his own behind a bush – where it would be forgotten!' With this badinage, they hastened back to be reunited with the main body of troops.

Denon regretted not being able to make records of the ancient monuments that he knew to be in the vicinity, especially those of Aphroditopolis and Crocodilopolis of the Ptolemies. Aphroditopolis was sited at modern-day Gebelein, about 30 kilometres south of Thebes. Here the rugged topography has thrown up two hills. The eastern one is known for the remains of a temple to the god Hathor. At the foot of the hill lies the largely unexplored site of the ancient township. The western hill contains a number of tombs whose wall paintings have been removed to Turin. Crocodilopolis was sited at modern-day Medinet El-Fayum and was the centre of worship for the crocodile-god Sobek. Here, in the midst of the Fayum region, Crocodilopolis and its temple complex served as the province of the capital. Graeco-Roman remains include baths and other public buildings.

The obstinate perseverance of Murad Bey in playing cat and mouse with the French army, and in evading direct military confrontation, was advantageous to Denon. The pursuit of their adversary offered him the prospect of travelling further into Egypt with an increased likelihood of being able to visit and record the great antiquities that were the daily object of his desire. Denon puts it more figuratively: 'We shall contrive to pursue him and this will lead us at last into the Promised Land from which my harvest will be reaped.'

Denon's 'Promised Land' was Upper Egypt, into which General Desaix had been leading his troops for the last two weeks. Murad Bey was thought to be in the vicinity of Girga and so it was to this township that the General and his men now made their way. This gave Denon the opportunity to record the following impressions:

> Girga, where we arrived two hours after noon, is the capital of Upper Egypt. It is a modern town that contains nothing remarkable. It is as large as El-Minya and Mallawi but smaller than Asyût and less beautiful than either. The name Girga . . . is derived from a large monastery, built earlier than the town, that is dedicated to St George. In the language of the country his name is pronounced *Girga*.
>
> The Nile encroaches on the walls of Girga and is constantly washing away part of them. It would require considerable expense to make these a harbour for boats. The town is therefore interesting only for being situated halfway between Cairo and Syene – and for being within very rich territory.

At Girga the French secured all kinds of provisions for a few sous – the equivalent of a few pennies. Bread was 1 sou per lb, twelve eggs cost 2 sous, two pigeons could be had for 3 sous and a goose, weighing 15 lb, could be purchased for 12 sous. Moreover, such was the abundance of these commodities that even after more than 5,000 French troops had remained there for three weeks, and had 'scattered out their money liberally', no rise in the price of these necessities had taken place.

A barracks was arranged at Girga to house 500 men. Despite Denon's words in praise of the fertility of the land, the army was in need of bread and ovens were set up to supply the soldiers with this, 'their most essential requirement'. Furthermore, with all their marching their boots were worn through. Replacements for these had to wait until the supply-boats arrived from Cairo.

At this time, Denon's eyes showed symptoms of being affected by Egypt's harsh light and desert conditions. This was probably some form of ophthalmia that was a common problem and many soldiers were, or became, similarly affected. To gain relief Denon had recourse to a remedy that has a modern-day, nature-cure connotation:

> Our time [at Girga] gave rest to us all and, in my case, I took advantage to strengthen my eyesight that had become so indifferent as to threaten serious inconvenience. I had indeed no remedy with me but I found a pot of honey and a jar of vinegar in the house of a sheikh in which I lodged. These did me great service for I ate abundantly of the former and cooled the heat of my blood with the latter that I drank largely mixed with water and sugar.

On 3 January 1799, the party received information that men living in neighbouring villages had been persuaded by the Mamelukes to rise up against them. The plan was for the locals to harass the French troops from the rear – a well-established tactic – while the Mamelukes would lead more orderly charges from the front. The French were aware that such threats had to be taken seriously. Only a month before a band of Mamelukes, with a group of local people, had adopted a similar tactic to plunder a caravan of some two hundred merchants from India. They had intercepted the caravan as it journeyed from

Quseir, by the Red Sea, to Qus on the Nile. Their success, it has to be said of a cowardly nature, against a lightly armed band of civilians, had emboldened the Mamelukes and villagers and given them a false sense of their military prowess. Taking on the French was an altogether different matter, as Denon's laconic comment on the incident confirms: 'They gave themselves great credit for their courage. Forty villages had assembled six or seven thousand men but our cavalry charged them, sabred ten or twelve hundred and put an end to their project.'

Not all visitors into Egypt met with such an inhospitable reception as that which befell the unfortunate Indian merchants. At Girga, Denon met a Nubian prince who was a brother of the king of Darsur. He was returning from India and planned to join another of his brothers who was accompanying a caravan of Nubians from Sannar, located far to the south on the Blue Nile. They had with them a cargo of elephants' tusks and gold dust which they intended to barter at Cairo for coffee, sugar, shawls, cloth, lead, iron, senna and tamarinds. Denon relates that also in the caravan were many women slaves. He had a long conversation with this young prince whom he describes as 'lively, gay, impetuous and clever', qualities evident in his physiognomy. His physical appearance also impressed Denon: 'His colour was deeper than bronze, his eyes very fine and well set, his nose somewhat turned up and small, his mouth very wide but not flat and his legs, like those of all the Africans, were bowed and lank.'

The prince informed the French that it was a 40-day journey by caravan from Darsur to Asyût during which time water was only to be met with once a week, either in the wells that had been sunk along the route, or when journeying in the vicinity of an oasis. Denon reasoned that the profits to be made from these caravans must be enormous to justify the great expense in fitting them out and to indemnify them for the great fatigues and risks to which they were daily subjected. He was told the slaves had been taken in war. The women had been exchanged 'for one indifferent gun and the men two' – there were male slaves in the caravan also.

Through an interpreter, the prince commented that at certain times in the year it could be very cold in his country but nevertheless his countrymen had no word for ice. He described ice as being 'a very hard substance when taken in the hands and which slips through the fingers when held for some time'. Denon regretted not having more time to converse with this interesting traveller and closes this part of his account with the observation: 'We could not indiscreetly burden him with questions although he seemed to be perfectly well inclined to tell us all he knew, having nothing of the gravity and taciturnity of the Muslim and expressing himself with ease and energy.'

There now occurred a period of inactivity in Denon's progress south. This was caused by the slow progress of the supply-boats that were following on behind the army. On board these were provisions, ammunition and clothing. General Desaix received news that his supply-boats had been delayed at Cairo. He had no alternative but to extend his sojourn at Girga and to delay his pursuit of Murad Bey and his forces. Denon filled his time with finding out more about the Arabs and their customs. The first thing to attract his attention was so pervasive it could not be overlooked: he and his soldier companions were perpetually subject to pilfering and audacious theft. So pernicious was this tendency that nothing seemed safe; arms, supplies and horses were spirited away even when the guard was doubled:

> Every night, the inhabitants stole into our camps like rats and, lurking about, they generally found an opportunity to seize some article of plunder and carry it away with them. Some of the robbers had been caught in the very act and were sacrificed to the rage of the soldiers on guard. It was hoped this [show of] discipline would prove a salutary example.
>
> The guard was doubled and yet, on the same day, two thieves were apprehended and immediately shot. In the night that followed this execution, the horse of the aide-de-camp of the General of the cavalry was stolen. The General laid a wager they would not dare touch any of his property – but the next day his horse also disappeared!

The nature of the climate then secured Denon's attention. On 11 January, he recorded in his *Journal*: 'The sky was cloudy and we suffered from it as if it was a sharp winter's day – although in Europe it would have been reckoned to be fine April weather.' Despite the relatively cool weather, Denon saw vines growing whose foliage was already as green as that of similar vines under cultivation in France in the month of July. Denon's observant eye further noted: 'The leaves [of the vine] in this country only harden and become red and dry while the end of the branch perpetually renews its verdure. The climbing peas do the same. Their stalk becomes woody and I have seen some that were forty feet high and had climbed to the tops of trees.'

Two days later, Denon's communing with nature was disturbed by the news that 'an innumerable troop of foot soldiers' was on its way by Quseir to join forces with Murad Bey. Their intention was to march with him and confront the French as soon as a favourable opportunity presented itself. General Desaix's response was swift. He dispatched a contingent of cavalry to engage with the would-be enemy and, in Denon's words, 'put to the sword a thousand of these deluded people'.

Several more days passed and still there was no news either of the cavalry or of the supply-boats. Denon spent the time listening to the Arabian storytellers. They frequented the streets and bazaars, first attracting the attention of passers-by and then recounting to them tales of imagination and valour – in return for which a small payment was expected. Denon has left the following impression of these imaginative and gifted narrators:

> The Arabs related stories so slowly that our interpreters could follow them without interrupting the narrative. The people retain the same passion for these tales as we have long been familiar with the *Thousand and One Tales* of the Sultana Scheherazade. I observed that if these narrations were not rich in natural images and proper sentiment . . . they abounded in extraordinary events, interesting situations and were occasioned by high and strong passions.
>
> The writers [of these tales] make abundant use of all the imagery of castles, iron gates, poisons, daggers, rapes, night adventures, mistakes and treachery. In short, all that can embroider a narration and appear to render the denouement impossible, and yet the story always finishes very naturally in the clearest and most satisfactory manner.
>
> It happens that the same story is told by several raconteurs successively with equal interest and success. One gives in a better style of declamation the pathetic and amorous part. Another

throws in more interest in the battle scenes and those of horror. A third makes the events humorous.

Denon noticed how it was common practice, at the close of a narrative, for a discussion of the tale to take place. The parts that had excited the audience the most, and had prompted applause, were critically analysed and, thereby, 'the talents of the performers were brought to greater perfection'. The best raconteurs were in greatest demand and were hired by families or groups of tradesmen to contribute to festive entertainments. On feast days, poets were engaged to proclaim verses in commemoration of the events being celebrated. Verses were sometimes improvised and ballads sung in honour of the occasion.

In a further attempt to improve the condition of his eyes, Denon spent some time in the public baths and claims he 'found much ease from this remedy'. Perhaps the steam and humidity were beneficial. Whatever the reason, Denon enjoyed the baths for their own sake and spent as much of his spare time as possible relaxing amid the torpid atmosphere of the heated chambers.

The morning of 15 January was sufficiently cold to make Denon wish for the comfort of a fire. He likened the weather to that of a chill May morning back home in France. This reflection prompted him to think more generally about the climate and the meteorological conditions of Egypt. He recorded the following interesting observations:

On putting my head out of my window I saw the birds alive and active and busy in making their nests. In the evening of this same day it thundered – a rare occurrence in this country. It happens hardly more often than once in a generation by a combination of circumstances perhaps not difficult of explanation.

The north wind, which is the most constant of all those that prevail in this part of the world, brings from the sea the clouds of a colder region. [It] rolls them along through the Valley of Egypt where a burning sun rarefies them and reduces them to vapour. When this vapour is driven into Abyssinia, the south wind, that crosses the lofty and cold mountains of this country, sometimes brings back a few scattered clouds. As they experience little change of temperature, when returning over the humid valley of the Nile in flood-time, they remain condensed and at times produce – without thunder or tempest – small hasty showers. But, as the east and west winds – that are in general the parents of storms – both cross burning deserts, they either absorb or raise the vapour to such a height as to be able to pass over the narrow valley of Upper Egypt without undergoing detonation [thunderclaps] by the operation of the waters of the river.

Thunder was so rarely heard that even the thinking people residing in the Nile Valley did not attempt to attribute its origin to a physical cause. General Desaix questioned a man versed in the law on the cause of thunder and received the following reply, delivered with perfect confidence and conviction:

We know very well that it is an angel but one so small in stature that he cannot be perceived in the air. He has, however, the power of conducting the clouds of the Mediterranean Sea into Abyssinia and when the wickedness of men is at its height he makes his voice heard – which is a voice of menace, reproach and of punishment. He opens the gate of Heaven a little way whence darts out the lightning. But the clemency of God is infinite. Never is His wrath carried farther into Upper Egypt.

General Desaix explained to the elderly sage the contemporary interpretation of thunder. At this the old man dismissed the theory as 'inferior to his own'. Indeed, so dismissive of it was he that he would not even condescend to hear any more on the subject.

Denon had occasion to observe Egyptian workmen at their trades. Being an artist he had a natural affinity for the skills of the craftsmen and he watched them intently as they carried out their work:

> The Egyptians are dexterous and industrious and since they have scarcely more tools to work with than any savage it is surprising how much they do with their fingers – the instruments to which they are commonly reduced. And [likewise] with their feet which assist their hands wonderfully. As workmen they have one great virtue which is that they are patient and unassuming and are ready to repeat their work until it is done to your satisfaction.

Reflecting on the nature and character of Egyptian workmen, Denon remarked: 'They are eminently sober, as active on their legs as couriers, centaurs on horseback and titans when swimming.'

On 20 January, Denon was at last able to record in his *Journal* that the long-awaited supply-boats had arrived. They brought with them the army's much needed materials and provisions – including new boots for the troops. There was also an unexpected pleasure in the form of a military band. On board one of the boats were the instrumentalists of the battalion's demi-brigade. They arrived playing favourite French airs and gave both officers and soldiers such a surprising sensation of delight that they were able to forget the frustrations caused by their enforced sojourn at Girga. Denon too enjoyed this musical reminder of his homeland but he comments in his *Journal*: 'Alas it was the song of the menaced swan', ominous words that anticipated future hardships and perils that will be described in due course.

The next day, brandy was issued to the men from the supply that had been transported from Cairo and they were also paid the arrears of money owing to them. Denon remarks: '[These] gave a new pleasure to the life of the soldier who, tired of eating his six eggs for a *sou*, set out with joy to meet further hardships.' Whether the latter observation is quite true, it is the case that the soldiers had languished at Girga for twenty-one days and were impatient for a more active life. Denon was also weary of the inactivity of his position. Furthermore, he had been studying the map of the Nile Valley and was keenly aware of how close he was to the sites of several great antiquities:

> I was near Abydos, where Ozymandias had built a temple and where Memnon had resided. I was constantly urging General Desaix to send a reconnoitring party as far as El-Arâba, where I daily heard there were several ruins. And, as often, Desaix said to me: 'I will conduct you there myself. Murad Bey is two days' journey from us. He will come up to us the day after tomorrow and we shall then give him battle and when we defeat him we can bestow as much time as you will on antiquities – and I will help you myself to measure them.'

Abydos, which Denon was so eager to visit, lies about 16 kilometres to the south of Girga on the west bank of the Nile. It was the sacred site and place of worship of the god Osiris. Today, the location is dominated by the ruins of the Temple of Sety (Sethos) I, and

The Propylon or ceremonial gate leading to the Temple of Dendera. Centuries of wind-blown sand shroud the structure and encroach upon the temple itself. This made survey-work for the French difficult. Stones have fallen from the portal, following earth tremors, and the ruins of mud-brick dwellings encumber the temple roof. The Commission excavated to the base of the portal and found much to admire: 'The north gate is remarkable for the beauty of its proportions and the richness of the sculptures with which it is decorated. In no other gate, with the possible exception of that at Karnak, does this member of architecture have so fine a proportion.' *(Dutertre, Author's Collection)*

those of his son Rameses I. In close proximity to the Temple of Sety I is the so-called Osireion that served as an object of veneration to Osiris.

Ozymandias, to whom Denon makes reference, is the Greek name for the mighty Rameses II who was the subject of Percy Bysshe Shelley's celebrated eponymous poem which begins 'I met a traveller from an antique land'. Rameses II is renowned for excavating the great rock-cut temple at Abu Simbel, the building of his mortuary temple known as the Ramesseum and for the completion of the breathtaking Hall of Pillars at Karnak begun by his father Rameses I.

Memnon, also mentioned by Denon, is the Greek name associated with Amenhotep III. He was commemorated at western Thebes in the form of two giant seated statues hewn from quartzite sandstone. These are now the only remains that survive at what was the location of Amenhotep's mortuary temple. The Greeks identified the site with Memnon who, in Greek mythology, was the son of Eos (Dawn) and was slain by Achilles at Troy.

Considering these many antiquities, with their glorious associations of past ages, it was little wonder Denon was anxious to make progress with his travels yet despite Denon's pleading with General Desaix to allow him to visit the ancient monuments, Desaix remained firm – even obdurate. Soldiers could not be spared to provide Denon with the security he required and, moreover, the time had come for the entire party to leave Girga. They did so at dusk on the evening of 22 January. With the approach of night, they passed directly opposite El-Arâba – one of the very sites Denon wished to see. General Desaix was clearly embarrassed and according to Denon 'he dared not look me in the face'. Although the circumstance was painful to Denon he had the good humour to make the following spirited remark: 'If I am killed tomorrow my ghost will forever be haunting you repeating in your ears *El-Arâba*'. General Desaix, who also had a lively sense of humour, noted Denon's remark. Five months later, when the party was once more in the same region, he provided Denon with the military escort he needed to make his survey of the architectural antiquities. These events will be described later.

By evening, the party arrived before the village of El-Besena. Not a single inhabitant was to be found. The residents, learning of the approach of the French soldiers, had deserted their homes, taking everything with them, circumstances which prompted Denon to comment: 'For my own part I was not sorry to find these villages empty. It spared me from hearing the cries of the inhabitants from whom we were obliged to exact our wants by force. As they were aware of our coming, everything was removed even to the door and window-cases. A village, thus stripped only two hours before, had the appearance of a ruin a century old.'

The next day, the army continued its march south with Denon himself at its head. He was among the first to catch sight of Mameluke forces advancing towards them.

> Our artillery fired on the whole front of the enemy, who made a false attack on our right in which several of their men were killed. One of their leaders, struck by a bullet, fell down too near us to be assisted by his own people. His foot hung in the stirrup and the horse, without abandoning his rider, would not let anyone approach him. This unfortunate chief was thus dragged from place to place by his horse and was made to suffer the horrors of death in many forms.
>
> Firing ceased at noon and by one o'clock none of our enemies were in sight. We directed our march to Farshut to which Murad Bey had retreated.

On arriving at Farshut, the French saw the town had been pillaged by Murad Bey and his Mamelukes. The sheikh and several leading members of the community were, however, still in possession of the town and received the French cordially. Having seen their tormentors flee, they regarded the Europeans as their avengers and, although in a state of weakness and reduced to poverty, they contrived to do their best to offer Denon and the French generals some hospitality. By midnight the army was once more on its way.

The darkness concealed new hazards. Marauders and villainous opportunists pursued the troops. They were so-called volunteers who regarded themselves as being noble and wore a green turban to indicate that they were descendants and followers of Mohammed Ali. In truth, they were no more than vagabonds who lived by plundering the caravans that journeyed along the coast of the Red Sea. For them, this was a period of inactivity since it was the dead time of year for the caravan trade. The presence of the French therefore offered a new temptation from their usual occupation.

Although the French eventually drove away their attackers, these remained a threat. How much of a threat these brigands posed can be judged from Denon's description of them: 'Armed with three javelins, a pike, a dagger, a brace of pistols and a carbine they attack with boldness and resist with obstinacy. Although mortally wounded they seem tenacious of life. In our last encounter, I saw one of them strike at and wound two of our men whilst they were holding him nailed against a wall with their bayonets.'

The French, fatigued by their marching and irked by their skirmishes with a largely unseen enemy, duly arrived an hour before sunrise at the township of Hiw, situated on the southernmost bend of the Nile below Farshut. In the Roman period, Hiw was known as Diospolis Parva. Denon made a tour of the area and considered the township occupied 'a fine military situation'. In antiquity, Hiw had formed part of a highly developed region extending for about 15 kilometres along the east bank of the Nile. In the modern era it has been excavated by the pioneering Egyptologist Sir Flinders Petrie who, with subsequent researches, found extensive traces of stone structures and signs of stone-working.

The French party remained at Hiw for a few hours and then, as was their habit, they set out once more on their march an hour before sunset to benefit from the cool of evening. From their experience of the previous day, they were aware that marching at night would once more expose them to the threat of brigands and their murderous attacks. Nevertheless, they were in high spirits and were confident that, sooner or later, they would meet up with their adversary Murad Bey and would vanquish him as gloriously as they had triumphed over the Mamelukes at the battle of the Pyramids.

Progress of a kind was made. The artillery was cumbersome, the infantry slow and the strong cavalry was too heavy for the party as a whole to advance effectively. Only the light cavalry was able to move with the speed required to overtake the Arab forces. At eleven they reached a large village where 'unfortunately for the inhabitants the soldiers misbehaved'. This place was departed at dawn – with many of its women violated.

Denon was keenly aware that he and his soldier-companions were approaching Tentyris. In Pharaonic times this was the capital of the sixth province of Upper Egypt. This site, situated on the west bank of the Nile, is directly opposite the township of Qena that lies about 50 kilometres north of Luxor. Qena was known to the Greeks as *Caene* and in ancient times was the hub of thriving caravan trading routes with Quseir. These brought prosperity to the region through the trade transacted across the Red Sea with Arabia, in dates and grain, and with India in spices and exotic goods. Qena provided Egypt herself with a rich supply of calcareous clay from which fine pottery was made. More importantly for Denon, in respecting his wish to make progress with his antiquarian researches, Tentyris was the site of the Dendera necropolis and the great

Temple of Hathor. Hathor was venerated as a sky-goddess and was also associated with the worship of the dead.

The party approached the ancient site of Tentyris and Denon could at last set his eyes on the celebrated remains:

> I found, buried in a heap of ruins, a gate built of enormous masses covered with hieroglyphics. Through this gate I had a view of the Temple of Hathor. I wish I could here transfuse into the soul of my readers the sensation I experienced. I was too much lost in astonishment to be capable of cool judgement. All I had seen hitherto served here but to fix my admiration. This monument seemed to me to have the primitive character of a temple in the highest perfection. Covered with ruins as it was, the sensation of silent respect it excited in my mind appeared to me proof of its impressive aspect. I may add that the whole army experienced similar feelings.
>
> I despair of being able to express all that I felt on standing under the portico of Tentyris. I felt I was in the sanctuary of the arts and sciences. How many periods presented themselves to my imagination at the sight of such an edifice! How many ages of creative ingenuity were required to bring a nation to such a degree of perfection and sublimity in the arts!
>
> What power! What riches! What abundance! What superfluity of means must a government possess that could erect such an edifice and find within itself artists capable of conceiving and executing the design, of decorating and enriching it with everything that speaks to the eye and the understanding! Never did the labour of man show me the human race in such a splendid light.
>
> In the ruins of Tentyris, the Egyptians appeared to me to be [a race of] giants!

Denon was particularly captivated by the beauty of what he called the 'gate' that closed the sanctuary to the temple. In Egyptian architecture, the ceremonial gate that gave access to the precincts of a temple is called a propylon. This structure, typically of imposing proportions, served as a form of ceremonial arch. In Greek architecture, a propylaeum fulfilled a similar purpose by forming a gateway to a sacred enclosure. More generally, this architectural form has been adopted in Europe, perhaps most notably in Paris in the form of l'Arc de Triomphe.

Having made a study of the outside of the Temple of Hathor, Denon next surveyed the interior and was moved to write the following words in appreciation of the Egyptian system of decorative ornamentation:

> I was confused by the multiplicity of objects, astonished by their novelty and tormented by the fear of never again visiting them. On casting my eyes on the ceiling I perceived zodiacs, planetary systems and celestial planispheres represented in a tasteful arrangement. I observed the walls to be covered with groups of pictures exhibiting the religious rites of the people, their labours in agriculture, the arts and their moral precepts.
>
> I saw the Supreme Being – the first cause – was everywhere depicted by the emblems of his attributes. Everything was equally important for my pencil and I had but a few hours to examine, to reflect on and to copy what it had been the labour of ages to conceive, to put together and to decorate.

Denon's reference to 'zodiacs, planetary systems and celestial planispheres' is worthy of particular mention. When he was exploring the roof of the Temple of Hathor, General Desaix discovered – to his delight and astonishment – a small temple now known as the

East Osiris Chapel. Its ceiling is decorated with a great circular zodiac in the form of a planisphere or map of the heavens. The original stone-engraved sculpture was transported to France where, today, it is a prized possession of the Louvre. The modern-day visitor to Dendera has to be content with a plaster-cast replica.

The bas-reliefs that so excited General Desaix, and likewise Denon when he was called up to see them, depict a large figure of Isis sculpted in captivating high-relief. The rest of the ceiling is composed of a great disc. Within this, six signs of the zodiac – Leo, Virgo, Libra, Taurus, Gemini and Cancer – spiral towards the centre. These reliefs, and their symbolism, have earned the universal admiration of all who have studied them.

Time did not allow Denon to undertake as complete a survey of the Temple of Hathor as he would have liked, and he made his departure with reluctance:

> With my pencil in my hand I passed from object to object distracted from one by the inviting appearance of the next. Constantly attracted to new subjects – and again torn from them – I wanted eyes, hands and intelligence vast enough to see, copy and reduce to some order the multitude of striking images that presented themselves to me. I was ashamed at representing such sublime objects by such imperfect designs, but I wished to preserve some memorial of the sensations I here experienced. I feared Tentyris would escape from me forever, so that my regret equalled my enjoyment.

Reflecting later that evening on the events of the day Denon recorded in his *Journal*:

> Since I have been in Egypt – deceived in all my expectations – I have been constantly heavy and melancholy, but Tentyris has cured me. What I have seen this day has repaid me for all my fatigues. Whatever happens to me, in the course of this expedition, I shall congratulate myself all my life for having embarked on it. I shall preserve the remembrance of this day forever.

CHAPTER 12

Thebes

The French party, marching in pursuit of Murad Bey, departed Dendera on 26 January 1799. They continued southwards following the direction of the Nile. The scenery in this part of Egypt was very different from in the Delta region. They saw palm trees much larger than any they had hitherto encountered and groves of tamarisks displaying their characteristic spiky flowers. Even the villages appeared to grow in proportion to the prosperity of the country – Denon describes them as extending for 'half a league'. He also noticed that while the countryside all around these villages received the benefit of the annual inundation – and was clearly very fertile from the rich alluvial deposits – it nonetheless remained uncultivated. This caused him to conjecture: 'Could it be the inhabitants choose to grow no more than required for their own consumption and thus deprive their tyrants of the profit from their superfluity?'

In the afternoon, Denon and General Desaix drew near to a part of the River Nile where several sandbanks and low islands projected from the waters. These were a favourite basking place for crocodiles – a species that fascinated Denon. The two Europeans had seen little of these formidable creatures and promptly searched the river for signs of them. They were soon rewarded:

> We saw something long and brown lying among a number of ducks. It was a crocodile asleep. He appeared to be about fifteen or eighteen feet long. We fired on him and he gently entered the water but some minutes after he came out again. A second shot made him again plunge in but he again returned to the island. His belly appeared much larger than that of animals of the same species I have seen stuffed. [Had the crocodile perhaps recently consumed an unsuspecting prey?]

Turning his attention to military matters, the General was told that a party of Mamelukes had recently passed along the right bank of the river and that another continued on its route to Esna and Syene. Desaix ordered the cavalry to set out at midnight in an attempt to catch up with the latter. The party as a whole departed on 27 January at two in the morning.

A few hours later, on rounding a projection in the chain of mountains, Denon perceived the site of ancient Thebes in all its majestic splendour. Here he was at last before the principal city of Upper Egypt and former capital of the fourth province. What he saw filled him with awe and elevated his spirits. He records: 'Suddenly, and with one accord, [the soldiers] stood in amazement at the sight of the scattered ruins. [They]

Interior of the Temple of Esna. The ram-god Khnum was venerated at the Graeco-Roman temple of Esna (ancient Latopolis). Khnum had associations with fertility and the creation of gods. The French were 'seized with admiration' by the massive grandeur of the twenty-four columns of the portico and the beauty of the temple interior. This was cleared of sand to be used, ignominiously, as a granary and then a store for gunpowder! *(Roberts, British Library)*

clapped their hands with delight as if the end and object of their glorious toils – the conquest of Egypt – was accomplished by taking possession of this ancient metropolis.'

Denon took a view of the panorama before him. The knees of an enthusiastic soldier served as a support for his drawing board and several others crowded round to shade him from the dazzling rays of the burning sun. The combination of the magnificent spectacle and the comradeship shown by his soldier-companions induced in Denon an 'electric emotion for the whole army of soldiers'. Later he confided to his *Journal*: 'The delicate sensibility of our soldiers made me feel proud of being their companion – and in the glory of calling myself a Frenchman!'

When his initial emotion had subsided, he made a visual interpretation of the vista before him. He considered the township to be as fine as any that could be imagined and the immense extent of the ruins such 'as to convince the spectator that fame and travellers' tales had not exaggerated their size'. With a touch of hyperbole he adds: 'The diameter of Egypt not being sufficient to contain it, the monuments rest upon two chains of mountains.' Denon is referring here to the Libyan range, to the west, and the Arabian range to the east.

At the time of the French visit to Thebes four large settlements were scattered among the ruins of the ancient monuments. The River Nile, curving on its eternal sinuous course, seemed to Denon 'to be still proud to flow amidst the ruins'. Soon after midday, the entire party crossed the desert and reached the region known as the Valley of the Kings – what Denon describes as 'the necropolis or City of the Dead'. Contemplating this resting place of the pharaohs of dynasties past, Denon and General Desaix decided to make a brief detour to gain a better view of the rock-cut tombs. They discovered this was not without its hazards:

> The rock, excavated on its inclined plane, presents three sides of a square with regular openings behind which are double and triple galleries that were used as burying places. I entered here on horseback with General Desaix, supposing these gloomy retreats could only be the asylum of peace and silence. But, scarcely were we immersed in the obscurity of these galleries when we were assailed with javelins and stones – by enemies whom we could not distinguish.
>
> This put an end to our observations. We learned later that a considerable number of people inhabited these obscure retreats and that, probably from the savage habits contracted there, they were almost always in rebellion with authority and had become the terror of the vicinity.
>
> Too much in haste to make a fuller acquaintance with these inhabitants, we left with precipitation. This time I saw Thebes only at the gallop.

Some time later Denon, General Desaix and the officers preceding the rest of the army on horseback, arrived at the great temple complex of Luxor. Denon wasted no time in making notes for his *Journal* and sketches for his portfolio:

> We arrived presently at a temple that I took to be of the highest antiquity from its ruinous appearance, its antique hue, its construction – which was less perfect than the rest – the extreme simplicity of its ornaments, the regularity of its outline and especially the coarseness of its sculpture. I made a hasty sketch of it and, galloping after the troops who were constantly marching on, I arrived at a second edifice that was much more considerable and in a better state of preservation.
>
> At the entrance of this temple two square mounds flank an immense gate. Against the inner wall are engraved, in two bas-reliefs, the victorious combats of some hero. This piece of sculpture is on the most irregular style of composition [being] without perspective, plan, or distribution – like the first conceptions of the unimproved human mind.
>
> At Pompeii, I have seen rude sketches on the stucco of the walls drawn by Roman soldiers. They entirely resembled, in style, those of which I am now speaking that are like the first attempts of a child – before it has seen anything whereby to arrange its ideas. Here, the hero is gigantic and the enemies, whom he is overthrowing, are twenty-five times smaller than himself.

Denon is here describing the Temple of Amun at Luxor. He was standing before the outer court and lofty pylon (temple gateway) built by Rameses II. It was adorned with

Entrance to the Temple of Luxor at Karnak. Two giant rose-coloured granite obelisks demarcate the entrance to the Temple of Amun. The one on the left was removed by the French to the Place de la Concorde in Paris. Beyond, half buried in sand, are two seated colossi of Rameses II, who erected the obelisks. Further still are the mud brick dwellings of the local people, described by Denon as 'a striking mixture of beggary and magnificence'. While he was making his sketch for this engraving, an elderly sheikh asked him: 'Was it the English or the French who built these ancient monuments?' *(Denon, British Library)*

four standing, and two seated, colossal statues of himself. A pair of obelisks further embellished the pylon. Denon's 'hero' is none other than Rameses II. The bas-reliefs portray the fierce battle fought in Syria between the Egyptians and the Hittites. Rameses II is, indeed, shown many times larger than his foe, whom he is portrayed dispatching with an axe.

Having completed his inspection of the façade of the temple, Denon undertook a survey of the precincts. Like others before him he was astonished to find the fallen remains of an enormous statue. This was the famed colossus of Rameses II.

> At some paces from this gate are the remains of an enormous colossus. It has been wantonly shattered. The parts that are left have preserved their polish and the [sharp] fractures of their edges. To give you an idea of its dimensions, the breadth of the shoulders is twenty-five feet which gives about seventy-five feet for the entire height. The figure is exact in its proportions. The style is middling but the execution is perfect. When overturned it fell upon its face which hides this interesting part. The drapes being broken, we can no longer judge by its attributes whether it is the figure of a king or a divinity.

Contemplating these colossal fragments, Denon was tempted to conjecture whether part of them could be removed to France: 'One foot of this statue remains which is broken off and is in a good state of preservation. It may be easily carried away and may [thereby] give those in Europe a scale of comparison of the monuments of this type.'

As so often, Denon did not have time to complete his examination of the antiquities. He perceived the cavalry was moving on and was obliged to follow or else, as he wryly observed, 'he would be stopped forever in his researches'. After journeying for some time, a flat expanse of territory was reached that offered the French party an unimpeded view. Denon's attention was caught by the sight of two large seated statues in the distance:

> The two statues still existing are in proportion of from fifty to sixty-five feet in height. They are seated with their hands on their knees. All that remains of them shows a severity of style and an upright posture. The bas-reliefs, and the small figures clustered round the seat of the southernmost of these statues, are not without elegance and delicacy of execution. The names of the ancient and illustrious travellers, who came to hear the sounds of the statue of Memnon, are written in Greek on the leg of the north statue.

These mighty seated statues were erected in honour of Amenhotep III and are all that now remain at this site of his mortuary temple. The diminutive figure standing by the knee of the southern colossus is that of Tiy (Tiye), his wife; a similar figure once adorned the northern colossus but has fallen away. Research has revealed the south colossus was hewn from a single block of grey siliceous rock. The north colossus is that popularly known as The Colossus of Memnon or the Singing Memnon.

As Denon observed, the legs of the north statue were marked with numerous inscriptions in Greek – and also Latin – bearing the names and testimonies of those who had heard the statue resonate. The sounds, or 'voice', of Memnon were usually heard at sunrise and were probably the result of air escaping from fissures in the body of the sculpture or by the resonance caused by the great pieces of stone expanding in the warm morning sunlight. Whatever the precise origin of the sounds, when repairs were made

to the statue in the third century by the Roman emperor Septimius Severus, the colossus
fell silent.

Denon was tempted to add his own name to those already carved on the colossus but
he busied himself, more productively, in making drawings of them. So absorbed did he
grow in his task that he failed to notice his companions were making their departure:

> I had hardly begun to draw these colossal figures when I found I was left alone with these
> stupendous conceptions – and the ideas these solitary objects inspired. Being alarmed at my
> unprotected situation, I hastened to rejoin my comrades whose eager curiosity had already led
> them to a large temple near to the village of Medinet Habu.
>
> I observed, as I passed by, that the ground about the tomb of Ozymandias was cultivated and
> I [assumed] the inundation [must] reach this far. [It appeared that] although the bed of the
> Nile was raised, there must formerly have been some form of dyke to prevent the water from
> flooding this part of the ancient town which, when we crossed it, was a vast field of green wheat
> promising an abundant harvest.

The Colossi of Memnon stand on what, in former times, was a flood plain of the River
Nile. Over the centuries, the encroachments of the inundation have contributed to
destablizing the great statues, causing them to lean backwards. This is particularly so in
the case of the north colossus (Singing Memnon) and may account for the cracks and
fissures it has sustained with the passing of time. Also of interest is the circumstance
that many of the inscriptions on this statue are found well above the present ground
level – evidence that the silt deposits, now cleared away, once reached high up the
seated figures.

The French convoy had now reached the western region of Thebes. In Pharaonic times,
this locality was the abode of the dead. On his death, the deceased pharaoh was ferried
across the Nile in his ceremonial barque to be buried in the large necropolis the
Egyptians named the Western City. Within the locality, on the Theban bank opposite
modern Luxor, is the temple complex known as Medinet Habu whose most distinctive
structure is the mortuary temple of Rameses III. Its principal architectural features are a
wide front pylon, together with entrance gate, leading to a series of outer and inner
courts that are separated by an inner pylon. Within the great pillared halls were
vestibules and sanctuaries, appropriate to the ceremonies and rituals of a king, together
with residential quarters. On leaving the Colossi of Memnon, Denon visited this temple,
where he recorded his impressions:

> Adjoining the village of Medinet Habu, at the bottom of the mountain, is a vast palace [that
> has been] built and enlarged at different periods. All that I could make of it on this, my first
> examination on horseback, was that the lower part of the palace – which abuts the mountain –
> is the most ancient in its construction. It is covered with hieroglyphics [that are] cut very deep
> and without any relief.
>
> In the fourth century [AD] the [adherents of the] Catholic religion converted it to sacred
> purposes. They made a church of it, adding two rows of pillars, in the style of that age, to
> support a covered roof. At the south of this monument there is a system of apartments with
> steps and square windows – the only building I had yet seen here which was not a temple.
> Beyond this are edifices rebuilt with old materials but left unfinished.

The hieroglyphics on the wall of the temple have now been deciphered. These tell of the various campaigns of Rameses III and his conquests over the neighbouring peoples. Other scenes depict religious processions and events from everyday life. Because of the impregnability of its great mud-brick outer defensive walls, the temple complex at Medinet Habu served as a stronghold and refuge in times of unrest. In addition, as Denon observed, the temple was also a place for Christian worship.

Denon's eagerness to satisfy his curiosity was curtailed by General Desaix who, as ever, was concerned to resume the march. Accordingly, he issued his command and led the cavalry away at full gallop. They journeyed in this manner across the plain for about two leagues until Hermonthis was reached.

The ancient site of Hermonthis is synonymous with modern-day Armant that lies south of Luxor on the west bank of the Nile. The antiquities at the site included the remains of a once great temple. These were still in existence at the time of the French occupation of Egypt, but time did not allow Denon to make an inspection of them. This agitated Denon who was already concerned at not having been able to spend more time investigating the ruins at Medinet Habu:

> At night I returned to my quarters. My head was confused by the profusion of objects that had passed before my eyes in so short a space of time. I could have found delicious and abundant food for my curiosity for a whole month in seeing what I had been obliged to pass over in twelve hours without, moreover, having it in my power to devote any part of the following day to reflection.

With the army's need to keep on the move the march south was once more resumed. On 29 January, early in the morning, the party arrived at Esna which is about 50 kilometres south of Luxor. This was the last township of any importance that had been occupied by Murad Bey in his dash south to evade and frustrate the French troops. All the signs were he had made a hasty departure only a few hours previously since a quantity of his tents and baggage were still burning. The French generals supposed Murad Bey had set fire to these possessions so as to be unencumbered when making his escape. They further conjectured that he was intent upon leading the French troops into the arid regions of Nubia, modern-day Sudan, in the hope of wearing them out. He knew this inhospitable region offered no succour whatsoever for a large body of men and their transport animals. Furthermore, it was probable Murad Bey intended to rally and augment his troops as a preliminary to mounting an attack on the French detachment.

Esna is the ancient Latopolis, celebrated for its Graeco-Roman temple dedicated to the ram-god Khnum. Although time was short, Denon had a few hours to visit and illustrate the architectural remains still standing within the township:

> Some remains are visible of the port or quay on the bank of the Nile which has been often repaired but, despite all that has been done, it still remains in a miserable condition. This town also contains the portico of a temple that appears to me to be the most perfect monument of architecture. It is situated near the bazaar in the great square and would make an incomparable ornament to this spot if the inhabitants had any idea of its merit. Instead of this, they have deformed it to the vilest purposes. The portico is well preserved and possesses a great richness of sculpture.

The famed Colossi of Memnon. These mighty seated statues are depictions of Amenhotep III sited on the Plain of Thebes. In the upper illustration they are portrayed at sunrise, casting their long shadows upon the mountains. In ancient times the warmth of the sun's rays caused one of the statues – 'singing Memnon' – to emit an ethereal sound. The lower illustrations are close-up details of their weathered forms. The diminutive size of the local people conveys the heroic scale of these awesome monoliths. *(Denon, British Library)*

The hieroglyphics in relief, with which it is covered inside and out, are executed with great care. They contain, among other subjects, a zodiac and large figures of men with crocodile heads. The capitals, though all different, have a very fine effect. As an additional proof that the Egyptians derived nothing from other people, we may remark that they have derived all the ornaments, of which these capitals are composed, from the productions of their own country such as the lotus, the palm tree, the vine and the rush.

The Temple of Horus at Edfu. The temple is shown encroached upon by desert sand and encumbered by mud dwellings – all of which have now been cleared. The Nile meanders in the distance. Edfu is the most complete of all Egyptian temples. Denon remarks: 'I took a journey of more than fifty leagues for the sole purpose of adding this view to my collection. I was about to quit the spot without having employed my pencil, so impossible was it for me to support the burning sun. Citizen Baltard [an accomplished artist] completed the sketch with my eyes smarting and dazzled with the sunshine and my blood in a violent ferment with the scorching heat of the day.' *(Denon-Baltard, British Library)*

It is probable that in its heyday the Temple of Khnum was connected to the River Nile by means of a processional route, remains of which still exist at the location that Denon took to be a quay. The temple itself, as Denon remarks, had been lost beneath the township of Esna. The surviving portico is decorated with twenty-four – not eighteen – great flower-headed columns that support a system of deep stone beams. At the time of Denon's visit, rubbish and wind-blown sand so encroached upon the temple that not all the columns were visible. The detritus has now been removed to reveal all the beautiful pillars with their magnificent over-arching capitals and their all-encompassing system of hieroglyphic decoration.

Denon worked rapidly at the temple site to make all the sketches he could before being called away once more to rejoin the cavalry. The infantry and artillery were left behind at Esna so that the men on horseback could make better progress.

Esna was the principal town of the most southern province of Egypt, situated on the western bank of the Nile between Thebes and the First Cataract. At this location the valley of the Nile had a width of about 8 kilometres. To the south the aspect of the town was picturesque. Here the soil benefited most from the irrigation-waters, promoting strong and vigorous vegetation. At Esna the river bank was lined regularly with rows of barques that offered the spectacle of an active and commercial port. However, the Nile at this location flowed with a rapid current that constantly impinged upon the waterline causing it to crumble and threaten the houses built nearby. During their stay at Esna the French saw this happen and observed its fearful consequences:

> The inhabitants of these houses, forced to abandon them, invaded the interior of the town that they crowded causing the plague to rise up and decimate the population. This scourge encroaches, little by little, every ten to twelve years. It typically follows after a great inundation. [The French records show that in the year 1801 the entire region had been overwhelmed and entire villages depopulated.]

Denon considered that Esna offered more luxury and out-reaching industry than the other towns of Upper Egypt. It was here that a great quantity of fine blue-cotton material was woven called *melâyeh*. Extensive use of this was made throughout Egypt, particularly in the form of the all-enveloping cloak worn by women. There were several potteries at Esna and numerous presses existed for the extraction of olive oil. Baskets were woven in large quantities and were decorated with interwoven palm leaves. A caravan trade brought rich goods to Esna such as gum arabic, ostrich feathers and ivory. These were purchased by the wealthy and powerful beys who included Hasan, O'sman and Sâleh who were implacable enemies of Murad Bey. Being so distant from Cairo they had little to fear from his oppressive regime and therefore exacted their own upon the local people. Denon observed: 'The veritable riches of [these] exiled beys and their Mamelukes are not of the nature to enable them to be easily subjugated. Their courage and the despotism they exercise over the people are inexhaustible.'

At the northern extremity of Esna was a picturesque garden belonging to Hasan Bey. This was adopted by the French as a pleasure garden and a place for their occasional rendezvous. It became known as the *jardin français* and one evening was the scene of a demonstration of oriental hospitality. In view of their loathing of Murad Bey, the principal sheikhs of the town regarded the French as being more like guests than conquerors and accordingly invited them to participate in a feast:

> All the officers of the garrison and the principal inhabitants of the town were assembled in the French Garden. The main avenue was covered with a tablecloth over all its length on which dinner was served on the ground with French and Muslims all intermingled. The Egyptians had some instruction in our language [such that] the conversation did not languish at any part of the table.
>
> The meal consisted of several entire sheep boiled and stuffed with rice and a multitude of small plates of sweetmeats which, by their delicacy, contrasted with the principal dishes. The servants, responsible for maintaining the service, placed themselves at each corner [of the table coverings] standing at intervals. Dressed in elegant costumes, they worked with energy. They served as much with their fingers as with their knives tearing and cutting from the quarters of the meat. They [also] served with such earnestness and solicitation that it was difficult to refuse them.
>
> Coffee being taken, the guests rose and the servants in the first row immediately replaced them. These were followed by their subordinates, the places at the table thus being occupied four times by new diners before the table was entirely depleted of all the meat with which it was covered. A fine fountain that Hasan Bey had built in his garden provided in abundance the refreshment that was offered to us.

As the French travelled further south, the country became progressively more barren and inhospitable. The resources of the land also began to diminish and 'with every league [it] dwindled to little or nothing'. After a march of 'three leagues and a half' the party camped for the night. On 30 January, it was resumed and soon brought the party within view of the ancient site of Apollonopolis Magna – modern-day Edfu. This is a site rich in Egyptian iconography. It was here the god Horus was venerated. Horus was a sky-god represented in hieroglyphics and sculptures as a hawk or falcon. His eyes were considered to be the sun and the moon.

The Greeks identified Horus with their own god Apollo and named Edfu Apollonopolis – Apollo's town. In Egyptian legend, Horus damaged his left eye – characterised as the moon – which, as it healed, gave a mythological explanation to the moon's phases. Horus was celebrated in a great temple, much of which still exists today. Indeed, the Temple of Horus at Edfu is one of the most complete of all Egyptian structures and provides tangible visual evidence of Egyptian attainments in the decorative arts. On arriving at Edfu, Denon recorded the following impressions of this justly venerated temple:

> We were struck with admiration at the fine and advantageous site of Apollonopolis Magna. It commanded the river and the whole valley of Egypt. Its magnificent temple towered over the rest like a large citadel that keeps the adjacent country in awe. This comparison is indeed so naturally suggested by the situation of this edifice that it is known only to the natives by the name of The Fortress. I foresaw, with regret, that we should enter the town late and quit it early in the morning. I pushed on to gain a little time to examine it before daylight left us entirely.
>
> During this visit I had time only to ride round this edifice – the extent, majesty, magnificence and high [state of] preservation of which surpassed all that I had yet seen in Egypt or elsewhere. It made an impression on me as vast as its own gigantic dimensions. This building is a long suite of pyramidal gates, of courts decorated with galleries, of porticoes and of covered naves constructed not with common stones but entire monoliths.

By the time Denon had completed his tour of the Temple of Horus, night had come on and he once again 'regretted the necessity of passing with such rapidity so much art that merited so much more attention'.

Below Edfu, the cultivated plain grows very narrow and, in Denon's estimation, there was only about 'a quarter of a league' of fertile ground between the desert and the river. The next day, the French party made their way along this strip of farmland and at noon halted on the banks of the Nile. The cavalry had gone on ahead of the detachment of soldiers. Messengers returned with the unwelcome news that in order to make further progress south 'a desert of some seven leagues extent must be crossed'. The day being too advanced to undertake such a gruelling march, the party stopped for the rest of the evening at a deserted village. They were fortunate to find wood for their fires and so were able to enjoy a cooked meal.

On 31 January, at three in the morning, the party resumed their march with the cool of night as their benefactor. The first hour was passed agreeably enough amid cultivated country, after which the terrain became more severe. The desert region was soon

The *pronaos* of the Temple of Horus at Edfu. A local man sits by one of the giant columns, his diminutive form conveying a sense of their enormous scale and materiality. Centuries of wind-blown sand obstructed survey-work in the temple forecourt – it was not cleared away until 1860 under the direction of Auguste Mariette. Edfu is the second largest Egyptian temple (after Karnak) and was dedicated to the celestial god Horus. *(Roberts, British Library)*

encountered where the alluvial soil gave way to a colourful but harsh combination of decayed freestone, white and rose-coloured quartz, brownish flint and white cornelians. After marching for five hours on this surface, the soldiers' boots were torn through and they were obliged to bind them with pieces of linen. The heat of day also began to take its toll and the men were tormented with a burning thirst. Denon describes the deprivations of the party:

> No water could be found except for the Nile which was a league out of our way and its banks were as arid as the desert. But the urgency of thirst prevailed and we arrived at the river exhausted with fatigue. However, the draught animals, bearing our camp equipage, had not had any food the night before and were so weakened by hunger that only a few of them were able to follow.

What was the general distress when it was announced there was nothing to eat! We looked at each other in mute consternation. After a while a camel with a light load of butter came up and

some others whose precious sacks had already been emptied. By shaking out every grain of meal from the bags – and rummaging in every corner – we found enough to make a distribution of a handful of flour to each. We got kindling from a neighbouring tree, made our flour into fritters and employment drove away our gloomy thoughts. French gaiety soon prevailed and restored our usual courage.

The inner court of the Temple of Horus at Edfu. Centuries of wind-blown sand has encroached almost to the capitals of the columns, each of which bears distinctive decoration derived from plant motifs. Brick structures encumber the interior and have now been cleared. A group of people take a meal within the precincts; Denon took pains to make friends with such local inhabitants and received many acts of kindness in return. *(Denon, British Library)*

An extended march under harrowing conditions brought the party to the ruins of El Silsila. These are noteworthy for the royal shrines dedicated to Rameses II and Sethos I. They were hewn from the living sandstone that was also used as a source of material from which to construct the great temples of Upper Egypt. Despite the hardships he had endured in reaching this place, Denon still retained sufficient self-possession to make a brief entry in his *Journal*:

The sandstone quarries of El-Silsila. On the march south, Denon explored the remains of these stone quarries from which great monoliths had been extracted for transportation to Lower Egypt – a Herculean undertaking. The quarries themselves had then been adapted as sanctuaries complete with ornate embellishments. Above is a general view of the site. Below are life-size figures carved into the rock face. *(Denon, British Library)*

The ruins of El Silsila consist of broken fragments, bricks and the remains of a temple whose highest walls are now not more than three feet above the sand. One can just observe that the nave of the temple, which is covered with hieroglyphics, was surrounded by a gallery to which in a later period a portico without hieroglyphics has been added.

El Silsila was soon passed and the route taken by the French led them once more into the desert. In this region of Egypt, the sandstone rocks give way to granite that shows flints of every colour. This rock was much favoured in Pharaonic times by sculptors for its inherent beauty and hardness, the latter quality enabling the stone to be burnished to a high polish. Denon found some cornelians, intermixed with jasper and serpentine. He also looked closely at the desert sand and found it to consist predominantly of small fragments of granite.

Shortly after he and his entourage arrived at an elevated position that offered a breathtaking panorama of the surrounding countryside. Below them the Nile could be seen meandering along its winding course. With the assistance of his telescope Denon thought he could see what he refers to as a *pharos*. This may have been some form of landmark or beacon to assist boatmen to navigate the treacherous course of the Nile in its many changes of direction.

Also in the distance Denon could make out the heights of Ombos that are situated about 40 kilometres north of Aswan. Today, the locality has the name Kom Ombo and is renowned for the temple dedicated to the veneration of the deities Sobek (god of the crocodile) and Haroeris (god of the hawk). Denon could only discern these from a distance and had to confine himself to describing them as 'the fine monuments of the summit'.

The principal temple of Kom Ombo occupies a sandy escarpment and is unusual in that it is divided along its width into two perfectly symmetrical parts, each side of the edifice having its own entrances and ancillary chapels where the respective deities could be worshipped.

South of Kom Ombo, the eastern tributary of the River Nile creates a great fertile plain from the beneficial effects of its annual inundation – a region Denon estimated to be 'more than twenty leagues in extent'. In fact, at the time of the French visit, the frequent flooding of this great plain turned the land into a veritable quagmire that served the local people as an island retreat from the incursion of the Mamelukes. Their cavalry could not secure a foothold in such soft terrain and, in consequence, the local people were able to live in relative peace and prosperity. The French also found it difficult to make an incursion into this territory with their own horses and heavy equipment, and so had to confine themselves to journeying along the firmer ground on the elevated banks of the Nile.

The local inhabitants fled with the approach of the French army, abandoning their village of Binbân, which skirted the desert, to their mercy. To Denon's critical gaze it was as gloomy in appearance as its name was unprepossessing. However, after a march of eleven hours the miserable mud dwellings of which the settlement was composed offered the welcome prospect of rest and refreshment. The more enterprising soldiers, despite the ruinous state of their boots, had managed to chase and herd together several oxen that guaranteed the army would not go without a supply of meat. In addition, the village was ransacked 'to its very foundations' in a relentless search for anything of use. Denon and his companions settled themselves for the evening.

Only one final push now remained for the French to reach the southernmost point on their journey into Upper Egypt.

CHAPTER 13

To the Cataracts

The French were now approaching the ancient township of Syene, modern-day Aswan. (The name Syene is a Greek derivative of the Arabic name Aswan.) Denon, his companions and the army were deep in the heartland of Upper Egypt and, being more than 600 kilometres south of Cairo, were dependent upon their own resources. Furthermore, they were in hostile territory and had to contend with the ever-present threat of attack from the forces of Murad Bey. Irrespective of these hazards, the region to which Denon and his companions were travelling offered the prospect of visiting some of the most spectacular and romantically sited temples in Egypt.

Syene is close to the first of the sequence of Nile cataracts, and borders what is today the northern tip of Lake Nasser. Denon could now anticipate setting his eyes not only upon the township of Syene but the nearby island of Philae and the quarries from the granite of which so many of Egypt's antiquities were constructed.

The rocky terrain through which they marched presented new deserts to the eyes of the troops for it consisted alternately of granite and decomposed freestone. This had weathered in the winds to give the sand a friable crust-like surface. They came upon deserted villages in which the sand had drifted. Here the surface was smooth and yielding like snow. The tracks of an animal that had passed since the last sandstorm could be perceived with ease. Denon's *Journal* resumes with an entry for 1 February 1799:

> We marched slowly and painfully stopping every minute to pull off our shoes and to take breath. In the middle of the desert I found the trace of a great antique road, bounded by large masses of cut stone, that led in a straight line to Syene. In the afternoon the troops were so much fatigued that, on quitting the desert, we halted at the first green spot that could provide food for our horses. I thought they would never be moved from the place nor our men ever again rise from the ground. As for myself, I was quite wearied and remained all night as if riveted to the soil.
>
> The next day we had but three-quarters of a league to march to rejoin our cavalry. They had gone before to consume all that the country would afford. At last we were in sight of Aswan, or Syene, the object of our destination. The soldier now forgot his fatigues as if he had already arrived at the Promised Land.
>
> I had the most reason to be satisfied. For the first time I was going to sit down and take a little breathing space in this country that abounded with interesting objects for my researches.

The route Denon and his soldier-companions had taken was that followed in ancient times by pilgrims making their way to the island of Philae, one of the most sacred places in Egypt. As Denon had noted, in the late eighteenth century this route still bore traces from antiquity. Lining the way were great stones inscribed with sacred characters and depictions of human forms. Also to be seen were the heads of animals accompanied by hieroglyphic inscriptions. Philae was still a distant prospect but Denon had the welcome opportunity of spending his time exploring the island of Elephantine.

First he made a tour of the countryside bordering the Nile. It was evident that the Mamelukes had passed this way. They had left behind several boats moored on the shore which they had been unable to haul over the cataracts. These would later assist the French in making their own progress down the Nile. On the morning of 2 February, Denon ascended the remains of the Christian convent of St Lawrence that served him as an observation tower. From here he gained his first view of the island of Elephantine set amid tumbling cascades of water:

> From the lofty summit . . . a most singular view presents itself to the eye. It seems to be at the end of the world, or rather a chaos, from which the air has already separated and the watery element appears to gush from the earth running in numerous channels that promise fertility to nature.
>
> The first effects of its bounties are seen around the granite rocks in the hollows of which the sand and slime, brought by the waves, are deposited forming a basis for vegetation that continues to increase and to embrace a larger and wider field. At Elephantine, the cultivation, the trees and the habitations exhibit a picture of perfection in the gifts of nature that have given rise to the Arabian name of *Kezivet-El-Sag* – Flowery Island – for this island.

A point of general interest can be made here. To Denon and his companions the giant granite rocks at this location in the River Nile, washed smooth by the action of the water, appeared to resemble the backs of large bathing elephants. In a word they were 'elephantine', from which the modern-day name for the island derives.

The next day the party crossed over to the right bank of the Nile to secure Aswan. By now Murad Bey had crossed the cataracts and had dispersed his forces over a considerable tract of countryside in search of forage for his animals and food for his retinue of Mamelukes. The French had to deploy themselves in much the same manner and for the same reasons.

They then endeavoured to make themselves at home. According to Denon the barbers were the first among the company to take the initiative. They set up their distinctive poles, established eating houses and became veritable restaurateurs offering their services 'at a fixed price'. These circumstances prompted Denon to reflect on the lively and spirited character of his soldier-companions:

> An army offers a picture of the most rapid exercise of every resource that industry can furnish. Every individual sets all his abilities to work for the common advantage. What peculiarly characterises a French army is to establish superfluities and amusements at the same time, and with the same care, as necessities. Thus, we had gardens and coffee houses in which we amused ourselves in games with cards manufactured at Syene.
>
> At one entrance of the village was a walk with straight rows of trees pointing to the north. Our soldiers set up a milestone here with the inscription: *Route de Paris No. Onze cent soixante sept milles trois cents quarante.*

Panoramic views of the island of Philae. The goddess Isis was worshipped at the temple illustrated here. This island temple was the largest dedicated to Isis. In legend, Osiris was buried at Philae which was also considered to be the mythological source of the Nile. The upper engraving is a view from east to west at sunset. In the centre is another view from the opposite direction. The lower illustration depicts the moment when the local inhabitants, mounted on the rocks, took up arms against the French in a futile attempt to prevent them from landing on the island. *(Denon, British Library)*

Nothing but death can put an end to valour combined with gaiety. The greatest misfortunes can do nothing towards it.

The position of the island of Elephantine, in the middle of the Nile on the border with Nubia, distinguishes it as among the most singular places in Egypt. The verdure and freshness of this region contrast so agreeably with the arid surrounding terrain that, in addition to being called the Flowery Island, it has also been named the Blooming Island and the Tropical Garden.

Edme-François Jomard, one of Denon's fellow savants, visited the island of Elephantine and was enchanted by what he found:

> The traveller promenades and rests with delight in the shade of the trees that are always green. The pure and fresh air induces inexpressible sensations that can be felt only by those who have experienced this tropic. The sweet impression of this environment is heightened by the contrast between the proximity of the rocks and the cultivated fields, between the desert sand – and the searing temperatures – and the verdure of the gardens. In a word, between the contrast of nature and of art that gives to this region a distinct physiognomy that is manifestly different in aspect to the monotony of other parts of Egypt.
>
> Amid all this varied picturesqueness, the traveller enjoys the spectacle of several ancient monuments that are still standing – fragmentary but precious vestiges of ancient Elephantine. Such is the first cultivated region of Egypt and such is the entrance of the Nile into this country, when it has traversed the chain of granite and rocks that cross it and the innumerable reefs of the First Cataract.

For a period, the island of Elephantine became Denon's 'country house and palace of delight, observation and research'. By his own testimony, he 'turned over every loose stone and questioned every rock on the island'. At its southern extremity was an Egyptian settlement and traces of Roman habitations together with the Arabian buildings that had succeeded them. The part occupied by the Romans could only be made out by piles of bricks, tessellated pavements and, remarkably, small images of porcelain and bronze that could still be found amid all the centuries of accumulated rubbish. Here is Denon's description of the island:

> The Island of Elephantine, defended on the south by breakers, has been doubtless much increased towards the north by alluvial soil. This soil soon becomes converted into cultivated lands and pleasant gardens which, being kept perpetually watered by means of wheels and buckets, produce here four or five crops yearly. Thus, the inhabitants are numerous, in easy circumstances and courteous. When I hailed them from the opposite shore they would come across for me in their boats and I was soon surrounded by all the children who offered me for sale fragments of antiquities and rough cornelians. With a few crowns I made a great number of these little ones happy and gained the good will of their parents who invited me to them [and] prepared me breakfast in the temples in which I had set up my drawing apparatus.
>
> In short, I appeared like a kind of master of a garden that contained, in reality, all that one seeks to imitate in our decorated gardens in Europe. Here were islets, rocks, deserts, plains, meadows, garden-ground, open groves, hamlets, dark woods, remarkable and numerous plants, a river, canals, mills and sublime ruins.

Top: A distant view of the island of Elephantine. Its river-washed boulders suggested the appearance of bathing elephants to the French explorers.

Centre: The approaches to Syene, modern-day Aswan. The construction of Lake Nasser has now changed much of the topography of this region.

Above: A large rock that appears to have been abandoned after the setting-out lines had been inscribed. As the French approached Elephantine and Syene, they discovered similar large rocks bearing traces of carving and hieroglyphic inscriptions. *(Dutertre, Jollois and Jomard, National Library of Scotland)*

I never passed hours more deliciously occupied than those that I devoted to my solitary walks at Elephantine – an island that alone is worth more than the whole territory on shore of the country that lies adjacent to the town.

Denon's stay at Elephantine enabled him to survey the island and devote time to making a study of its monuments:

An ancient temple is left standing surrounded with a pilastered gallery and two columns in the portico. Nothing is wanting but two pilasters on the left angle of this ruin. Other edifices have been attached to it in a later period. Some fragments are remaining that give an idea of their form when [it was] perfect. [This] proves these accessory parts were much larger than the original sanctuary. This latter is covered both within and without with hieroglyphics in relief – very well cut and in a good state of preservation.

I copied the whole side of the inner figures. The corresponding side appears to be nearly a repetition of the same. This kind of picture is both interesting and curious. It possessed a unity of design that I had not before met with in this sort of decoration, which is commonly divided into distinct compartments.

I also took [a view of] one side of the outer wall and a single pilaster. All the rest are nearly similar. The view of the whole of this small edifice will give an idea of its importance and high state of preservation.

The edifice Denon had discovered was the Temple of Amenophis III, dedicated to the ram-headed god Khnum. His description of it is historically important since it was destroyed about twenty years after his visit to Elephantine. The two columns he saw were conceived to resemble papyrus buds in the style of the kind adopted at several other temples throughout Egypt. Still existing at the time of Denon's visit was a seated statue to the deity Osiris that was wrought from a monolithic block of red granite – about 2.5 metres high. Denon's colleague Edme-François Jomard also visited this temple and considered it to be 'a model of simplicity and purity' and remarked how 'the eye is satisfied by the harmony that prevails between the architectural members'.

Due to the exposed position of the island of Elephantine in the middle of the River Nile, the ancient temple builders had, of necessity, turned their ingenuity to constructing defensive works to prevent the flood waters from encroaching upon the farmland. Notable among these was a great quay wall that rose some 15 metres above low-water level. This impressive structure was more than 150 metres in length. It is a tribute to the engineering skills of the Egyptian masons that this quay had the capacity to resist the mass of water forced against it, with great rapidity and turbulence, at the height of the seasonal inundation.

A staircase had been built against the side of a portion of the quay that led down to the water. This was graduated with a scale that served to give an indication of the water level and could thereby show the extent of the encroachment of the flood waters. This staircase functioned as a Nileometer and was one of several such constructions that were sited along the course of the Nile at certain strategic locations.

The French found the township of Syene supported 'a numerous population' and was bustling with activity. A Turkish garrison was also maintained at Syene. There was a prosperous trade in senna and dates, the income from which was sufficient to provide for

The Hypostyle Hall of the Temple of Isis. The monuments on the island of Philae captivated Denon. He discovered columns and wall decorations still resplendent in their original coloration of blue, green, red and yellow. The motifs depict the pharaohs making offerings to Isis who was venerated at Philae. The colours were washed away in the nineteenth century by the encroaching waters of the Nile. *(Roberts, British Library)*

the primary needs of the people and the levies imposed by the governor of the district. Senna was grown both as a cultivated crop and was harvested from the wild. In the case of the latter, it was brought in from the neighbouring districts by members of the local tribe, known as the Barâbras, to whom reference has already been made. These jet-black people came from Nubia and were of a warm-hearted, genial disposition. They endeared themselves to the French travellers by reason of their 'gaiety which pleases and touches', the French finding in them more genuineness and reliability than in the other local people whom they had encountered in Egypt.

On the island of Elephantine, whole families of Barâbras occupied themselves in collecting the cornelians and precious agates that were washed down by the Nile 'in great numbers'. By their efforts Denon and his fellow savants were also able to acquire engraved stones, amulets and ancient lamps that the local people foraged by searching through the ruins. Denon considered that the goods he purchased, particularly senna, would cost 'one hundred times more' back home in France. Senna, he recorded, was taxed heavily at the ports of Alexandria and Cairo. Dates grew in abundance and were exported in huge quantities. Large boats were loaded with them daily for transport down the Nile to Lower Egypt.

Although the French sojourn on the island of Elephantine was idyllic, it was overshadowed by the realization that the Mameluke forces were in the neighbourhood and continued to pose a threat. Spies were sent out who reported they had navigated upriver and were camped a little distance above the cataracts. Here they could obtain forage for their animals and acquire supplies of flour and dates – by extortion – from the local people. The Mameluke forces were considerable and the French spies estimated that they extended for perhaps as much as 'ten leagues on each bank'. Their rearguard was known to be no more than 'four leagues distant' and, in consequence, was familiar with every step the French took – as the French were informed of all their movements. Denon suspected that some of their spies, who were local people, were also employed by the Mamelukes and 'served both parties equally faithfully and with exactness'.

Mention has been made of the great polished granite boulders that had suggested to the French explorers the forms of elephants bathing in the water. More particularly, the region of Syene was renowned for the high quality of its granite and had been used as a source for this material for centuries by generations of temple builders and quarrymen requiring giant blocks of stone from which to carve obelisks and colossal statues. The granite quarries at Syene are located on the east bank of the Nile, a few kilometres south of the island of Elephantine. They were the subject of Denon's next excursion:

> I encountered the quarries in the granite rocks from which were extracted the blocks that form the material of the colossal statues. [These] have been the object of admiration to so many ages and the ruins of them still strike us with astonishment. It seemed as if the quarrymen desired to preserve a memorial to the masses [of stone] that produced these blocks by leaving, at the place [where they were extracted], hieroglyphic inscriptions that perhaps record the event.
>
> The operation by which these blocks were detached must have been nearly the same as is employed in the present time. A cleft is first cut out and then the whole mass is split off by means of wedges of different sizes, all struck in at one time. The marks of these first operations

Top: A group of young people who lived beyond the cataracts in the border region of Egypt with Nubia. The costume of the men was absolute nudity unless modified with a drape of cotton. They anointed their frizzy hair with oil of cedar wood the strong odour of which 'repelled all vermin'! Women and children wore decorative ornaments and collars made from coloured glass. Denon observed how married women had 'a palpable love of their husbands'.

Above: This is the last drawing Denon made on his journey into Upper Egypt, some 300 leagues south of Cairo. He encountered this Arab family scratching a living from the arid region with little more than a few goats, pigeons, a bread oven and straw for a bed. *(Denon, British Library)*

are preserved so fresh in this malleable material that to look at them one would suspect the work had been interrupted only yesterday. I took a sketch of them.

Denon continued his journey south in the direction of the neighbouring island of Philae. Once more he was captivated by the picturesque nature of the countryside:

After passing the cataracts, the cliffs grow loftier and on their summit rocks of granite are heaped up appearing to cluster together and to hang in equipoise [as if] on purpose to produce the most picturesque effects. Through these rough and rugged forms, the eye all at once discovers the magnificent monuments of the Island of Philae that form a brilliant contrast and one of the most singular surprises that the traveller can meet with.

The Nile makes a bend here, as if to come and visit this enchanting island, where the monuments are only separated by tufts of palm trees or rocks. These appear to be left merely to construct the forms of nature with the magnificence of art and to collect, in one rich spot, everything that is most beautiful and impressive.

By the time Denon had drawn closer to the island of Philae, the inhabitants had fled to the relative safety of the nearby island of Biga. From there they emitted 'loud and savage cries' that the French were given to understand, through their interpreter, were more a demonstration of the islanders' fear than of their hostility. Denon and his companions tried to persuade them to send over a boat so that they could explore the island, but to no avail. Denon therefore had to content himself with sketching the island of Philae from across the river.

During this period this branch of the Nile was very narrow and so Denon was able to get a good view of his subject. He returned to camp well satisfied with his day's work, although he remarks: 'This cursory view did not appear to me sufficient for objects of such quality, of such importance and for monuments of such an extent and high [state of] preservation'. He resolved to make a return visit as soon as possible to gain a more detailed understanding and better description of subjects he knew 'would be attended with so much interest'.

On reaching camp, Denon and his officer-companions learned that the Mamelukes were now within a mere 2 leagues of the French forces and the decision was taken to set out immediately to engage them. Their route was along the highway taken by the pilgrims in ancient times. It was marked, once more, by great blocks of stone decorated with hieroglyphics.

The island of Philae was one of the most sacred places in Egypt. In Egyptian mythology this island sanctuary was the abode of the goddess Isis while the adjacent island of Biga was the resting place of Osiris, the consort of Isis. The cult of Isis survived into Roman and Christian times, as is evident from the architectural remains from these periods found on these islands. In the modern era, with the building of Lake Nasser and the Aswan High Dam, the surviving temple structures on the island of Philae have been transferred to the nearby island of Agilqiyya to protect them from the rising waters – one of the great achievements of contemporary archaeology and civil engineering.

On reaching Philae, the French found the inhabitants had returned to their island retreat but were in a hostile frame of mind and were resolved not to offer hospitality. Denon attributed their demeanour to a combination of the strange and unfamiliar appearance his party presented, clothed as they were in European military uniforms, and, more significantly, to the sight of their threatening weapons. In view of this show of ill-will the French decided to continue the journey south.

Beyond Philae, the River Nile presented an open stretch of water and for some distance was quite navigable. On the banks could be seen an Arab fort and a mosque. Further on, the Nile became impracticable for travellers and yielded views only of 'barren

soil, left to itself, and rocky places bearing a few habitations that resembled the huts of savages'. The party next entered an inhospitable desert region through which they trudged for several hours. This in turn gave way to terrain composed of valleys and deep hollows that suggested to Denon that 'the landscape was constantly exposed to storms and torrents'.

Their route returned to the bank of the Nile. Once more it presented an open stretch of water. Journeying along a ravine they came to a village located on its banks by the

The great Temple of Abu Simbel. The majestic rock-cut temple of Rameses II was unknown to the French explorers – it was discovered later by Johann Ludwig Burckhardt. It is included here to complement the selection of images of Egypt's antiquities. The head of one of the colossi has fallen to the sand that for centuries shrouded the monuments. The site was cleared by the explorer-showman Giovanni Belzoni – he was himself a colossus and could support the weight of eleven men. The subsequent removal of the great structures, to escape the waters of Lake Nasser, is one of the memorable archaeological achievements of UNESCO. *(Roberts, British Library)*

name of Taudi, occupied by the very Mamelukes whom they were pursuing. Observing the approach of the French, the Mamelukes made such a hasty departure they left behind them their plates, kettles and even the soup they had prepared.

A spy was sent out during the night. He returned at daybreak to report that the Mamelukes had retreated 'about 4 leagues further beyond Taudi' to another township called Demiet where they were resting and feeding their horses. The French generals had achieved part of their object in driving the enemy further off. Denon was out of humour and remarked: 'I had seen enough of Ethiopia, the Gublis [the people of the region] and their wives whose extreme ugliness can only be equalled by the savage jealousy of their husbands.'

Denon had the opportunity to observe a number of local women at close quarters. A group of them had been taken by surprise at the arrival of the French and were caught hiding behind some rocks – their more agile companions had plunged into the river and had swum to safety. Those taken captive were placed under Denon's personal protection. He has this to say of them and their menfolk:

> They appeared to have the sullen stupidity of downright savages. A rugged soil, fatigue and indifferent food must doubtless impose on them, even in youth, the marks of decrepitude. But the men seem to be of another species. Their features are delicate, their skin fine, their countenance lively and animated and their eyes and teeth admirable. Alert and intelligent, they appear to impart so much clarity and consciousness to their language that a short phrase is always a complete answer to questions that are put to them.
>
> Their inactivity more resembles ours than that of other oriental nations. They are quick in understanding and seeing and have a greediness for money that keeps pace with their frugality and can only be justified by their extreme poverty. Their leanness is not connected with ill health. Their colour, though black, is full of life and blood but their muscles are only tendons – absolutely without fat – so that I did not see a single person among them who was even plump.

Had Denon and the French army journeyed another 250 kilometres further south, it is conceivable they might have discovered the great rock-cut statues of Abu Simbel. These seated figures are representations of Rameses II and remained unknown to Europe until they were found by Jean-Louis Burckhardt in 1813. As it transpired, Aswan was the furthest south the French reached in their exploration of Egypt.

It has been remarked upon how Denon had left the island of Philae behind several days earlier, expressing regret that he had not been able to survey the monuments with the care and thoroughness they deserved. The return journey north the French were now about to undertake offered him the prospect of gratifying his wishes.

CHAPTER 14

Upper Egypt

On their return journey from the Cataracts, the French were mindful of the threat presented once more by Murad Bey and his Mameluke forces. When marching south the presence of the French army had been sufficient to drive him and his cavalry deep into Nubia but now, as the French retraced their steps, the wily Murad emerged from his retreat to harass them again. The response of the French was to adopt a policy of attrition with respect to the land to deny their pursuers all possible advantage of its resources: 'We could keep our persevering enemy at a distance from us, only by starving the country between them and us. We therefore bought up all the cattle, paid for the green crops on the land and the inhabitants themselves assisted us in pulling up from the ground every source of provision and then followed us with their domestic animals. Thus carrying off with us the whole population, we left behind us nothing but a wilderness.'

Denon was, however, less concerned with military matters than with the prospect of seeing the island of Philae :

> On returning, I was again struck by the sumptuous appearance of the edifices of Philae. I am persuaded that it was to produce this effect, upon strangers entering their territory, that the Egyptians had erected upon their frontier such a splendid group of monuments. Philae was the entrepôt of a commerce of barter between Ethiopia and Egypt and, wishing to give the Ethiopians a high idea of their resources and magnificence, the Egyptians raised many sumptuous edifices on the frontier of their empire.

As noted, Osiris and Isis were worshipped at Philae. Osiris was the god of fertility and the dead. According to Egyptian mythology, he was murdered by his brother Seth after which his body was scattered to the winds, collected together by his wife Isis and given renewed life. As king of the underworld, Osiris was the personification of all the pharaohs. Isis was associated with the rich plains of Egypt, made fruitful by the annual flooding of the Nile. The island of Philae, with its splendid temple structures, was therefore more than a symbolic demarcation of the old boundary between Egypt and Nubia. It was a sanctuary of the utmost significance where the worship of Isis continued until the reign of the Roman emperor Justinian in the sixth century AD.

When the French arrived back at the island of Philae, they attempted once more to negotiate with the inhabitants. The islanders were both obdurate and impertinent. They let it be known that even if the French were to come every day to the island for two months, and plead their case each day, they would still not be allowed to set foot on Philae.

Top: Ruins on the island of Philae, where Denon spent many happy hours at his researches. He identified shrines indicating Egyptian, Roman and Christian occupation.

Middle: The north side of the island with the Temple of Isis towering above its defensive works. The annual inundation impacted considerably upon Philae, prompting Denon to record in his *Journal*: 'The traveller cannot help being struck with astonishment at finding, on the frontier of Ethiopia, so many monuments of such magnificence which have for so long resisted the injuries of time.'

Above: A granite rock, to the east of Philae, which has been carved into the form of a great chair together with hieroglyphic inscriptions. Denon conjectured it may have been intended to receive a colossal statue. *(Denon, British Library)*

The French, whose intentions towards the people were amicable, were incensed that 'a handful of peasants', as Denon describes them, should respond to French courtesy with such effrontery. Denon tells us what happened as a consequence:

> We resolved the next day to try to make them change their mind. On the morrow we returned with two hundred men. As soon as they saw us, they put themselves in a posture of defence and defied us in the manner of savages, with loud cries, that the women repeated. The inhabitants of the neighbouring larger island immediately collected in arms that they made to glitter in the sun like sword-players. Some of them were quite naked, holding in one hand a sabre and in the other a shield. Others had rampart-muskets with matchlocks and yet others had long pikes.
>
> In a moment, all the east side of the rock was covered with enemies. We still called out to them that we were not coming to do them any harm and that we only wanted to enter amicably into their island. They answered they would never let us approach, or furnish us with the means of landing on their shores, and that they were not Mamelukes to fly before us.

This bragging speech terminated with loud shouts of defiance that resounded on all sides of the riverbank. At this, the order was given for the French sappers to level some huts, built near the shore, from which to construct a raft to carry the military across the river to the island. This was taken as a declaration of war by the islanders, who 'kept up a brisk and well-directed fire'. The French then moved their heavy guns into position 'which carried the rage of the natives to the highest pitch'.

The French sappers discovered that the palm wood, from which they were attempting to construct a raft, absorbed water and was not therefore very buoyant, a circumstance which compelled them to defer their attempted crossing of the Nile until the next day. In the meantime, the troops remained on the shore and a thorough search was made for driftwood and other materials sufficient to make a raft to hold forty men. The work employed them a whole day and was carried out under the gaze of the local people who, from the security of the island, continued to taunt the French with insolent remarks. They even proposed the General should pay 100 piastres to go over to the island on condition he was unarmed! However, their demeanour soon changed with the arrival of a large contingent of soldiers who gathered on the banks of the river and discharged volleys of grapeshot in the direction of the islanders. Denon relates:

> Terror succeeded, as usual, to headstrong rashness. Men, women and children threw themselves into the river to escape by swimming. Preserving their ferocious character, we saw mothers drowning their children – whom they could not carry away with them – and mutilating the girls to save them from the violence of the victors.
>
> When I landed on the island, the next day, I found a young girl seven or eight years old who had been cut with brutal cruelty in such a manner as to prevent her from satisfying the most pressing necessity of nature. It was only by a counter-operation, and a bath, that I was able to save the life of this unfortunate little creature who was very pretty.

According to Denon's *Journal*, the next day was the most rewarding to him of the whole time he spent travelling in Egypt. He was able to visit seven or eight monuments, in the space of 600 metres, and moreover could examine them at his ease. He remarks: 'I did not have by my side any of those impatient companions who always think they have seen enough and are constantly pressing you to go to some other object. Nor had I in my ears the beating of drums as a signal to muster, or to march, nor the Arabs, nor the peasants to torment me. I was alone, at full leisure and could make my drawings without interruption.' This was Denon's sixth visit to the island of Philae but the first that afforded him an opportunity to make detailed visual records of the ancient monuments:

As soon as I could set foot on the island I began by going over all the inner part to take a general survey of the various monuments and to form a topographical chart containing the island, the course of the river and the adjacent scenery. I found convincing proof that this group of monuments had been constructed at different periods by several nations and had belonged to different forms of religious worship. The union of the different forms of these various edifices – each of them in itself regular and crowded together in this narrow spot – formed an irregular group of the most picturesque and magnificent objects.

I could here distinguish eight sanctuaries, or separate temples, of different dimensions built at various times. The limits of each had been respected in the construction of the succeeding ones which has impaired the regularity of the whole.

What could be the meaning of this vast number of sanctuaries so contiguous to each other and yet so distinct? Were they consecrated to different divinities? Were they votive chapels or places devoted each to particular ceremonies of religious worship? The innermost temple contained still more mysterious sanctuaries such as monolithic temples and tabernacles, of a single stone, containing perhaps what was most precious and sacred to the worshippers.

On the ceilings . . . were painted astronomical pictures [representing] the theories of the elements. On the walls were religious ceremonies, images, priests and gods by the side of the gates and gigantic portraits of certain sovereigns. There were also emblematic figures, of strength or power, threatening a group of suppliant figures whom they held with one hand by the hair of the head. Could these be rebellious subjects or vanquished enemies?

Denon is here describing the Great Temple of Philae that was dedicated to the deity Isis. The ruinous state of the temple structures was indicative of the effects of earth tremors experienced in previous ages. Despite these, sufficient of the fabric remained intact to convey the grandeur and beauty of the edifices. The monuments at Philae were constructed from sandstone but their exteriors exhibited a brilliant white appearance without showing any signs of deterioration. To the eyes of the French artist-illustrators, the massive inclined walls of the temple resembled European fortifications with no other opening than the gates. Their solidity imparted to them 'a grave and mysterious character' that was further enhanced by their island location. On closer inspection, Greek and Latin names were found inscribed on the obelisks adorning the temple – testimony to the records left by travellers from previous ages. In due course the French also left inscriptions commemorating their expedition in the spirit that 'in all ages men have wished to attach their names to something that survives them and which speaks of them in their absence'.

Approached from the south, the visitor to the Temple of Isis first encountered the majestic outer pylon that formed an integral part of the ceremonial entrance to the temple complex. Before this pylon were obelisks hewn from red granite that lay almost buried in sand. One bore the inscription:

I, Trebonius Oricula, have lived here under Emperor Caesar, Consul for the third time.

It was close by the fallen obelisk that the French left their own text carved on the great door of the pylon. This consecrated the conquest of Egypt by Bonaparte, his defeat of the Mamelukes and the entry on to the island of Philae by Lieutenant General Desaix. On passing through the gate of the first pylon a second one was encountered, set back from a peristylar courtyard or forecourt. Here ten columns were found still showing their original coloration of green, red, yellow and blue 'in the greatest vivacity'.

On the island of Philae, the legacy of temple building from the Roman era was embodied most perfectly in a small temple structure known to the French explorers, for reasons of its location, as the Eastern Edifice – called, more correctly, the Kiosk of Trajan. This was a form of small open-work structure with supporting pillars that afforded a shady retreat for the king and his officials. Denon paid a visit to the Kiosk of Trajan for which he provides the following description:

> The Kiosk of Trajan is one of the most beautiful that can be conceived. It is in a perfect state of preservation and is so small it almost gives one the desire of carrying it away. If ever we should be disposed to transport a temple from Africa to Europe, this of which I am speaking should be selected for the purpose. Besides the practicability of such an operation – afforded by its small dimensions – it would give palpable proof of the noble simplicity of Egyptian architecture and would show, in a striking manner, that it is character and not extent alone that gives dignity to an edifice.

Denon's desire to carry away the Kiosk of Trajan to France is understandable. It was picturesquely sited on the eastern shore of the island of Philae where it could be seen from all vantage points by those approaching from the river. It was decorated by an array of fourteen majestic columns that stood more than 11 metres high. Bas-reliefs on the walls portrayed offerings to the gods. Further decoration was found on the wall panels whose refinement prompted the French artists to comment: 'The Egyptians have excelled in the art of distributing ornaments in such a manner as to fill all the spaces without sacrificing the purpose of the decoration.'

As Denon completed his tour of the island, he was enchanted to find more Greek and Roman architectural remains interspersed with the Egyptian antiquities. To the southeast he came upon what he thought was a small port. In fact it was a landing quay that also served as a defensive structure to protect the island from encroachment by the river. It was decorated with attached columns and arcades in the Doric style – evidence of the later Grecian influence on the Egyptian temple builders. He also discovered a gallery where fragments of columns could be seen still standing. To the north of the Temple of Isis he came upon the foundations of a Catholic church whose antique fragments were mixed with crosses and Greek ornaments from later ages.

Pages 180–1: The 'Kiosk of Trajan' on the island of Philae. This *hypaethral* (open to the sky) temple was built at the period of the emperor Trajan (AD 98–117) from whom its name is derived. It was sited picturesquely on the eastern side of the island of Philae from which this view was composed. The elegant structure was used in ceremonies to venerate the goddess Isis. Its lotus-headed columns are quintessentially Egyptian. Although unfinished (its inter-columnar walls were left undecorated), Denon was captivated by this temple and wanted it transported to Paris. Some 150 years later it was dismantled and relocated as a consequence of the building of the Aswan High Dam. *(Roberts, British Library)*

Ruins at El-Kab on the east bank of the Nile, about 80 kilometres south of Luxor. The sandstone temples were dedicated to the deities Nekhebt and Thoth. Denon was only able to view them from the river through his telescope. A French artist can be seen at work, drawing board on his knee, while a sentry keeps guard. (*Dutertre, National Library of Scotland*)

The monuments on the island of Philae captivated Denon through their diversity, the refinement of their workmanship and their picturesque location. He wrote a characteristically exuberant tribute, in his *Journal*, in praise of the treasures he found all around him – combined with an equally characteristic touch of humanity:

> What a profusion of objects of curiosity! But time was gliding by so fast that I wished to stay the course of the sun. Having employed many hours in observation, I began to make drawings and measurements . . . [but] I at last quitted this spot with my eyes tired out by so many objects and my mind filled with the various recollections attached to it. I left at night loaded with treasures and bringing with me my little girl whom I entrusted to the Sheikh of Elephantine to restore her to her parents.

The French marked the most southerly point reached on their march into Upper Egypt with an inscription cut into a large granite rock located just beyond the First Cataract. Denon took advantage of the time this required to join a reconnaissance party that was venturing into the bordering desert region. His object was to visit the famed granite quarries that had been described by the English traveller and orientalist Richard Pococke. He had explored Egypt in 1737 and 1739 and a copy of his resulting book was among the French library of works of Egyptology that the scholars had taken with them on the Egyptian Campaign.

After marching for an hour, Denon discerned the remains of a monument that had also been visited by Pococke some fifty years before. With typical impetuosity – and little regard for his personal safety – he left the detachment of soldiers to make an inspection of the sombre ruins: 'Nothing indicated the remains of the habitation of man but some sentences written on the walls. I fancied I could trace in these inscriptions their last sentiments and the only memorial they would leave to those who were to succeed them – a vain attempt which time, that destroys everything, has entirely frustrated.'

With their return north imminent, the French needed to secure the upper reaches of the Nile to ward off the threat of attack from the Mamelukes who were still in the region, to which end it was decided to fortify Syene with such means as were available. This work was entrusted to the engineer Citizen Garbé who constructed a defensive esplanade on an escarpment to the south of the city. This commanded all the approaches and overlooked the adjacent country.

When the defensive works were completed, the French commenced their departure from Upper Egypt on 25 February 1799. Denon would willingly have remained there for at least two more weeks to complete his survey-work, but even his enthusiasm was tempered by the realization that the weather was changing. In this region of Egypt, with the onset of spring come burning winds that can sear the body. In addition, Denon was feeling the strain of the long marches he had endured with the army. Furthermore, three days of a strong east wind had made the atmosphere oppressively hot. These had been followed by a cold north wind that had left Denon with a fever. In the hope of securing some rest, he put himself on board one of the barques that was about to transport the troops back along the Nile. Despite his indifferent health, Denon was motivated to make the journey with the troops in the hope of visiting Kom Ombos and the quarries of Gebel El-Silsila.

Kom Ombos is the site of ancient ruins that occupy a sandy escarpment on the east bank of the River Nile, about 40 kilometres to the north of Syene. The name translates as 'the hill of Ombos' and the elevated position meant the township and surviving monuments were shrouded in sand that had blown in from the great plain lying below the Arabian Mountains. At the period of the French exploration of the region, sufficient of the antiquities were visible to stir Denon's desire to inspect them.

The principal architectural monument at Kom Ombos was the great temple dedicated to the deities Haroeris (Horus) and Sobek, the former identified with the hawk and the latter with the cult of the crocodile. Gebel El-Silsila offered Denon the prospect of visiting the Pharaonic and Graeco-Roman sandstone quarries and rock-cut shrines for which this site is renowned. He therefore embarked with the soldiers in his usual state of enthusiasm and eager anticipation. The journey, though, proved to have its frustrations:

I was hardly embarked when I experienced all the inconveniences of this mode of conveyance. The contrary wind, the stupidity of the natives – who could not be made to work the vessels – and the fruitless cries of our *provençals*, everything conspired to torment us.

We were a long while working up to Kom Ombos. [As we approached] the wind became favourable for passing it. Our flotilla was in too much haste for me to suggest stopping there for even a single hour. I just had time to give it a glance, in sailing by, and to take a hasty sketch of the general site and the fine position of the mountains.

Despite the cursory nature of Denon's visual survey, he was able to take in sufficient of the scene to provide a description of the site:

The ancient Ombos, where the crocodile was revered, is still called Kom Ombos – The Ombos mountain – and is situated on an eminence that commands the country. It projects out to the very margin of the river. If all the fragments that are seen here belonged to a single edifice it must have been immense. In the centre is a grand portico of columns with wide capitals in very large proportion. On the south one gate is preserved entire. It joined a surrounding wall that is now destroyed.

The double Temple of Horus and Sobek was unusual in that it combined two temples within one enclosure. The boundary of the site was protected by an immense brick wall some 8 metres thick with a perimeter of over 700 metres. The outer portico of the temple had an array of sixteen great columns that enclosed a large courtyard. Within was a second portico having ten additional columns of which several had fallen or were buried in sand, making survey-work difficult. The temple had been constructed from sandstone that had weathered to a grey-yellow colour and all the surfaces had been worked to achieve a high polish so as to provide a smooth surface for the numerous bas-reliefs with which they were adorned.

Between the joints of some of the fallen stones could be seen traces of a reddish cement and the remains of tenons cut from sycamore wood. Egyptian builders were not averse to

View of the quarries of Gebel El Silsila from the River Nile. It was here that much of the beautiful red sandstone was quarried for the temples and monuments of Lower Egypt. The rock-cut remains were often decorated as shrines. A boat passes by with a group of Frenchmen on board. (*Balzac, National Library of Scotland*)

resorting to such measures in order to provide stones with greater bonding properties than could be achieved by sheer weight alone. Throughout the temple were signs that it had been plundered as a source of building materials by the local people. Even so, the French artists were sufficiently moved by the quality and refinement of the surviving ornaments and decoration to confer upon the edifice the epithet 'this beautiful temple'.

The following day Denon was more fortunate when sailing down the Nile. The barques anchored at a location on the river close to the freestone quarries at Gebel El-Silsila which were cut into the banks on both sides of the river. The principal quarries are to be found on the east bank, while those on the west bank contain catacombs that have been adapted into shrines. Denon left the protection of the barques to inspect these excavations:

> The stone of these quarries, being of an equal grain and uniform texture throughout, [is such that] blocks may be cut out of them as large as can be desired. It is doubtless to the beauty and unalterability of this material that we owe the vast size and fine preservation of the monuments that are the cause of our admiration at the present time – so many centuries after the date of their construction.
>
> From the immense excavations, and the quality of fragments that may still be seen in these quarries, we may suppose they were worked for some thousands of years. They alone might have supplied the materials employed for the greater part of the monuments of Egypt. The distance would, in fact, prove no obstacle to the working of these quarries since the Nile, during its inundation, would constantly come and float the boats that were loaded, during the dry season, and carry [the building stones] to the place of their destination.

When quarrying operations had been completed at a particular rock face, catacombs and caves were left behind where the supply of building stone had been exhausted. Such grottoes were subsequently adapted as shrines, or monuments, to the gods by recourse to carving and decorative embellishments. Denon inspected these shrines; his detailed descriptions are of considerable antiquarian interest since they provide an account of their state of preservation at the close of the eighteenth century, before their subsequent decay:

The enthusiasm for erecting monuments among the Egyptians shows itself on every side in these quarries. After having furnished materials for the erection of temples, they were themselves consecrated as monuments and [were] decorated with religious edifices. On the shore of the Nile may be seen porticoes with columns, entablatures and cornices, covered with hieroglyphics all cut out of the solid rock and, likewise, a large number of tombs are also hollowed out of the mountain.

In several of these tombs, small private chambers are found, many of which contain large figures. These chambers are adorned with hieroglyphics, traced out on the rock, and are terminated with coloured stucco [decorations] representing offerings of bread, fruit, liquor and fowl. The ceilings, also of stucco, are ornamented with painted scrolls in an exquisite taste.

The choice of this situation for the habitations of the dead shows that at all times in Egypt the silence of the desert has been the asylum of death. Even now the Egyptians carry their dead into the desert, three leagues from their habitations, so that the dryness of the sands may preserve them from corruption. They go there every week to pray over these tombs.

I had hardly drawn the most interesting of these quarries when a favourable wind summoned us back on board.

Denon sailed north to Esna. As the party approached the town they once more caught sight of crocodiles. They had not been seen in the region of Syene although they were to be found in the calmer waters above the cataracts. Denon concluded they seemed to prefer certain reaches of the river, particularly those from Tentyris to Kom Ombos. Most of all they frequented the banks of the river near Hermonthis. Here, Denon saw three. One of them, much larger than the rest, he estimated had a length of nearly 25 feet! They were all asleep and so could be approached to within a few paces, enabling Denon and his companions to distinguish all the peculiarities that give them, as Denon remarks, 'such a hideous aspect'. He considered they resembled a dismounted cannon! He shot at one with a musket. The ball struck the crocodile and rebounded from its scales after which the ferocious creature made a leap of 10 feet and dived into the river.

As Denon approached Esna a quay, faced with dressed stone, attracted his attention. It ran alongside the river for a length of 200 metres. At its termination he could see a pyramidal gate, in ruins, together with six columns. These, he thought, formed part of the portico of a temple and once more the instincts of the artist within him were roused. He wanted the convoy to halt for a moment but this was impracticable: 'We had a good wind and it would have been a crime of treason against the army to request a delay for the purpose of making a drawing. I could only take a sketch as we passed by.' At daybreak on 27 February the flotilla arrived at Esna. On landing, Denon heard the beat of drums to muster the forces. By now he had had enough of travelling by water and so, within ten minutes of setting foot on shore, he was more than eager to get back in the saddle once more.

He had to quit the monuments of Apollonopolis and Latopolis with many details left unexamined. At Esna he received news that the coalition of the Arabs was in some disarray but that Murad Bey himself still had the personal support of more than three hundred Mamelukes. He had taken the road north to Eluah where there was an oasis sufficient for him to water his animals and to sojourn for a while until he received news of the French and their position. He was still waiting for chance to turn in his favour. It was clear that the threat to the French from the Arabs remained.

CHAPTER 15

Tribulations of an Artist

During his brief sojourn at Esna, Denon had good reason to reflect with pride upon his achievements. He had journeyed with the army to the most southerly point in the Nile Valley which the French reached during their Egyptian Campaign. A civilian, he had shown himself capable of enduring the rigours of military life. More significantly, he had seen and recorded many of the ancient monuments of Upper Egypt. Travelling north his mind turned to the antiquities he had viewed but briefly on his journey south and which he now wished to revisit and inspect with greater care.

On the evening of 4 March 1799 he arrived at Armant, the site of the ancient township of Hermonthis. He was once more in the company and protection of the army and the halt at Armant was precipitated by the military's need to gather news of the Mamelukes and their Meccan supporters. The French detachment with which Denon had ventured south was also in need of intelligence as to the disposition of the main body of the French army which was thought to be deployed at various locations in the region of Cairo. However, important as these considerations were for Denon's personal wellbeing and that of his soldier-companions, they took second place to his wish to survey the antiquities in the region. At Armant, the principal attraction for Denon was the temple dedicated to the war god Montu, now largely destroyed.

When Denon visited the edifice it was still a majestic structure. Many of its slender columns stood upright, silhouetted against the sky. It was constructed from a particularly durable sandstone and several of its great beams were in their original locations having resisted the earth tremors experienced in previous ages. Inside, the edifice was well preserved and displayed numerous bas-reliefs and wall decorations. In one tableau, Osiris could be seen kneeling to receive the embrace of Isis. In places, on the ceiling, were tableaux in the form of a celestial zodiac. Denon's attention was captured by these images and he spent the time available to him sketching them. The site of the ancient town proved less rewarding. The state of its impoverishment caused Denon to lament the loss of so many antiquities:

> I now had a better opportunity of observing the site of the ancient town that [originally] had a perimeter wall and several temples. As for the temples not a single public edifice, not a single house, nor even a royal palace has been able to resist the ravages of time. The famous canal, of which history speaks so grandly, preserved no magnificence: neither causeways nor sluices and the only facings and quays that I met with on the Nile, are trifling works compared with those of the colossal and immortal temples.

In the meantime they had received word that a contingent of Mameluke forces, under the command of Osman Bey, had been sighted. It was thought they were about to attempt to cross the Nile at Qena. In an effort to thwart them, the French army left Esna on 8 March. Denon was once more agitated, this time at the prospect of journeying close to Thebes but with little prospect of examining the monuments:

> I again had the mortification of crossing the ground occupied by ancient Thebes, with still less opportunity of examining it than at first. Without measuring a single column, without taking a single sketch, without approaching a single monument we followed the course of the Nile avoiding both the temples of Medinet Abu, the Memnonium, the temples of Qena – that I passed on my left – and those of Luxor and Karnak on my right.
>
> Still temples! – Nothing but temples! – And not a vestige of the hundred gates so celebrated in history! No walls, quays, bridges, baths, or theatres! Not a single edifice of common utility or convenience!
>
> Despite all the pains that I took in my research, I could find nothing but temples and walls covered with obscure emblems and hieroglyphics. These attested to the ascendancy of the priesthood that still seemed to reign over these mighty ruins and whose empire constantly haunted my imagination.

The party halted at a settlement on the west bank of the Nile in the vicinity of the Necropolis of Thebes. As they approached the rock-cut tombs the local people turned hostile. They had appropriated these former resting places of the dead as their retreats and mistrusted the motives of the European intruders. Despite the attempts made by the French interpreters to reassure the leaders of the Anchorites of their good intentions, it became clear that a dispute was inevitable. And so it proved. The French resorted to chasing the tomb dwellers back into their sanctuaries while a reconnaissance was made of the area to verify the whereabouts of Osman Bey and his forces. Amid the ensuing commotion Denon found a moment to sketch the desolate scene and the rock-hewn habitations of the dead.

No signs were found of the marauding Arabs and the French troops reconciled themselves to billeting where they were for the night. On 10 March the journey in search of the enemy was resumed. In due course this led to the township of Qus on the east bank of the Nile.

Historically Qus was important as the location of the Temple of Heket who was associated in Egyptian mythology with childbirth. But Qus held other, more pressing, attractions for the French contingent than antiquarian remains. Being so close to the River Nile, and enjoying the advantages of a fertile plain, the settlement had numerous productive gardens and immense plantations of watermelons. These afforded the troops a welcome source of refreshment after their days spent tramping along the borders of the desert – the problems experienced earlier in the campaign with diarrhoea contracted from eating watermelons appear to have been overcome! Qus was no less hospitable to thirsty traders arriving from the shores of the Red Sea via the port of Quseir.

A few hours after passing through Qus, the French arrived at Koptos – modern-day Qift. Its situation, on the east bank of the Nile, had favoured Koptos as the principal trade route across the Nile Valley and also to the east and the coastal regions of the Red Sea.

Two views of the Ramesseum or mortuary temple of Rameses II (Rameses the Great), known to the French as the Memnonium or Tomb of Ozymandias. It was a place for the performance of funerary rituals and cults dedicated to Amun, the supreme god of Thebes. Top: The ruined peristyle (columnar arcade) with the shattered remains of the colossal statue of Rameses II to the west (right). Above: A view down the nave of the temple before which a group of local people has gathered. *(Denon, British Library)*

Trading missions passing through Koptos departed by sea to and from the east coast of Africa, which was a rich source of exotic goods such as African blackwood and ivory.

As Denon surveyed Koptos, nothing of its ancient splendour could be discerned. It merely presented desolate heaps of ruins that served only to demarcate the boundaries of the ancient city. The settlement had become as dry, inhospitable and uninhabited as the desert.

Scarcely had the French passed through Koptos when their scouts informed them their enemy had been sighted. This prompted the generals to pause and consider their strategy. They decided to confront the Arabs and the troops were ordered to resume their march to meet them. The French were taken by surprise at the versatility shown by the Mamelukes in the manipulation of their field guns, and Denon himself was, for a moment, in great danger:

I now saw death close at my side. In the short time of ten minutes that we stopped, three persons were killed while I was speaking to them. I dared no longer speak to anyone for the last was struck by a cannon ball. We both saw it coming, ploughing up the ground before it. Appearing to be almost spent, my friend lifted up his foot to let it pass him. With a sudden leap the ball struck him on the heel and tore the muscles of his leg. This made a wound which, the next day, proved fatal to this young officer since we lacked the necessary instruments for amputation.

The Mamelukes took up a defensive position in a village situated close by. The French were occupied for upwards of two hours in attacking this and sixty of their men were killed or wounded. To the good fortune of the French, one of the Mameluke magazines blew up and flames extended in every direction. Denon saw what followed:

As they were without water, they extinguished the fire with their feet and hands and even endeavoured to smother it by throwing themselves upon it. They were seen, black and naked, running through the flames and resembling so many devils in hell. I could not view them without an emotion of horror blended with admiration.

An amusing incident occurred amid these harrowing and dramatic events. Towards the middle of the night two donkeys entered the French quarters at full speed. In a moment the soldiers were on their feet and at their posts – only then to realise the identity of the intruders! The silence and military order were as striking as the occasion was ridiculous. The light relief was, however, short-lived. The conflict was soon resumed with ferocity on both sides:

At daybreak our troops entered by the breaches that the fire had made and put to the sword those who, even though they were half roasted alive, still offered resistance. One of them, who appeared to be a chief, was brought to our General. He was in so swollen a state that, in endeavouring to seat himself, his skin cracked in every part. [He said] 'I beg that you hasten to put me out of my misery.'

He was accompanied by a slave who regarded his master with so deep an expression of grief that I felt an esteem both for one and the other. The dangers . . . could not draw aside for a moment his affectionate concern for his master. He lived for him alone. How good must he have been who was thus cherished by his slave! However deplorable his lot, I could not help envying him who was thus so beloved.

A contented Muslim. Denon took delight in observing local people and captured their likenesses whenever he could. He noted how many old men were content to pass their hours of leisure smoking at their door. Of this typical gentleman he wrote in his *Journal*: 'Seated beneath a tree with his pipe, his coffee, his cat and his birds, he is tormented – but never annoyed – by his little children whom he adores'. *(Denon: University of Edinburgh)*

The Mameluke stronghold was secured on the morning of 23 March – at a high human cost on both sides. General Belliard pardoned the prisoners he had taken, a show of compassion that so impressed the captives – who were expecting to be put to the sword – that they asked if they could follow the French army. Their wish was not granted since many of them had been severely wounded in the conflict and, in any event, their loyalty could not be relied upon.

Despite the French success, Murad Bey's army was still intact and continued to pose a threat to the French. General Belliard's next course of action, therefore, was to make a reconnaissance of the immediate desert region to gain an idea of the extent of the enemy's forces. A short march proved sufficient. On reaching the brow of a hill the French had a full view of the Arab army. According to Denon, the enemy had at least a thousand men on horse, as many supply camels and perhaps two thousand foot soldiers. In addition, their numbers were augmented by a considerable body of Meccans who had been forcibly conscripted into the conflict. The sight of so many men in battle array was daunting and disposed General Belliard to caution. His men were already weary from their recent conflict and, moreover, the enemy was in an advantageous position occupying territory with which they were familiar. Denon remarks:

> We felt more than ever how useless it was to pursue them, when they would not fight, and how impossible it was to surprise them in a country where they had, on each side of the river, a retreat always open to them. We therefore gave up a useless pursuit and wisely returned to secure and protect our barques.
>
> The remainder of the day was spent by the General in collecting together and putting on board the guns, ammunition and warlike implements we had captured.

In the villages the French had conquered, Denon was surprised to find a number of local women in the company of French soldiers. Their fraternizing with his countrymen prompted him to comment:

> Each of them had made her choice freely and they all appeared perfectly well satisfied. Some of them were very pretty. It was so novel a thing to be fed, attended and well treated by their conquerors that I am of the opinion they would willingly have followed the army.
>
> When the French departed, these women were reunited with their own men without altercation. Concerning what had passed, they justified themselves: 'It was owing to the war'.

On 11 April, the French army resumed its march north towards Qena. Progress was interrupted by sandstorms. The soldiers had not experienced this particular phenomenon, which Denon describes as 'those particular winds which, however that the sky is clear and unclouded, fill the air with so much sand that it is neither day nor night'.

At nine in the morning of the following day they reached Qena. The advance party had freed the city of Mameluke forces and the grateful inhabitants of the town came out to greet the French. They found Qena to be a prosperous town that, at the time of the occupation, had superseded its neighbour Koptos (Qift) in importance. Qena was favoured both by being 'at the entrance to the desert' and close to the River Nile. It was from here that pilgrims obtained their supplies before journeying north into Lower Egypt and, likewise, Nubians travelling south to their homeland via Upper Egypt.

Traders also replenished their supplies at Qena before embarking across the eastern desert for Medina and Mecca.

General Belliard was unable to pursue the Mamelukes due to his army's lack of ammunition. He decided instead to lodge for a while at Qena and fortify the town's defences against a surprise attack. A few days later, his men now rested, General Belliard gave the order to commence the march. The army quitted Qena during the night, as was its custom, to take advantage of the cool of evening. Signs of a Mameluke encampment were discovered but the enemy was no longer present, having departed at about the same time the French had left Qena. They had taken to the desert to seek refuge at the nearby township of Kittah. The French were reluctant to give chase since the Mamelukes had the advantage of being acquainted with the region and, importantly, of knowing where to find the oases.

Experience of marching through the desert had impressed upon the French the vital necessity of being able to locate a supply of water. As Denon phlegmatically remarks: 'The latter is of great importance when the desert is to be occupied'. Instead, therefore, of following the Mamelukes into the desert, General Belliard held his forces close to the banks of the Nile, thereby confining his opponents to the inhospitable regions of the desert while, at the same time, cutting off their lines of communication and generally impeding their movements.

Some three hundred men and several field guns were left behind at Qena to secure the defences of the town. General Belliard's army was reinforced, to his considerable relief, by the 21st Brigade light infantry sent from Cairo. The plan of action now was to forego the pursuit of the Mamelukes and to return south to Thebes. On hearing this Denon records: 'The hope of seeing Thebes in the direction of which we were to march made me once more joyful.'

Before Denon could commence his survey of Luxor and Karnak, he had a number of farewells to make to certain of his colleagues. Their military obligations, and subsequent destiny, lay elsewhere. In particular Denon had final meetings with General Desaix and a young officer called Latournerie. The emotional nature of Denon's remarks bear testimony to the close attachment he felt for these men:

> On the evening before we departed we formed a thousand projects for the future. Our adieus were, however, of a melancholy cast and on this occasion our separation was to me more distressing than ever.
>
> Our detachment had proceeded a league when the brave Latournerie galloped to me. He came back to bid me adieu. We had a great affection for each other and, moved as I was by this mark of his tenderness, I was struck by his emotion. We did not embrace each other without shedding a few tears.

Denon concludes this passage of his *Journal* with sentiments that many men must have felt when engaged in great conflicts and trusting their lives to each other:

> The possession of arms may burden those whose temperament is cold and frigid but its horrors do not weaken the sensitivity of tender souls.
>
> Connections formed amid the hardships and dangers of an expedition, such as that of Egypt, become unchangeable. The parties enter into a bond of fellowship and, when this union is cemented still more by a conformity of character, fate cannot destroy it without embittering the remainder of life.

CHAPTER 16

Karnak and Luxor

The march south to Thebes not only filled Denon's imagination with the prospect of seeing Karnak and Luxor once more, it also offered him the chance to visit the ruins at Qus. When he had first passed through this region with the army time had not allowed for a detour to be made, but now the direct route taken by the military gave him the opportunity he required.

On reaching the town Denon found the upper part of a large construction protruding from the ground. It was sited in the middle of the square. From its decorative cornice he conjectured it to be the remains of a great gate, or portal, that had once formed part of an ancient edifice. He remarks: 'The bulk and magnitude of this ruin present a contrast with all the objects that surround it. They say more about the nature of Egyptian architecture than would twenty pages of praise or a dissertation. This fragment alone appears larger than all the rest of the city.' To his disappointment, Denon was not able to undertake any excavations at this site and pressure of time obliged him to continue the march with the army.

Half a league beyond Qus the party came upon a village called Elmecia. Here Denon discovered the bases of several ancient structures, constructed from local freestone, that bore traces of hieroglyphics. Further on he visited other remains whose sombre nature and remote location oppressed his senses:

> We proceeded to an enclosure that had once been a convent inhabited by Copts. Latterly it has been used as a burial ground. After taking up our lodging within this enclosure, we employed ourselves in driving away the bats and throwing down the tombstones. A fortress, a desert and tombs! We were surrounded by the most dismal objects in the world! Moreover, if we occasionally went out at night to banish the melancholy impressions these scenes had imposed upon us – and to breathe the fresh air for a few moments – our respiration was the only sound that disturbed the tranquillity of the void by which we were terrified.
>
> The wind fleeting over this vast horizon, without meeting with any other objects than ourselves, brought to our perception by its silent motion the immense and dismal vacuity by which we were surrounded.

In the morning Denon and his party encountered a caravan of merchants who had been fortunate to evade the Mamelukes. At first they were fearful of the French since, noting their dishevelled appearance, they took them to be a band of robbers. They were clearly wealthy since Denon records 'it was impossible for them to conceal their riches'. The meeting with these merchants was fortunate for the French since they had lost many of their possessions in their recent conflict and these merchant travellers now afforded a welcome and unexpected opportunity to replace some of their items. It also gave the French an introduction to the eastern custom of bargaining – and hospitality – as Denon explains:

> We were in need of linen and requested the merchants to open their bales. Their hope now vanished. [The merchants thought they were about to be robbed.] We made a selection of what would suit us and asked them the price of the quantity of each article we required. They replied that they left this entirely to ourselves but we persisted on knowing the lowest price. As soon as they had satisfied us, we paid them – at which they were surprised. They thought their money was lost and were certain that what had passed was a dream.
>
> [We were] armed men with power in our hands – who paid! They might have passed through every part of Asia and Africa without meeting with anything so extraordinary. From that moment, we acquired their full esteem and confidence. They came to prepare our breakfast, brought us Indian and Arabian sweetmeats, cocoanuts, and made us the best coffee it was possible to drink. This combination of wretchedness and luxury, this motley state in which we lived, was not without its share of interest.

Refreshed and sartorially refurbished, Denon and his companions reached Nagadi, which Denon describes as being 'at the entrance of the desert'. This was appropriate since the township occupied a favoured position from which the camel trade could depart for Quseir on the west coast of the Red Sea. The journey from Nagadi, across the eastern desert, was a full day shorter than that by any other route. Denon tells us: 'A messenger who sets out from Quseir may reach Nagadi in two days, with the help of a camel, and three days on foot'. Nagadi was favoured for other reasons. Since Quseir was a relatively austere and inhospitable town in the late eighteenth century, merchants arriving there by ship with their goods from the Far East sent to Nagadi for their camels and such other supplies as they required to cross the desert to the Nile.

When Denon was at Nagadi he observed the workings of the camel trade and provides the following information. A hundredweight of merchandise could be transported for the cost of a *dollar* – Denon's expression – and a single camel could carry as much as 4 hundredweight. However, the sojourn of the French at Nagadi had unfortunate consequences for the caravan traders, as Denon explains: 4/21/2010

> We boasted we were more just than the Mamelukes but we committed daily, and almost necessarily, a great number of iniquitous acts. The difficulty of distinguishing our enemies by their exterior form and colour was the cause of our continually putting to death innocent peasants. The soldiers, who were sent out on search parties, frequently mistook the poor merchants belonging to a caravan for Meccans. Before justice could be done, which in some cases time and circumstances would not allow, two or three of them had been shot and part of their merchandise was either plundered or pilfered and their camels exchanged for those of ours which had been wounded.
>
> The [spoils] resulting from these outrages invariably fell to the blood-suckers of the army [namely] the civil commissaries, the Copts and interpreters.

The local people, caught up in the misery of war, fared little better than the innocent caravan traders:

General Belliard, seated in the centre, interrogates prisoners at Nagadi. The meeting took place within a local sepulchre that the French had made their headquarters. Denon, seated to the left, found 'this gloomy habitation a great relief in the desert and preserved us from the heat of a most scorching sun'. He also informs us that the torches which illuminate the scene were those used at night when the army was on the march. *(Denon, Author's Collection)*

The situation of the inhabitants, for whose happiness and prosperity we were no doubt come to Egypt, was no better. If, through terror, they had been obliged to quit their houses on our approach, on their return – after we had withdrawn – they could find nothing but the mud of which the walls were formed. Utensils, ploughs, doors, roofs – everything in short of a combustible nature – had been burned for cooking. Their earthen pots were broken, their corn consumed and their fowl and pigeon roasted and devoured. Nothing was to be found except the bodies of their dogs, killed in endeavouring to defend the property of their masters.

If we made our stay in a village the unfortunate inhabitants, who had fled on our approach, were summoned to return. [They were] under penalty of being treated as rebels who had joined the enemy – and of being made to pay double contributions. When they submitted to these threats, and came to pay the *miri* [tax], it sometimes happened they were so numerous as to be mistaken for a body of men in arms and their clubs were considered to be muskets. In such cases, they were certain to be assailed by several discharges from our riflemen and patrols before they could offer an explanation.

The locals who chose not to oppose the French – and who paid the taxes levied by them – fared better. They were spared fleeing into the desert and having all their possessions appropriated by the army and were allowed to retain a portion of their rations and to sell eggs to the soldiers. If they were lucky, the doors and window frames to their houses were not burnt as firewood. Denon adds, with a chilling reminder of the atrocities of war, 'few of their wives or daughters were ravished'.

On making their eventual departure from Nagadi, the French were harassed by marauding patrols of brigands. In their predatory excursions they followed the French like so many wolves. Sometimes, however, bravado got the better of them and they fell into the hands of the French patrols. No mercy was shown to them: 'They were collected together, shot and destroyed like animals obnoxious to society'.

Despite their skirmishes with brigands, the French made progress to their destination. By noon on 2 April they were in the region of Thebes. At three-quarters of a league from the banks of the Nile the ruins of a large temple came into view. These were Denon's longed-for sightings of the great temple complex at Karnak:

> At length we arrived at Karnak, a township built on a small part of the site of a single temple the circumference of which would require half an hour to walk round – which has been remarked upon [by previous writers]. Herodotus . . . has given a correct idea of its grandeur and magnificence. Diodorus and Strabo, who examined it in its ruinous state, appear to have described it in its present condition.
>
> All the travellers who have copied them have taken the great extent of the masses [of the ruins] as the measure of beauty and [thereby] have allowed themselves rather to be taken by surprise than charmed. On an inspection of the largest ruin in the world [they] have not dared to prefer this temple to that of Apollonopolis at Edfu, that of Tentyris or the simple portico at Esna.

Having made his preliminary observations, Denon proceeded to conjecture about the origins of these celebrated temple structures and those who created them: 'It is probable the temples of Karnak and Luxor were built in the time of Sesostris – when the flourishing condition of the Egyptians gave birth to the arts among them – and when these arts were perhaps displayed to the world for the first time.' [Sesostris is known today as Sensuret. He embellished the temples at Karnak.] Denon considered the great obelisks at Karnak to be 'sublime' with regard to both their dimensions and the skill which their workmanship displayed. He found the style of the ornamentation of the outer gates to be 'admirably chaste' and the overall plan of the temple to be 'noble and grand'. Concerning the latter he provides the following description:

> Of the hundred columns of the portico alone of this temple, the smallest are seven feet and a half in diameter and the largest twelve. The space occupied by its perimeter contains lakes and mountains. To be enabled to form a competent idea of so much magnificence, it is necessary that the reader should fancy what is before him to be a dream – as he who views the objects themselves rubs his eyes to know whether he is awake. With respect to the present state of this edifice it is, however, necessary at the same time to observe that a great part of the effect is lost by its degraded state.
>
> The sphinxes have been wantonly mutilated – with a few exceptions that barbarism, wearied with destruction, has spared. On examination, it is easy to distinguish that some of them had a woman's head, others that of a lion, a ram and a bull. The avenue that leads from Karnak to Luxor was of this latter description. This space, which is nearly half a league in extent, contains a constant succession of these chimerical figures, to the right and left, together with fragments of stone walls, small columns and statues.

This point, lying in the centre of the city, is the most advantageously placed and there is reason to suppose therefore that the palace of the grandees or kings was situated there.

Journeying further south Denon glimpsed the ruins of Luxor. From a distance he perceived the elevated pylons, obelisks and arrays of columns that bore testimony to the vast extent of the temple site:

Luxor, the finest township in these environs, is also built on the site of the ruins of a temple. [It is] not so large as that of Karnak but is in a better state of preservation [since] the masses [of stone] have not yet fallen through time or by the pressure of their own weight. The most colossal parts consist of fourteen columns, nearly eleven feet in diameter, and two statues in granite – at the outer gate – buried up to the middle of their arms and having, in front of them, the two largest and best preserved obelisks known.

The gateway leading to the Temple of Khons at Karnak. An avenue of mutilated sphinxes precedes the south propylon beneath which French surveyors are taking measurements. The temple is in the distance (see also below). Arab women approach bearing pitchers of water while soldiers prepare a meal over a fire. (*Cécile, Author's Collection*)

Notwithstanding the excessive heat of the sun at midday, I made a drawing of the gate of the temple which is now become that of the township of Luxor. Nothing can be more grand, and at the same time more simple, than the small number of objects of which this entrance is composed. No city whatever makes so proud a display, at its approach, as this wretched village, the population of which consists of two or three thousand souls. [They] have taken up their abodes on the roofs and beneath the galleries of this temple which has nevertheless the air of being in a manner uninhabited.

After completing his survey of the ruins of Luxor, Denon was once more obliged to resume the march with the army. They set out at two o'clock in the afternoon and trekked continuously through the inhospitable terrain for thirteen hours, eventually reaching the township of Salamieh. This offered only a brief respite and the next day the party once more continued its march through the desert. They reached the outskirts of Esna where the ruins of a temple caught Denon's attention:

A view of the sand-encroached interior of the Temple of Khons at Karnak. Khons was a moon-god whose sanctuary was within the precincts of the Temple of Amun. Depicted here is the hypostyle hall with its system of clerestory lighting. *(Dutertre, National Library of Scotland)*

We found a small temple in a very ruinous state but nevertheless picturesque and singular in its plan as well as in several of its parts. It consists of a portico, with four columns in front, two pilasters and two columns in depth with a sanctuary in the middle. [It had] two lateral apartments one of which, on the right hand, is scarcely to be traced. This building is in a more ruinous state than any other I have seen in Egypt. The decay has undoubtedly arisen from the nature of the freestone with which it was built.

Denon is here describing the ruins of the Temple of Khnum that have now been lost. This temple was of interest to the French expedition since it was still brilliantly coloured and was decorated with several zodiacal signs. The temple appeared to have been constructed in haste and, uncharacteristically, with some negligence. It was not well sited and some of its great stones were irregularly shaped and poorly bonded. Time did not allow Denon to make a full survey of the ruins, obliging him to remark: 'I regretted I had not a better opportunity to study the details of the plan of this temple and of the buildings that had been posteriorly added'.

The Great Hypostyle Hall forming part of the Temple of Amun at Karnak. The French, like others since, were in awe of its immense size and grandeur. The over-arching capitals are so enormous that a horse and chariot can turn round on them. Karnak wonderfully exemplifies the concept of 'the mansion of god [and] his earthly home where he lived, ate and drank and was worshipped by his priestly assistants'. The French surveyors found traces of water at the site that had begun to undermine the stability of some of the columns. Extensive restoration work has since been undertaken to correct this. *(Roberts, British Library)*

The party proceeded south, in the direction of the mountains, encountering such severe terrain that Denon remarks: 'Our artillery was conveyed with difficulty and the greater part of the day was lost'. Despite this hardship, progress was made and easier ground was reached. Several interesting quarries were encountered whose workings suggested they had been used to supply stone for temple building. The township of Chenubis was next reached. This provided a resting-place for the troops and a welcome opportunity for Denon to inspect the monuments nearby:

> Within a quarter of a league of this city are two tombs hewn out of the rock and a small sanctuary, surrounded by a gallery, having a portico in front. I next proceeded to view the temple, or temples, of Chenubis the ruins of which – as well as those of the city itself – are in so disjointed a state and so varied in their proportions it is difficult to form any correct idea of their plan.
>
> There is a block of granite that seems to have belonged to a colossal statue. In an eastern direction, I met with a basin of water the circumference of which is lined and decorated by a gallery formed of columns.

In the western part of the city Denon chanced upon various architectural ruins and pieces of sculpture, the latter lying abandoned with their heads broken off – further testimony to the neglect into which these treasures of antiquity had been allowed to decline. Denon reached the city boundaries that were demarcated by immense walls constructed from unburnt clay bricks. Here, his researches were curtailed by the unwelcome sound of the bugle summoning him and the soldiers to resume their march, a circumstance which led him to curse the war, the soldiers and the necessity for the military operations that compelled him to abandon his most interesting projects. He had no alternative but to obey the call and rejoin the troops.

The next day, with the march well under way, they approached the Redifi pass. It had a bad reputation as a location where a convoy might be attacked. Confirmation of this occurred when Denon and his party entered the pass and chanced upon a distressing scene. A caravan train had been set upon and laid to waste. The harrowing sight prompted Denon to write one of the most sombre passages in his *Journal*:

> This march was traced by [the caravan's] disasters and by what they had left behind them – tents; arms; clothing; the carcasses of horses, starved to death; camels that were no longer able to support their burden; and attendants and their women whom they had abandoned to their fate.
>
> I imagined to myself the sufferings of a poor wretch, panting with fatigue, expiring with thirst, his tongue parted and breathing with difficulty the hot air by which he is consumed. He hopes that a few minutes repose will enable him to recover his strength. He stops and sees his companions pass by – calling on them in vain for help. The misery to which each one is a prey has banished every compassionate feeling. They proceed on their way without casting a look on him and follow in silence the footsteps of those who precede them. Soon, they are no longer in his view. They are departed and his benumbed limbs, already overpowered by their painful existence, refuse their office and cannot be stimulated to action either by danger or terror.
>
> The caravan has passed. It appears to him like an undulating line in the wild expanse and, becoming at length a mere point, disappears altogether like the last glimmer of an expiring taper.

The central nave in the Hypostyle Hall of the Temple of Karnak. The twelve columns illustrated were assembled from massive stone drums – a considerable feat of engineering. These were smoothed, tapered and then embellished with bas-reliefs and coloration – the latter now faded or completely effaced. The ceiling beams have fallen down but part of the clerestory lighting structure can still be seen. When surveying here, the French engineers heard the stone beams creak as they expanded with the heat of day. *(Roberts, British Library)*

He casts around him with wild and frantic looks but can see nothing. He turns them towards himself and then closes his eyes, to shun the aspect of the terrible vacuity by which he is surrounded. He hears nothing but his own sighs and fate hovers over him to cut the final thread of his existence.

Alone, and without a companion to do him the last offices, he is about to expire, without a single ray of hope to administer comfort to his departing soul. His corpse, consumed by the parched and burning soil, will soon become a bleached skeleton. It will serve as a guide to the uncertain steps of the traveller who shall dare to have the fate that has befallen him.

Such was the picture which the vestiges of the passage of the Mamelukes presented to us. It was by such terrible spectacles as the above that we ascertained the direction of their march.

With these frightful scenes behind them, Denon and his companions reached the bank of the Nile where they camped amid the shelter of some ruined tombs and withered acacia shrubs. Fresh orders were issued by the military. All those who could be spared were instructed to proceed further south to Edfu. Denon volunteered to join this party to see once more the great Temple of Horus. His wish was granted. On arriving at the site of the majestic ruins, he lost no time in recording his observations:

Being built at a period when the arts and sciences had acquired all their splendour, the workmanship of every part is equally beautiful. The hieroglyphics are admirably executed, the figures more varied and the architecture [is] of a higher order than in the Theban edifices – the building of which must derive from an earlier age. My first task was to take a general plan of the building.

Nothing can be more beautiful than these outlines. Nothing can be more picturesque than the effect produced in the elevation and by the various dimensions belonging to each member of the harmonious whole. This superb edifice is seated on rising ground so as to overlook not only its immediate vicinity but the whole valley.

Denon enjoyed two full days exploring Edfu until he was interrupted by General Belliard. There was little prospect of engaging with the Mameluke forces and he instructed his men to return north to Esna. This curtailed Denon's investigations but he could content himself in the knowledge that his portfolio was enriched with the drawings he had made of the hieroglyphics decorating the temple friezes.

The prospect of journeying north promised further opportunities for him to revisit the monuments which the previous constraints of time had only allowed him to study in haste.

CHAPTER 17

Dendera

The French army commenced its journey north on 13 April 1799, setting out once again early in the morning to take advantage of the cool of the day. Esna was eventually reached, but only after the men had experienced hardships and fatigue. The following day was spent crossing the Nile, an operation which took so long to accomplish that by the time all the men were safely over, the march had to be resumed in the full heat of the rising sun. The conditions became so oppressive that a halt was called and the party rested until nightfall. By late evening the troops arrived at the township of Salamieh where a halt was called for the night. The next day, after marching for a few hours, Denon caught sight – for the fourth time – of the majestic ruins of Thebes. He wasted no time in making a drawing of them from his vantage point on the bank of the river – he estimated the great temple complex to occupy 'an extent of two leagues'. Denon was in luck. The army was to rest here for a while which provided him time to study the temple decorations.

> Not being able, of myself, to outline the plan or draw comprehensive views of this mighty mass of ruins – that at first sight resembles a heap of sculptured mountains – I employed the two hours of my stay in delineating the historical bas-reliefs and in acquiring an accurate idea of the style and composition of this primitive sculpture. The state of [this] art is from so remote a period as to make it probable these are some of its most ancient productions.
>
> The fragments in the highest [state of] preservation are the following. A hero – perhaps a pharaoh, Memnon, Ozymandias or Sesostris – is seen waging solitary combat from his chariot in pursuit of people, at a distance, with beards and clothed in long tunics. He forces them into a marsh and obliges the rest to take shelter in the fortress. He overthrows their chief [who is] already wounded with an arrow. He returns bringing back the captives. He presents them fettered to the three divinities by whose protection he has obtained the victory.

Although Denon was allotted two hours to undertake his survey-work, by the time he had completed his drawings the general in command realised the day was now so far advanced, and the heat still so oppressive, that to resume the march would unduly tax his men. Furthermore they had not yet had anything to eat and, as Denon remarks: 'Heroes of romance might have done without refreshment but to modern soldiers food is no luxury'. The decision was therefore taken to pass the night at Karnak. Being free to continue his survey-work Denon returned to the temple site where he made further observations:

I surveyed the ruins and was convinced that a whole week's application would not be too much to construct a plan of the edifices contained within the single boundary wall. I had not time to measure, by rule, the extent of the ground occupied by these buildings but I found repeatedly that twenty-five minutes were required to encompass them on foot.

The heat was so intense that my feet were squashed through my shoes and I was unable to sit down for the purpose of drawing, until I had placed my servant between the sun and myself – in order to intercept the rays and to procure myself a little shelter. The very stones had become so hot that wishing to collect some carnelian agates – which are found in great abundance in the outskirts of the town – I was obliged to lay each hastily in my handkerchief as if it was a hot coal.

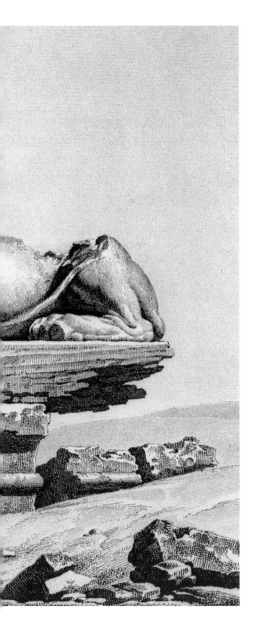

A defaced and eroded sphinx from the Avenue of Sphinxes linking the Temple of Mut with the sanctuary of Amun at Karnak. Two local men are in conversation with a French savant – useful information was often gleaned this way concerning the whereabouts of various antiquities. *(Balzac, Author's Collection)*

Harassed and fatigued, I betook myself to a small Arabian tomb that was to serve for my night's lodging. It appeared to me [to be] a delicious *boudoir* until I was told that, in our former march through this place, a French soldier – who had loitered behind his detachment – was stabbed at this very spot. The marks of the assassination, still visible upon the walls, filled me with horror. Nevertheless I lay down and slept. So weary was I that I could even have reposed on the very carcass of this ill-fated victim.

As soon as it was light, Denon and his attendant made their departure from Karnak. For once Denon felt content with his researches. He noted: 'This time I carried with me more drawings and fewer regrets'.

By the time he returned to camp, his imagination had turned to the possibility of making a visit to the tombs located in the Valley of the Kings. He was aware he could not make such a hazardous journey unaccompanied and that he would need a military escort. On raising this possibility, he was reminded that the troops were utterly fatigued by their repeated marches. Denon was therefore 'obliged to trust to future favourable circumstances' for the fulfilment of his wishes.

Despite his disappointment, Denon did not let time weigh upon him. The troops were billeted at Qus – the ancient Apollonopolis Parva. That gave him the opportunity to make a drawing of the upper part of a great portal that he discovered projecting from the wind-blown sand. Even though it was partially buried, its immense size prompted him to observe: 'This great fragment appears larger than all the rest of the town and offers a striking picture of the eternity that characterises Egyptian architecture'. The extent of the drifted sand prevented Denon from making a more detailed examination of the rest of the structure that lay beneath the rubbish of the modern town. He did, however, take advantage of the mounds of debris to clamber to the summit of the portal, which would otherwise have been inaccessible, where he made a drawing of an inscription engraved on the lintel.

A sphinx from the principal avenue leading to the great Temple at Karnak. In Egyptian iconography the sphinx was a mythical beast with the head of a man and the body of an animal – in this case a ram. The representations were sculpted from a single block of stone. An inscription, of uncertain meaning, defaces the monument. The juxtaposition of two local men convey a sense of its great size. *(Balzac and Jomard, Author's Collection)*

When the troops were suitably rested the march resumed. The party left Qus and headed north for Qena, a journey of about 30 kilometres. On reaching the town Denon was delighted to find that a number of merchants 'of all nations' had just arrived. Discoursing among them with the help of an interpreter, he was prompted to pen one of his philosophical reflections:

> When we converse with visitors from different countries, remote distances seem to contract. When we begin to reckon the days required for the journey, and the means of effecting it, the space to be travelled over ceases to be immense.
>
> Many difficulties, formidable at first, progressively diminish and at length disappear. The Red Sea, Jeddah and Mecca seem like places neighbouring to the town where we are and India itself [appears] but a short way beyond them.

Some of the merchants had journeyed from the township of Beneadi and Denon had cause to witness one of the more sobering events on his travels in Egypt. The traders had with them a number of women, some of whom were slaves brought in by the caravan. It was the misfortune of these poor women to be sold in the open market, in a series of complex transactions, as though they were commodities:

> They were passed from one to another rising in value with every change of master until, at length, they were purchased from their last owners by their fathers or their husbands. Meek and modest, they submitted with impassive resignation to their lot and were reinstated in their domestic relations without any questions being asked.

This was conduct so untypical of the usual Mohammedan custom that it induced us to express our surprise. We were answered very sensibly: 'What fault of theirs is it that we have not been able to defend them?'

Shortly after witnessing this scene, Denon had an opportunity further to gratify his fascination for crocodiles. At the time of the French occupation of Egypt, these fearsome creatures abounded along the River Nile. They were little known then to naturalists in the West, and Denon shared their curiosity to learn more about them. Whenever the opportunity arose to examine one he took advantage of it:

> While at Qena I had to regret the death of a crocodile that some peasants surprised asleep and had bound and brought alive to the officer who was in command during the absence of General Belliard. The animal being yet young, and fettered by an iron circle between the shoulders and belly, could not be very formidable. We might have observed and become acquainted with his habits which are unknown in his native country – so much so that he is an object of terror!
>
> It would have been curious to see his manner of eating, to ascertain what kind of food he lives on, whether mastication is necessary to him and, if so, how it is achieved in an animal possessed only of cutting teeth and how his throat takes the place of a tongue and whether advantage might be taken of his voracity to render him tame. He might perhaps have been brought alive to France and there have been submitted to the examination of the naturalists and the curiosity of the Parisians – doing homage to the nation as a trophy of the conquered Nile.

From the window of his room at Qena, Denon could see the majestic ruins of Dendera, 'no more than two leagues distant on the other side of the Nile'. This prospect stirred the recollections of his previous sight of the celebrated Temple of Hathor and of his regret at not having had an opportunity to make a drawing of the famous astronomical ceiling and its zodiacal characters. Since the temple was only some twenty minutes journey away, Denon did not have difficulty, this time, in securing permission to visit the site with an armed escort:

> We arrived at the town in the evening. The next morning, with a guard of thirty men, I went to the ruins and this time took possession of them in the plenitude of repose and quiet. I was, first of all, delighted that my enthusiastic admiration of the great temple was not an illusion. It still appeared the most perfect in its execution and constructed at the happiest period of the arts and sciences. Everything in it is crafted, is interesting and is important.
>
> It would be necessary to draw the whole, in minute detail, to possess ourselves of all that is worth carrying away. Nothing has been made without some end in view, without contributing in a greater or lesser degree to the perfection and harmony of the whole. As my time here was very limited, I began with what had been the principal object in my previous journey, namely, the celestial planisphere that occupies part of the ceiling of a little apartment built over the nave of the great temple.

Denon is here referring to the East Osiris Chapel that is situated on the roof of the Temple of Dendera. The planisphere, to which he makes reference, is the famed circular zodiacal ceiling. Denon resumes his narrative with a description of the chapel and its famous ceiling:

> The floor being low and the room dark I was able to work for only a few hours of the day. Neither these difficulties nor the multiplicity of the details – and the great care required in not

The portico of the Temple of Hathor at Dendera. The roof is supported by twenty-four great columns surmounted by representations of the goddess Hathor (these were defaced by Coptic Christians). As 'lady of the sky' she had astrological associations and was also identified with music and love. The French had difficulty in surveying the interior, which was filled with wind-blown sand. This had, however, preserved much of the original brilliant coloration – now faded or lost. *(Roberts, British Library)*

The circular zodiac found in the chapel dedicated to Osiris on the roof of the Temple of Dendera. This large carved stone portrays astrological scenes – striking evidence of mankind's early attempts to interpret the cosmos. Four pairs of falcons and four divinities support the heavens. To the right Isis, devoted wife of Osiris, extends her arms across the heavens. The complete artefact was removed by the French in 1822 – an undertaking that required four weeks – and was transported to the Louvre. Out of respect for antiquity, a plaster cast was left in its place. *(Jollois and Dutertre, Author's Collection)*

confusing them in so inconvenient a posture – abated my ardour. The desire of bringing to the philosophers of my native country the copy of an Egyptian bas-relief of so much importance made me patiently endure the tormenting position required in its delineation.

I also copied the rest of the ceiling, which is divided into two equal parts by a large figure that seems to be of Isis. Her feet rest upon the earth, her arms are extended towards heaven and she appears to occupy all the space between.

His survey of the Chapel of Osiris complete, Denon next investigated an adjacent chamber: 'Behind the first chamber is a second that receives light only through the door. This is also covered with the most interesting and admirably executed hieroglyphical pictures. Despite the darkness, and the difficulty of getting what little light there was to fall at the same time on this bas-relief and my paper, I made drawings of almost all that was contained on the ceiling or the walls.' Denon reflected on the nature of the symbolism and meaning of the wall decorations he had taken such pains to copy:

> It is difficult to imagine what could be the use of this little edifice that is so carefully finished and ornamented with pictures and is so evidently scientific. Those on the ceiling appear to relate to the motions of the heavenly bodies and those on the walls have probably some reference to the earth and the influences of the air and water.
>
> The earth is universally represented by the figure of Isis, who was the presiding divinity in all the temples of Tentyris, and whose emblem figure is found in every part. Her head is seen forming the capital of the columns belonging to the portico and the first chamber of the great

The Temple at Dendera dedicated to the sky goddess Hathor. Her image was celebrated in the capitals surmounting the central columns. French soldiers patrol while artists survey the fabric. When undertaking his own investigations, General Desaix discovered the celebrated planisphere (see above) on the roof of the temple – encroached at the time by mud-brick dwellings. *(Denon, Author's Collection)*

temple. It is also sculpted in gigantic proportions on the outside of the foundation walls and is the distinguishing object in the ornaments of the frieze.

Denon employed all the time available to him in measuring the capitals and columns of the temple, in drawing plans and elevations and taking views of the gates. As he explains, because of the lack of light he was unable to complete his work on the celestial ceiling and had to be content with making outline sketches.

His researches were cut short by the unwelcome news that the sheikh of the local village had made it known to the French that he wished to be rid of them from his district. General Belliard, not wishing to provoke an unwanted conflict, sent word to Denon and his companions that they must depart without delay. Indefatigable as ever, Denon made some final hasty observations:

Just before setting off, I took a view of the site of Tentyris [Dendera] and the group of monuments that overlooks the town with the mountain in the distance. I also copied an inscription, in beautiful large Greek characters, carved on one of the outer gates to the temple. The following is the inscription [in translation] taken as correctly as the mutilated state of some of the letters would admit:

On account of the Emperor Caesar, God, the son of Jupiter the Deliverer, in the govenorship of Publius Octavius, Marcus Claudius Posthumous Commander-in-Chief, and Tryphon General, the deputies of the metropolis consecrated, in the virtue of the law, the propylaeum to Isis, the greatest of the goddesses, and to the associated gods of the temple, in the thirty-first year of Caesar.

Taking a final view of Dendera, Denon noted wistfully: 'These few Greek characters, in the midst of innumerable Egyptian inscriptions, form an extraordinary and striking contrast'. With that he made his departure.

CHAPTER 18

To the Red Sea

A few days after his return to Dendera, Denon learned that a detachment of French cavalry was required to accompany a military chest that was to be transported from Esna to Qena. He took advantage of the opportunity this presented to request permission to join the party so that he could visit Koptos, modern-day Qift. He had already passed the town three times without having been able to stop. Now he saw his chance to make a visit and survey the antique remains.

Koptos originally owed its importance and prosperity to the gold and porphyry mines in the neighbourhood. The town was also associated with the worship of Isis who, according to tradition, found the body of Osiris there. In the Roman period the township flourished as a centre of trade but was heavily taxed as a consequence. In AD 292, the township rebelled only to face savage retribution from the emperor Diocletian. He had the town laid to waste. Following its recovery it became the centre of a thriving Christian community from which the Coptic Christians derived their name. On arriving at Koptos Denon recorded his observations:

> On entering the town I was struck by the good state of preservation of its different monuments. The ancient part still remains in the state in which it was left by the conflagration that terminated the long siege that destroyed it in the third century. The old limits of the city have been abandoned and have been succeeded by an Arab town with a boundary wall of unbaked bricks. Beyond this, verging to the west, the village of Qift was built that still exists.
>
> One may distinguish the different ruins of two temples of high antiquity and those of a Catholic church in which taste and art in the construction were certainly less remarkable than the magnificence and richness of the materials employed. The fragments of porphyry, granite columns and pilasters, scattered over a vast space of ground, remain to attest to the opulence and luxury of the first believers.
>
> All these monuments lie without form and order on the ground, excepting a few portions still left standing. None of them furnished me with a single subject for a drawing.

Although Koptos did not yield any significant monuments for Denon to illustrate for his portfolio, it was during his visit to the town that he had occasion to experience the phenomenon of a sandstorm. He had heard local people speak of this as the *Khamsīn*, or fierce wind, that he knew to be 'equally terrible by the frightful spectacle that it exhibits, when present, as by the consequences that follow it'. On the evening of 18 May, Denon was out walking when he felt himself overcome by a suffocating heat. It was as if the very fluctuation of the air was suddenly suspended. Unknown to him a sandstorm was approaching:

I went out to bathe, to overcome the painful sensation [of heat], when I was struck at my arrival at the bank of the Nile with the changed appearance of nature around me. This was a [quality of] light and colours that I had not seen before. The sun, without being concealed, had lost its rays. It had even less lustre to the eye than the moon and gave a pale light without shadow. The water no longer reflected its rays but appeared in agitation. Everything had changed its usual aspect.

The yellow horizon showed the trees on its surface to be a dirty blue and flocks of birds were flying off before the cloud. Frightened animals ran loose in the country, followed by the shouting inhabitants who vainly attempted to collect them together again.

The wind, that had raised an immense mass of sand and was urging it forward, had not yet reached us. We thought that by plunging our bodies in the water that was then calm, it would prevent the baneful effects of the mass of sand that was advancing from the south-west. But we had hardly entered the river when it began to swell, all at once – as if it would overflow its channel. The waves passed over our heads and we felt the river bed heave under our feet. Our clothes were carried away, along the shore, that seemed to be swept by the whirlwind that had now reached us.

We were compelled to leave the water whereupon our wet naked bodies, being beat upon with the sandstorm, were soon encrusted with black mud that prevented us from dressing ourselves.

With only a red and gloomy sun to light us, with our eyes smarting, our noses stuffed up and our throats clogged with sand – so that we could hardly breathe – we lost each other and our way home. We at last arrived at our lodgings, one by one, groping our way and guided only by the walls that marked our track.

We could now easily appreciate the dreadful situation of those who are taken by surprise by such a phenomenon of nature when crossing the exposed and naked desert.

The next day the trail of the sandstorm could still be discerned as it progressed through the Libyan desert. It followed the mountain chain and, just when Denon and his companions thought they were rid of this excoriating scourge, the west wind brought it back and, once more, the French were overwhelmed with the 'scorching torrent'. According to Denon:

Flashes of lightning pierced the dense sandstorm [but] only with difficulty. All the elements seemed to be still in disorder. The rain was mixed with whirling winds of fire. Wind and dust and, in this time of confusion, the trees and all other productions of nature seemed to be again plunged in the horrors of chaos.

Paradoxically, while the desert winds of Libya were sending Denon and his companions searing clouds of dust, the winds to the east were bearing a deluge of rain. This became apparent when a band of merchants arrived from the borders of the Red Sea telling how, in the valleys they had crossed, the water had reached up to their knees. Two days later Denon was told the plain was carpeted with birds 'that were in close files like an army moving from east to west'. He went to investigate:

From a distance the files appeared to move like a broad torrent flowing through the country. Thinking they might be some foreign species of birds, we hastened out to meet them. But, instead of birds, we saw a cloud of locusts that just skimmed over the soil, stopping at each

blade of grass to devour it and then flying off for new food. If it had been the season in which the corn was young and tender this would have been a serious plague.

The wind, changing again in a contrary direction to their march, drove them back into the desert. These locusts are a rose colour and are speckled with black. They are very strong, shy and difficult to catch.

Shortly after this event Denon learned that he and his military detachment were to journey west to the port of Quseir on the shore of the Red Sea, because Bonaparte had decided it was necessary to establish a fortress in anticipation of possible attack from the

The rugged countryside encountered by the French on their march east to Quseir. Despite the many obstacles the French army had to overcome, the region was a veritable paradise for the geologist-members of Bonaparte's Commission. They explored ravines veined with basalt, feldspar, gypsum, granite, limestone, mica and quartz which presented 'all manner of colours'. *(Raffeneau–Delile, National Library of Scotland)*

English. The time allowed to make his preparations afforded Denon the opportunity to satisfy his curiosity as a naturalist. He turned his attention to one of Egypt's quintessential symbols, the camel.

In his travels along the Nile Valley he had depended upon the camel as a means of transport and had developed a fascination for the creature by reason of its remarkable attributes. Immensely strong, dependable, able to bear considerable loads and, of course, capable of journeying for long distances without the need for taking water, he and his soldier companions had come to rely upon their camels almost – if not more than – their horses.

The caravan bound for Quseir was composed of 360 French soldiers each of whom had a camel. The camels served for personal transport and to carry the baggage and water necessary for each individual. In addition, 200 camels, with attendants, were loaded with the heavy articles and equipment required to establish camp. Hearing that the French were departing for Quseir, several Arab chiefs made an alliance with their erstwhile enemies. Hoping to ingratiate themselves with the French in the expectation of deriving benefits for their services, they volunteered to act as guides.

When the French and their escorts were finally assembled 'the whole party amounted to between one thousand and eleven hundred men – and as many camels'. The sinuous company of men and their heavily laden beasts made a remarkable spectacle as they wended their way across the Arabian desert.

Although Denon and the senior officers had by now acquired some experience of handling their camels, mounting them still proved a challenge:

It was entertaining for us to see each other mount our beasts. The camel, which is in general deliberate in all his actions, first rises very briskly on his hind legs as soon as the rider leans on his saddle. He then springs up and throws the rider forward and then backward. It is not until the fourth motion, when the beast is entirely on his legs, that the rider can find his balance. None of us had been able to resist the first shake and we each had occasion to laugh at our neighbour, until we were all well fixed on our saddles.

I had been apprehensive of the swinging gait of the camel and the prancing of the dromedary had made me fear being thrown over its head. I was soon agreeably reassured. When fixed in the saddle, one has only to give way to the motion of the beast and one soon finds it is impossible to be more pleasantly mounted for a long journey. No attention is required to guide the animal, except in turning him out of his straightforward direction, which very seldom happens in the desert [particularly] amid a caravan. The camel rarely trips and never stumbles, except when the ground is wet.

Since the camel was little known to the West in the late eighteenth century, Denon provides the reader with further information:

The dromedary is among the camel tribe what the greyhound is among dogs. They are used only for the saddle. A ring is passed through their nostril, to which a thong is tied, and this serves as a bridle to guide and stop him or to make him kneel when the rider wishes to dismount. The pace of the dromedary is light, the opening of the angles of his legs – and the flexible spring of his lean foot – renders his trot easier than that of any horse and at the same time still as swift.

On quitting their encampment on the Nile, the company turned east and entered a long, wide valley that led to an extensive plain. At its extremities appeared rocky projections indicative of the chain of hills along which they were travelling. They marched until ten at night maintaining good military order. This was essential so that the soldiers could form a defensive military array as quickly and effectively as possible, such precautions being necessary since the party was now moving into open country and hence was vulnerable to attack.

On setting up camp, each officer spread his own blanket by the side of his camel, consumed his rations and settled down for the night under the starry sky. At one in the morning, with a full moon, the drum was beat. It was the signal to resume the march. Within five minutes everyone was ready to depart 'without any confusion or trouble'. Denon adds the following remarks, once more in praise of the camel:

In the desert one's respect is redoubled for the camel, that worthy animal. However hard is his condition, he knows it and conforms to it without impatience. He is a truly bountiful gift of Providence and nature has set him down in a country in which his place could not be supplied to the service of man by any other animal whatever. The sand is truly his element. As soon as he quits it – and touches the mud – he can hardly keep upon his feet and his constant trips alarm the rider for the safety of himself and his luggage.

French troops rest at a fountain on their march to Quseir by the Red Sea. They found water in a declivity beneath the rocks which was 'fresh and good'. Note the heavy gun-carriage that had to be hauled up several steep ravines. Denon informs us: 'This is a faithful portrait of a halt'. *(Denon, British Library)*

The march resumed and as the party progressed the nature of the hilly countryside began to change. Denon grew interested in the geology of the region. He had noticed that the mountains they had passed the day before were composed of freestone. These now gave way to alluvial pudding stone – a mixture of granite, porphyry, serpentine and other primitive stones aggregated in green schist. The valley along which they journeyed continued to grow narrower and the rocks on every side more lofty. By noon the first half of the journey had been achieved.

The party began to descend until they reached an oasis called El-More. Although this was little more than a small hole under a rock, the quality of the water was judged to be excellent but not sufficient in quantity for the large numbers in the caravan. A search was made for a second watering place, and that was fortunately soon discovered. This consisted of several wells once more sheltered below a rocky outcrop. Denon records: 'the geological stratum was a rock of very green schist, mixed with white quartz, that gives it the appearance of antique green marble'.

The pass along which they were now travelling became so narrow and difficult it became troublesome to manoeuvre the heavy artillery pieces. However, this terrain soon gave way to an easier route which Denon describes as being like 'a well-sanded walk in a garden'. This appearance may be explained by the fact that from time to time this part of the pass was swept by torrents precipitated by flash floods. Since these only ever lasted for a few hours the level of the valley was maintained without it being turned into a ravine.

As the party carried on its way, Denon continued with his observations of the nature of the terrain through which he and his companions were travelling:

The variety of form and colour in the rocks began to break the sad and monotonous uniformity of the desert and gave it almost a rural appearance. The country became sonorous. The noise of our party began to echo in the valleys and disappeared, like the wakening of nature, for our troops had crossed the sandy plains in silence. They had conversed little when in the valleys but, when arrived among the rocks, they made them resound with mirth and gaiety and the gloom of the desert evaporated.

As they descended from the heights which they had scaled, the aspect of the mountain ranges altered. They no longer exhibited the same beds of magnificent breccia but once more appeared as siliceous rock veined with quartz. Having been on the march for eighteen hours, and overcome now with fatigue, the party stopped to sleep. The journey was resumed at daybreak and, within a short while, they entered a large valley. Here, an oasis was encountered known locally as the fountain of Ambag. Although there was water in abundance, when Denon tasted it he judged it to be 'only drinkable for camels'. He adds:

> It possesses the quality of a mineral spring and would perhaps be as beneficial in the cure of diseases as spa [water] but here – owing to the sterility of the soil and the sobriety of the inhabitants – there are but few diseases and no physicians. This spring creeps inglorious under a blank and mephitic [noxious] mud. It purges those who can endure the detestable taste that it leaves in the mouth but it increases instead of satisfying thirst. It passes for the most malignant spring in the country.

Denon and his companions were made aware they were nearing the coast when they noticed the lightness of the air and the brightness of the sky. Following the course of a ravine for a short distance, they saw waves breaking on the reefs that skirted the line of the shore. Looking beyond, Denon could see mist on the horizon that he conjectured concealed the coast of Asia. The tribe of Ababdes Arabs, who had accompanied the French, went on ahead to parley with the elders of Quseir who were now approaching. Soon afterwards they returned with several sheikhs from the town who, together with their followers, brought with them a flock of sheep – 'the first offering of peace and homage'.

Denon observed that the costume of the most senior emissaries from Quseir was much the same as that of the people of Mecca. The people of a lower class were almost naked except for a girdle around their loins. Each held a lance in his hand and had a dagger attached to his left arm. They sat on the saddle of their camels – which were sickly-looking beasts – with their legs crossed beneath them. Denon noted that, in contrast, the Meccans had a graver demeanour, wore an elaborate headdress and were wrapped in long garments decorated with broad stripes. They were mounted on well-fed, sturdy-looking camels. As soon as the different parties met everyone dismounted and the French troops disposed themselves in their customary defensive battle order. After a few minutes of amicable conference, the French went away to take possession of the fort of Quseir from which the tricolore was soon waving in the fresh coastal breeze. Denon made a preliminary survey of the port and neighbouring coast:

> [The town] is open on the east and south-east. The headland, or cape, is entirely of late formation and is composed of nothing but madrepores [corals] the greater number of which are of an enormous size. Nothing can describe in adequate terms the deep melancholy of the country, the rigid aspect of the soil and the insupportable dazzling reflection of the sun from the white shell-covered shore.
>
> The Arab houses are composed of a few pieces of wood that support some miserable mats. The inhabitants live on shell-fish and form all their household utensils from the shells – and

even work them into boxes that are not without elegance. Quseir will only hold a small number of merchant ships, of inferior size, since the depth of water is only two fathoms and a half where it is the deepest. To load the vessels, they are obliged to carry the goods in the arms of men a hundred and fifty paces from the shore and to put them on board boats that afterwards have to take them to the vessels that are to be freighted.

When Denon explored the coast in the vicinity of Quseir, he found it to be desolate and barren. The sea in contrast was evidently rich in fish, shells and coral, the latter so plentiful and brightly coloured that Denon wondered if it was for this reason the whole sea had acquired its name – Red – while the sand everywhere on the shore was such a brilliant white.

Denon regretted not having time to make a collection of the shells that appeared to be 'as numerous as varied'; it was a pleasure he had to forgo since he had drawings he wanted to complete. He also had to devote time to the preparations required for making his return journey. However, he did find time to make an excursion along the shore with his new allies the Ababdes Arabs. Having mounted one of their camels and seated himself, in the fashion of the country, on its lofty saddle, he soon delighted in the beast's light and easy pace.

Denon so won the trust of his companions that, oblivious to the passage of time, they spent the rest of the day travelling along 'in the bond of friendship'. They made such good progress that they achieved the rate of 'a league in less than a quarter of an hour'.

As Denon journeyed back to Quseir his respect for his Arab companions grew. He appreciated their ability to live from the land even though it was so inhospitable. Nothing was left to waste nor was any opportunity allowed to pass unheeded, as Denon's account of the following incident reveals:

> We perceived two gazelles fleeing into the desert, upon which four of our allies set out in pursuit of them with indifferent matchlock guns. Some minutes after, we heard just two shots fired and we saw them return with both the gazelles that were as fat as if they had been fed in the richest pasture. I was invited to partake of them and, being curious to know how their cookery was carried on, I went to their quarters.
>
> The leader, who was as proud as a sovereign, had no other decoration than the belt we had given him. His kitchen utensils consisted of two plates of copper and a pot of the same metal. Butter, flour and two sticks of wood completed his table equipage. In a few minutes he had struck a light, collected old camel dung for fuel, made dough with his flour and cooked some fritters that were very good when hot. These, with the soup of the flesh, the bouillie [stew] and grilled meat made up a very tolerable repast for one who had any appetite. However, this was not so in my case for I had not the least hunger. In the desert I lived almost entirely on lemonade that I generally made when riding on my camel – by putting slices of lemon in my mouth together with sugar and washing it down with water.

The Arabs' management of their camels provided Denon with further evidence of their skill in surviving amid the unforgiving terrain of the desert:

> Our Arabs were acquainted with every corner of pasturage. They knew to what state of growth such and such plants should have attained – at a league's distance from the regular track – and sent their camels to feed upon them.

These poor animals had nothing else in the whole day but a single feed of beans that they ruminate for the remainder of the day, either on their journey or lying down on the scorching sand without evincing the least impatience. The passion of desire alone gives them some violence in their actions, particularly the females who appear more irritable. What is extraordinary is that fatigue seems to inflame their temperament instead of exhausting them.

The return journey from Quseir was accomplished more rapidly than the outward journey, the party now being unencumbered by the heavy artillery pieces. These had been left behind to help with the defence of the town and consequently the men were free to step out more briskly. Halts were still required, to gain a moment's respite, but within two days the banks of the Nile were once more within sight. The last half-day of the journey was achieved, however, only after overcoming considerable fatigue and with the troops' supply of water exhausted. On reaching the Nile they quenched their thirst by consuming great quantities of watermelons and finally plunging into the river itself – Denon included.

Denon had now spent eight days travelling in the desert. The experience had heightened his awareness of nature:

I still remember the delight I felt on again spending the night reclined on the banks of the Nile, hearing the wind rustling in the leaves of the trees and feeling the refreshing coolness that it acquires in brushing through the long leaves of the palm that it gently agitates. Everything was alive and gave animating sensations. Life was in the air and nature seemed to respire. However, I became fully convinced by this journey – made in the hottest time of the year – that undertaking it requires the effort of courage and that danger flies from those who brave it.

The journey east to Quseir had isolated Denon and his military companions. They were eager to receive news of the affairs of the rest of the army and particulars of their operations. The news, though, was not always favourable, as Denon remarks in his

French troops assemble on the beach at Quseir as their officers are greeted by a procession of local people. The party of 360 men had marched over 160 kilometres to reach the coast hauling their heavy equipment. This was used to strengthen the fortress (left) in case of invasion from the Red Sea by the English. The vessels in the distance are trading ships. In the foreground a camel has expired from the rigours of the journey. *(Denon, British Library)*

philosophical style: 'Intelligence was often clouded with grief in learning of the loss of some one or other of our brave companions. These fatigues of mind, combined with those of the body, recalled in a melancholy way our thoughts towards our native country and made us feel our forlorn situation and the necessity we felt of being near human beings to whom we were bound by the ties of affection.'

To add to Denon's feelings of sadness the weather was taking an unfavourable turn:

It is at this period that residence in Upper Egypt is almost intolerable. The winds are variable and are constantly changing from the east to the south, or the south-west. This latter is terrible for it troubles the atmosphere, obscures the sun – with a white, dry and burning vapour – parches with thirst, dries up everything, inflames the blood, irritates the nerves and makes life itself painful. It also oppresses the lungs so severely that one involuntarily seeks cooler air to breathe in, feeling as if the mouth is an oven of fire. If one inhales the air by the nostrils, it affects the head and, in again exhaling it, it feels like a gush of blood rushing over the air passages. Everything one touches is burning and – even in the night – iron acquires the same heat to the touch as it would have in France in the dog days exposed to the noon-day rays of the sun.

Not only was the weather intolerable but the French found themselves tormented by an additional burden in the form of numerous camp followers. They pursued the French army like flies, progressively insinuating themselves into their ranks and eventually finding roles for themselves as servants or assistants of all kinds. The process was insidious and one that Denon and his companions had little power to resist:

In the east [servants] are a kind of vermin who multiply at every step and feed upon you without your being able to defend yourself from their importunities. Scarcely have you engaged a single domestic than you are served by another. As soon as you give him livery, he must have his horse and this introduces a third officious fellow and so on.

It must be acknowledged that, by degrees, we rendered ourselves accomplices to this corruption for we caught the spirit of the Orientals – in breathing the same air with them. We became so accustomed to an entourage that we soon could not do without a large train of attendants.

Following his exertions marching with the army through the desert, Denon was content to spend the next few days relaxing with the soldiers on the banks of the Nile. But it was not in his nature to be inactive. And there was much he still wished to record. It was not long, therefore, before he was actively seeking further opportunities to enrich his portfolio.

CHAPTER 19

The Tombs of the Kings

On his return from Quseir, Denon set about making plans to search for further antiquities. His deliberations were interrupted when he learned that an assembly of sheikhs was about to take place. In effect, this was an Arab council whose principal members were the headmen of the local villages of the region where Denon and the French army were billeted. Denon was told that the purpose of the council was to make decisions concerning the cultivation of the land the following year. His curiosity aroused, he asked permission to attend to find out more about the proceedings and how they affected the management of the land and the planting of crops.

He was told premiums were offered, in the form of distributions of the most favourable land, to those farmers who had the best record of cultivation. The agricultural year commenced with the preparation of the canals and waterways. It was by means of this irrigation network that the flood waters from the annual inundation were distributed across the fields and pastures. When these preparations were complete, the planting of the crops could commence. If the inundation was strong the flood water could be several feet deep, yielding a rich deposit of nutrient-bearing mud that soaked and enriched the ground below. In the flood season typical crops were maize, wheat, barley, clover, beans, flax, onions and lentils. During the period of the lower-water level, typical crops were cotton, sugar cane, sesame and millet.

While the local sheikhs were in counsel, Denon learned that a party of engineers and surveyors – members of Bonaparte's Commission of Sciences and Arts – was about to proceed north to chart the course of the Nile. The head of the party was Citizen Gerard. He consented to Denon travelling with him who lost no time in making his preparations. This expedition afforded Denon the opportunity to renew his travels of exploration, something for which he had been hoping for several days.

The survey party arrived first at Dendera for which Denon was particularly grateful as it gave him the opportunity to verify the drawings he had made there previously of the zodiacal ceiling. He was also able to enrich his collection of hieroglyphs that, on this occasion being free of the pressures of military discipline, he was able to study in relative tranquillity.

At the time of Denon's visit to Dendera, many of the decorations adorning the inner walls of the temple were preserved in a state of pristine freshness, their colours almost as vivid as on the day they had been painted. The first subjects to claim his attention were representations of human forms. He discovered figures traced in outline with red chalk

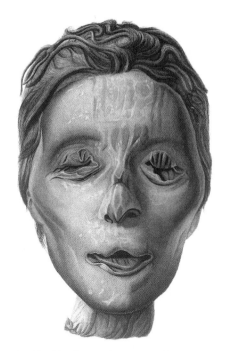

Two views of the head of the mummy of a woman. The French savants were astonished to discover human remains preserved so perfectly. Denon offered a large sum to anyone finding an entire mummy but was unsuccessful. This head was found by the illustrator Delile. It later formed part of Denon's Paris collection of Egyptian artefacts. *(Dutertre and Redouté, National Library of Scotland)*

which had been filled in with a covering of white stucco upon which colour had been applied. He studied the Egyptian system of proportion of the human figure which he thought 'corresponded with the heroic style of the Greeks'. Next, he completed a collection of drawings of animals. Denon considered that the Egyptians excelled at these representations and that the grandeur and simplicity of their lines often attained the ideal of abstract beauty. Moreover, he was astonished by the minute exactness of the details, the care and execution of the work and the perfect finish achieved. He recorded in his *Journal*: '[In this work are] the hallmarks of the determination and perseverance that characterise the monastic spirit whose zeal neither perishes nor cools and whose pride is not individual but corporate.'

After completing his study of the wall decorations adorning the Temple of Hathor, Denon enjoyed a moment's respite from his artistic survey-work. He noticed that the waters of the Nile were rising and he made some observations:

On 26 June [1799] the Nile began to rise and on this and the following two days [it] attained [an increase in] height of three inches. It increased at the rate of two inches a day and afterwards at three inches. The water now filled the banks and ceased to be green without, however, becoming muddy. The Nile, after rising for some time at the daily rate of two inches, came at length to an increase of a foot each day – at which period the water began to be muddy.

[This] appears to show that the course of the Nile traverses some large lakes whose limpid

waters are forced down the stream by the torrents of rain from the Abyssinian mountains. The discoloration of the Nile does not happen until the arrival of the fresh water in Egypt.

Not only was the Nile transforming itself but the weather was also changing. The heat had become insupportable. The dry west wind, in particular, oppressed everyone and caused bleeding from the nose. It also induced painful eruptions on the surface of the skin. These covered all parts of the body and then dried and hardened the skin. This in turn impeded perspiration, and gave rise to further discomfort. Denon attributed the affliction to the direct heat of the sun, remarking: 'The rays of the sun, the principal, perhaps the sole cause of these evils, raised on every pore a pustule similar to smallpox that became intolerable [particularly] when lying down when it was necessary to rest on these inflamed points.'

Wall decorations from a rock-cut tomb. The scenes depict the ritual sacrifice of an ox. A priest secures the animal, another prepares to cut its throat, his companion carries a bowl to collect the blood and another finally dismembers the hapless creature. Despite the harrowing nature of the subject, the mural is a minor work of art – originally rendered in full colour. *(Jollois and Dutertre, Author's Collection)*

Despite the intense heat the march was resumed. A detachment was to return south to Karnak. This raised Denon's spirits again since it increased the likelihood of him being able to visit the Valley of the Kings to inspect the ancient rock-cut tombs. When the military orders were given, he readily fell in line and set out with the detachment:

The heat was extreme on 1 July and our blood was inflamed by the solstitial sun. Two soldiers fainted while we were leaving Qena and, the next morning, fifteen others were obliged to remain behind. If we had not by this time been a little accustomed to the climate, not an individual would have been able to resist it. As it was, we were obliged to make shorter day journeys and to march only in the morning.

The country in spite of the heat was quite alive. The whole population, under the direction of the sheikhs, was busily employed in clearing out the canals and opening them to admit the inundation. The restoration of public confidence and tranquillity had brought back the herds from the passes of the desert. The fields, abandoned four months ago, were now covered with animals feeding in peace.

The party rested a whole day at Qus and on 3 July, late in the evening, Karnak was reached. Since Denon had by now made several visits to Karnak, he was able to act as a guide for the members of the party who were seeing the temple ruins for the first time. This also enabled him to verify the measurements he had made previously – taken in haste due to the limitation of time – and to add several more descriptions to his existing records.

On this visit time allowed Denon to inspect the Ramesseum, or mortuary temple, of Rameses II that was known to the French as the Tomb of Ozymandias. Mortuary temples were designed for the performance of funerary rituals and cultic practices. At Karnak they were dedicated to Amun, the supreme god of Thebes. In the New Kingdom the temples of successive pharaohs rivalled each other in size and magnificence. Denon provides the following description of the outer peristyle or courtyard:

On the south side of the first court there is a particular edifice, within the general circumvallation [perimeter], consisting of a boundary wall and a gate – opening into a court. [This is] surrounded with a pilastered gallery in front of which are figures, with their arms crossed, holding in one hand a scourge and in the other a kind of hook. There are, in addition, two lateral galleries and five antechambers with five [more] chambers behind them.

Perhaps this was the palace, or rather the splendid prison, of the kings? [This] idea is rendered probable by the sculpted figures. On the side of the gate [portal] they represent heroes, holding conquered prisoners by their hair, [to whom] the divinities present new arms for future victories.

While completing his survey work at Karnak, Denon learned that another military detachment was to make a journey south to Edfu. Although this presented a distraction from his wish to visit the Valley of the Kings, he decided to accompany the army to better acquaint himself with the great Temple of Horus. This was his third visit to the ancient Apollonopolis Magna – 'Apollo's Town'. On arriving, his enthusiasm was undiminished:

At Edfu the temple appeared more magnificent than ever. If that at Tentyris [Dendera] is more learned in its details, this at Edfu has more grandeur as a whole. I had the promise of being allowed an entire day here but was obliged to content myself with an afternoon. The air was still so scorching that I could scarcely endure it in order to make the drawings that were the express object of my journey. Being by this time accustomed to regulating my movements by those of others – and to conform to [their] circumstances – I completed the business I came for as well as I was able.

I added more than thirty figures to my hieroglyphic alphabet and also discovered a way through the ruins into one of the interior chambers. [This] appeared to be the second behind the portico – and immediately preceding the sanctuary. All that the heaps of ruins [here] allowed me to see of the inner sanctum was highly finished in excellent good taste. The freestone from which the building was constructed was finer than any other I had seen. All the work engraved upon it had retained its original boldness and delicacy, as if the material had been marble.

When the work of the military at Edfu was completed, it was time for the detachment to journey north once more to Esna. The party set out at night but much of the journey had to be undertaken the following day in the full heat of the sun. This prompted Denon to remark on the measures he adopted to maintain his health and wellbeing:

I could not allay the smarting of the eruptions, caused by the weather, in any other way than by frequent bathing – which I did in the presence of the crocodiles that I had learnt by this time to despise. To these repeated ablutions, I added a vegetable diet wholly abstaining from flesh-meat and taking little of anything else. Yet, even with this regimen, I could with difficulty procure but a few hours of broken sleep.

Returning to Esna, Denon made for the ruins of the Temple of Isis – the so-called Temple of Contra-Lata (Contralopolis) that was sited on the east bank of the Nile in the locality of Esna. Although by Egyptian standards the Temple of Isis was a modest construction, it provided the French artists with some fine examples of the

Harpists from the Tomb of the Harps in the Valley of the Kings. These captivating representations are details from the wall decorations in the tomb of Rameses III. The French artist-illustrators were struck by the similarity of the Egyptian harps with instruments of their own times – complete with multiple strings, tuning pegs and sound boards. *(Dutertre, Author's Collection)*

date-palm capital. The structure has now been lost which makes Denon's account of particular interest:

> The temple is in the plain to the right of Armant [Hermonthis]. The moving sands, or a defect in the foundation, have caused partial sinking by which several of the columns are thrown out of perpendicular and the ceiling of the portico is much damaged. I made a plan, however, of the building in order to gain a clear idea of the distribution of its parts and of some peculiarities such as the double walls that form the sides of the porticos.
>
> The parts behind the portico are trivial and negligent as to their decorations. The sanctuary is totally destroyed but, from what remains of the outer wall, there seems to have been an exterior gallery around the temple. Some of the rubbish has lately been removed by Assan Bey [in search of treasure] and this has revealed underground buildings which show that the temple formerly extended beyond the portico. The remains of the latter consist of eight columns, with broad capitals, differing from each other in the ornament they bear. In one is the vine, in another the ivy and in the third the palm leaf.

Pressure of time compelled Denon to cease his study of the portico of Esna which he regarded as 'the purest fragment of Egyptian architecture and one of the most perfect monuments of antiquity'.

On 9 July he departed Esna at daybreak in the company of the detachment of troops with which he had been travelling for the last few weeks. Their road took them past the township of Asfun that appeared to be built from 'a vast heap of rubbish'. They marched for most of the day, in the full glare of the sun, and eventually arrived at Hermonthis. According to Denon the air was less dry and suffocating but the heat of the sun continued to scorch him and his companions. Commenting more generally on the weather he remarks:

> The season of the inundation, during which the north winds are prevalent, is that in which the summer temperature of Egypt is the most endurable. It is enough [for wellbeing] to avoid the rays of the sun . . . from noon until three. For the rest of the day, the air is light and the nights are clear and cool. The object of our journey, however, being a survey of the canals and the establishment of a regular system of husbandry, obliged us to travel in the heat of the day in order to find the labourers at work.
>
> Several of our people died of heat in this expedition. Nothing is more frightful than this kind of death. A person suddenly falls sick which symptom, in spite of every assistance, is succeeded by fainting following which the patient soon dies. Our horses also were subject to like accidents.

Despite the harsh conditions, to Denon's delight the party approached Thebes. He now had the prospect of visiting the Valley of the Kings to survey the royal tombs cut from the living rock. Benefiting from the security provided by the troops he rode ahead of the party to make preliminary sketches.

Catching sight of the Colossi of Memnon rising majestically from the Plain of Thebes, he could not resist taking another look at them. Once more negligent of his personal safety, he hastened in their direction. It was still early morning and he was anxious to experience the impression travellers had, in ancient times, of seeing the great seated figures bathed in the first light of dawn.

Denon became so absorbed in contemplation of the huge statues that he quite overlooked his isolation; only when he saw his military detachment 'half a league ahead of him' did he become aware of his vulnerable situation. He galloped at once to rejoin the troops. Safely among them he noticed they were extremely fatigued. To his dismay, there was discussion as to whether the march to the Valley of the Kings should be abandoned. Despite his strong feelings – and wish to protest in favour of continuing with the expedition – he remained silent, a tactic that worked to his advantage. He remarks: 'Vexed as I was, I said not a word and profited more by my silence than I should have done by giving loose rein to my feelings, for we at length resumed our journey without further discussion'.

The party soon reached the Valley of the Kings where they experienced the hostility of the local people who used the rock-cut tombs as their 'subterranean habitations'. According to Denon: 'For the third time [on our journey] we were saluted by the incorrigible inhabitants with a volley of musketry'. The occupants of the royal tombs were in a well-nigh impregnable position. Denon explains: 'This was the only place in Upper Egypt that held out against our forces. Strong in their sepulchral retreats, they came out like spectres only to alarm [other] men. Culpable, by their many crimes, they concealed their remorse and fortified their disobedience in the obscurity of these excavations. They are so numerous that of themselves they bear testimony to the immense population of Egypt.' The presence of so many soldiers finally restrained the combative nature and hostility of the cave dwellers and checked them from attacking the French party. Denon and his companions were therefore able to march on without further dispute into the Valley of the Kings. Denon was jubilant. At last he could undertake the researches of the tombs he had so long desired.

The description that follows is Denon's account of the great Royal Necropolis, the final resting place of the pharaohs of the New Kingdom. It is an important document for a number of reasons. It is one of the earliest writings by a European to provide a detailed description of the tombs. Denon's observations are of additional importance since they were made at a time when the majority of the wall decorations were in a pristine state.

It was not until after marching for three-quarters of an hour in the desert valley that, in the midst of the rocks, we observed all at once some openings parallel to the ground. The first of these openings displayed no other architectural ornaments than an entrance [cut] in a simple square frame. As soon as the threshold of the first entrance was passed, we discovered long galleries twelve feet wide and twenty in height cased with stucco, sculptured and painted. The arches, of an elegant elliptical figure, are covered with innumerable hieroglyphics. [These are] disposed with so much taste that, notwithstanding the singular grotesqueness of the forms, and the total absence of demi-tint [shadow] or perspective, the ceilings make an agreeable whole and a rich and harmonious association of colours.

It would have required a stay of some weeks to discover, or form any system concerning, the subjects of so many and such serious paintings. Unfortunately, I was allowed only a few minutes and even these were not granted to me with the best possible grace. I asked [myself] questions on all sides with impatience. Preceded by torches, I had merely time to pass on from one tomb to another.

Lateral chambers, hollowed into the rock, are covered with a fine white stucco on which are coloured hieroglyphics. [These are] in a most wonderful state of preservation except for two of the eight tombs that I visited, which have been injured by water trickling down them. All the rest are still in a full [state of] perfection and the paintings [are] as fresh as when they were first executed. The colours of the ceilings, exhibiting yellow figures on a blue ground, are executed with a taste that might decorate our most splendid salons.

While undertaking his researches, Denon was mortified to hear the sound of the trumpet summoning him and his guides back to camp. He had just discovered a chamber in which were represented all kinds of arms such as bows, arrows, quivers, pikes and javelins. In another was a collection of household utensils including chairs, sofas and beds – 'all of exquisite form such as might well grace the apartments of modern luxury'. In yet another chamber was a figure, clothed in white, playing on a harp with eleven strings that Denon thought to be similar to the modern ones of his day. He was allowed a further twenty minutes to make his final drawings. He concludes: 'One person lighted me while another held a taper to every object that I pointed out to him and I completed my task in the time prescribed with spirit and correctness'.

Denon quitted the tombs with regret. Although he had remained three hours he could easily have found subjects to occupy him for as many days. Reflecting on his visit, and the all too short a period of time available to him, he noted in his *Journal*: '[My] visit to Thebes was like an attack of fever. It was a kind of crisis that left behind the impression of indescribable impatience, enthusiasm, inanition and fatigue.'

CHAPTER 20

The Splendours of Mid...

Marching north with the troops Denon arrived for... was populated by Christians, and a Coptic bish... the French party. Following him was a grou... the commanding officers to his house... Denon supposed this show of courtesy wa... ...ered his township from the oppression of th... ...aving freed the bishop from captivity. The party... at El Balass, a region famed for the high quality of its... transported to the whole of Egypt and as far afield as Syria... an exceptionally fine consistency, the jars enabled water to be kept c... process of evaporation.

These pots were made at little expense and sol... ...ly they were sometimes used to construct the walls of houses. Even the poorest in...bitant could supply himself with them in abundance. Nature provided the clay material in the neighbouring desert. This was compact marl that only required moistening and working in the hands to be perfectly ductile and tenacious. The vessels formed from it, when dried in the shade and baked in the sun, only needed kilning for a few hours with a little straw fire to be ready for use. The people made rafts of these pots that they floated down the Nile. Part of the cargo was sold on the way, and the remainder was embarked at Rosetta and Damietta to be sent abroad. The use of these jars can be traced back to antiquity and Denon saw them represented in hieroglyphic paintings and in ancient manuscripts. He describes their use as follows:

> The spongy nature of the clay makes the water transude [evaporate] while the particles suspended in it are attracted to the side of the vessel. The outer surface is always moistened by the transudation. When there is the least breath of wind to promote evaporation, the water within the jar becomes as cool as if it were iced. They are sometimes spiced with benzoin [a fragrant juice derived from a tree that grew in the locality] or perfumed with orange flower or other aromatics to vary the taste of the water which, when drunk from these vases, is the best in the world.

Continuing their journey, the party arrived at Qena where they found the level of the Nile had risen fully 6 feet higher than when they were there previously. It was while he was at Qena that Denon learned of Bonaparte's march into Syria with a substantial army. Following the loss of the French fleet at the battle of Abukir Bay, he had decided it was

Two views of the palace of the Mameluke leader Alfi Bey. When established at Cairo the French commandeered several fine houses that were abandoned when the Mameluke leaders fled into Upper Egypt. This fine house, with its verdant pleasure garden, was occupied by Bonaparte who drafted many of his military orders from within its shaded apartments. Wind scoops on the roof helped to keep the interior cool. On completion of his travels, Denon showed his portfolio to Bonaparte who promptly encouraged its publication and authorised the wider survey of Egypt's monuments and culture by Denon's fellow savants. *(Dutertre, National Library of Scotland)*

necessary to reconnoitre a possible land route back to France, in the event of his army having to be evacuated from Egypt. This information had personal significance for Denon:

> The news of the return of our army from Syria was now announced. I reasoned that as Upper Egypt had been conquered and secured by us, and as Lower Egypt was about to be covered with water – and would therefore be secure from threat of invasion – Bonaparte would find himself without any [military] operation of great importance on his hands. He would [therefore] turn his mind towards Europe. I had not, however, begun to look that way myself. [Moreover] since Bonaparte had brought me with him and had promised to take me back again when he returned, the recollection of this gave me some disquiet and impatience.

Denon's reflections on the circumstances of the French in Egypt exaggerate the extent of the achievement of the French army. Upper Egypt was never, as he remarks, 'conquered and secured' and the threat of attack from Murad Bey's forces, and those of his allies, remained with the French throughout their occupation of Egypt. Of greater significance to the narrative is Denon's speculation that Bonaparte would shortly set his sights on returning to Europe – with the immediate likelihood of Denon returning there himself. Both of these predictions were to come about, as I shall soon relate. For the time

being, Denon was still secure in the heart of Middle Egypt surrounded by its antiquities which he was determined to investigate.

It was the prospect of further military conflict that provided Denon with an unexpected opportunity to undertake further researches. General Belliard was intent on subjugating a band of troublesome marauders who had fired on his troops as they approached Qena. His plan was to send out a detachment of soldiers on an expedition calculated to take the enemy by surprise and then, in Denon's words, 'to take their flocks, blow up their retreat, expel them [from the neighbourhood] and carry off their sheikh'. It was for this reason that this expedition was to journey north – to the region of Thebes – and so aroused Denon's enthusiasm:

> Thebes! – Thebes! At the mention of which I was agitated by conflicting emotions. However, this uncertainty soon ceased and my passion for the arts, which appeared to me in the light of duty, prevailed. I therefore returned to visit, for the seventh time, this great Diospolis [funerary settlement] which I had always seen in such haste that regret was mingled with the gratification that I received.
>
> I hoped this time to at least increase – if not complete – my collection [of drawings] relative to this most important object of curiosity and to verify the accuracy of my former observations of this metropolis of the ancient world – this focus of vision and knowledge which, for so many ages, enlightened every nation that wished to emerge from barbarism.

Denon departed south by the River Nile in the company of General Belliard and his military detachment. The party progressed as far as Luxor where they moored their barques. The following day the troops marched in the direction of the Valley of the Kings. On arriving they met with resistance again with stones and javelins. Since the catacombs communicated with each other they afforded the combatants numerous hiding places. A gunpowder charge was detonated that sent some men fleeing into the desert. Those who remained started to parley with the French. Denon remarks disparagingly: 'It was like making war with gnomes and our terms and articles of accommodation were shouted through the vaults in the rocks'. A messenger was sent into the desert to negotiate with those who had fled and the conflict was soon suspended.

The cessation of hostilities provided Denon with the opportunity to explore the rock-hewn tombs the local people had inhabited. Despite having suffered the depredations of tomb robbers and pillage by generations of local inhabitants, Denon found much to marvel at as he examined the subterranean retreats by torchlight.

He began his researches with the help of volunteers, starting at the vaults near the entrance. These were carved from the living rock 'without magnificence'. Here and there great pillars had been left to support the roof – evidence that the Egyptian masons had acquired an intuitive knowledge of the principles of mining engineering. The height of the tombs – Denon describes them as 'grottoes' – increased the deeper they went into the mountainside. They also become more richly decorated: 'I was soon convinced I was among the tombs of great men or heroes by the magnificence both of the paintings and sculptures and by the subjects they represented'.

Throughout the maze of catacombs, Denon considered the quality and finish of the workmanship to be comparable to that he had seen in the temples: 'It was like the work of the chisel itself and I stood in astonishment at the high perfection of the art and of its singular destiny to be fixed in places devoted to silence and obscurity.'

In the working of the galleries, the masons had to cut through beds of fine-grained calcareous stone. Despite its hardness, lines of hieroglyphic characters were found 'cut with a firmness of touch and a precision of which marble offers but few examples'. All the figures depicted in the wall decoration had 'an elegance and correctness of contour' that reaffirmed Denon's respect for the skill of the Egyptian artists. Progressing by torchlight the party descended further and deeper into the tombs:

> We penetrated together these subterranean labyrinths which, indeed, they resembled by their mysterious passages and windings. After passing the apartments, adorned in the elegant style I have just described, we entered long and gloomy galleries that wind backwards and forwards in numerous angles and seem to occupy a great extent of ground.
>
> [The galleries] open into other chambers, covered with hieroglyphics, and branch out into narrow paths that lead to deep perpendicular pits. We descended by resting our arms against the sides and fixing our feet into steps cut in the rock. At the bottom of these pits we found other adorned chambers and, lower still, a new series of perpendicular pits and horizontal chambers. At last, ascending a long flight of steps, we arrived at an open place that we found to be on a level with the chambers we first entered.

Denon emerged from the rock-hewn tombs satisfied with his survey work. He was one of the first Europeans to explore these former abodes of the dead, and posterity owes much to him and his fellow artist illustrators for recording their observations with such care. In the intervening two hundred years since they undertook their survey work, much that they saw has been lost through a combination of human negligence and the natural processes of attrition.

Returning to camp to be reunited with his colleagues, Denon observed some kites and vultures. These had previously caught his attention and their behaviour now provided him with another subject for his *Journal*. During the whole of their expedition they had been followed by a flight of kites and small vultures that had become as familiar with the army as they were naturally voracious. They fed on what the military left behind – typically the skins and carcasses of animals – and always rejoined the troops whenever they halted. In the days of battle, instead of being alarmed by the noise of cannon fire, they took this as a signal and flocked about from all sides. Denon adds:

> We were much entertained by their address and familiarity. Sometimes we threw a piece of meat down from the steep banks of the river that they always caught before it touched the water. Now and then they would carry off the rations the servants were carrying on their heads to the advanced posts. I have seen the kites, while our soldiers were cleaning fowls for the table, gently twitch from their hands the entrails and parts that were rejected.
>
> The vultures however had not the same dexterity, but their impudence equalled their voracity. They fed on the vilest and most corrupted offal that fell their way. Their nature partook of the infection of their food. I frequently attempted, but without success, to endure the stench of the carcasses of these birds [even] though I flayed them the moment I had killed them, either with a gun or pistol, and whilst they were yet warm.

Denon arrived at the soldiers' encampment by evening and was delighted to learn that he was to be allowed more time to survey the catacombs. He negotiated with his guides to meet again the following morning – urging them to be punctual! His account continues:

> The next day I was conducted to new tombs and galleries that were less winding and would serve as very agreeable habitations from their situation that enjoys daylight, pure and healthful air and a fine prospect. These [tombs] were no different from the others in any point of decoration. They had similar ornaments and paintings.
>
> The rock, which is of a gravelly nature, is coated with a smooth stucco on which are painted – in every colour – subjects of funereal processions. [These are] much less laboured than the bas-reliefs but are equally interesting by reason of the subjects that are here represented. I regretted that the part which had been injured [decayed] prevented me from following the whole order of these ceremonies, but the remains that are still perfect attest to their extreme magnificence.

In the course of his investigations, several fragments of mummies were brought to Denon – he had made it known that these remains were of particular interest to him. He even promised 'an unlimited reward to any who should procure one whole and untouched'. This was not to be. Generations of tomb robbers pre-empted him. Mummified remains were valued by the robbers, not as precious artefacts but for the resin that had been used in the process of embalming:

> They sell at Cairo the resin they find in the belly and skull of these mummies and there is no preventing them from committing this violence to them. In addition the fear of selling one that

might contain some treasure – though they have never found any in these antiquities – makes them always break the outer wooden covering and tear that of the painted cloth, which wraps the whole body, whenever such pains have been taken in the embalming.

With his survey of the rock-cut tombs complete, Denon was free to continue his researches of other notable monuments in the locality. Concerning these, the reader will recall how Denon's survey of the great mortuary temple of Rameses III at Medinet Habu had been curtailed by General Desaix because of the need of the army to continue on its march. Now free of such obligations, Denon seized the chance to revisit the temple complex.

He made a study of the wall decorations and attempted to interpret their meaning. The scenes of a martial nature disturbed him: 'One person is counting out before him the hands cut off from the enemy killed in battle. Another image depicts a pile of severed male sexual parts. A child appears, with his hands tied behind his back, who is about to be immolated before the conqueror who has stopped to receive this horrible sacrifice.' It was while he was conducting these sombre researches that Denon made one of the most significant archaeological discoveries of the French expedition. Until that time he and his fellow savants had found only fragments of ancient Egyptian texts. These consisted mostly of a few hieroglyphic symbols, painted on pieces of wood, recovered from the shattered remains of pillaged sarcophagi. No manuscripts had been discovered and Denon assumed that either they had never existed or that they had long since been lost or destroyed. Imagine, then, his delight when just such a find came into his possession.

Denon was brought the remains of a mummy that had escaped detection by earlier tomb robbers. He was initially outraged by this violation of the sanctity of the remains when he noticed what appeared to be a roll of papyrus clasped in the hand of the corpse. At the sight of this Denon records how he 'turned pale with anxiety'. He continues:

> I then blessed the avarice of the Arabs and my good fortune that had put me in possession of such a treasure. I hardly dared to touch for fear of injuring this sacred manuscript – the oldest of all the books in the known world. I could not venture to trust it out of my sight and all the cotton of my bed was devoted to wrapping it up with the utmost care.
>
> What could be its contents? Was it the history of this personage – the remarkable events of his life? Was the period [of the text] ascertained by the date of the sovereign under whom he lived or did this precious roll contain maxims, prayers, or the history of some discovery?

Denon's precious manuscript was carried safely back to the Institute of Egypt, at Cairo, where the linguists who had accompanied Bonaparte studied it. The text would remain unread until Jean François Champollion, with others, had learned how to decipher the Egyptian system of hieroglyphic characters. It is now known that Denon's papyrus, the first ever to be found in its original location by a Western observer, consists of a collection of writings from the *Book of the Dead*, a funerary compilation dating from the period of Ptolemaic rule.

For the time being, Denon had to be content with the survey of the tombs he had now made. However, always the opportunist, on learning a detachment was making the journey to Kurna he resolved to go with the party in the hope of making 'further discoveries in a country so rich to the artist and amateur'. His journey allowed him to make another visit to the temple of Medinet Habu. This time Denon and his companions were well received by the local people. They remembered Denon in particular for the kindness he had shown them:

> They recollected me by some little gifts I had made them and, instead of resisting us with weapons, they brought us fresh water, bread, ripe dates and grapes. I had leisure to draw everything that I had only glanced at the evening before. I took candles that gave me an opportunity of penetrating into the darkest places and those [also] I could not see in my former visits to this spot.

Next, Denon's party explored a small neighbouring temple where, in his words, 'we met with a little adventure'. They entered a sanctuary which they were about to examine when all at once a large beast jumped out. It scratched the face of the member of the party lighting their way with his torch. As for Denon and the other members of the group:

> I had just time to cover my head with my hands and to stoop my shoulders on which I received the first spring of the animal. With the next it threw me down by rushing between my legs. He also overthrew my two companions who were hastening to the door and thus, in a moment, he defeated us all. We came out laughing at our alarm without being able exactly to make out what beast it was that had caused it.

After recovering from this incident, Denon journeyed north to see once more the remains of the great seated statues of Amenhotep III – the Colossi of Memnon. This further visit stirred Denon to reflect on the aesthetic nature of Egyptian sculpture:

> I then went to the two colossi, supposed to be those of Memnon, and took an accurate drawing of their actual state of preservation. These two pieces of art, that are without grace, expression, or action, have nothing which seduces the judgement. But their proportions are faultless and this simplicity of attitude – and want of decided expression – has something of majesty and seriousness that cannot fail to strike the beholder.
>
> If the limbs of these figures had been distorted in order to express some violent passion, the harmony of their outline would have been lost. [Moreover] they would be less conspicuous at the distance at which they begin to strike the eye, and produce their effect on the mind of the spectator, for they may be distinguished as far as four leagues off.

To complete his survey of the great monolithic sculpture of Thebes, Denon made a second visit to the remaining fragments of the Colossus of Rameses, known from Greek times as Ozymandias: 'I again examined the block of granite that lies between these two statues. I am still more convinced it is the ruins of the famous statue of Ozymandias who, on the inscription, braved both the ravages of time and the pride of men.' The inscription to which Denon refers is that immortalised by Percy Bysshe Shelley in his already mentioned celebrated verse 'Ozymandias':

> My name is Ozymandias, king of kings:
> Look on my works, ye Mighty, and despair!

Shortly after making his study of the great Colossus of Rameses, Denon was unexpectedly joined by a number of his artist colleagues who had journeyed from Kurna. He was eager to show them the rock-cut tombs and proposed they should visit the Valley of the Kings. He led the way, now having some experience of exploring the dark passageways by torchlight.

They began their search in the hope of finding a chamber that had not been ransacked. This proved fruitless but they did reach a pit 'scattered with numerous

Fragments of the Great Colossus, at the Memnonium, Thebes.

Fragment of the colossus of Rameses II. The remains of the shattered colossus lie in the forecourt of the Ramesseum, the mortuary temple at western Thebes. They portray Rameses the Great and were hewn from a single block of red Aswan granite weighing over 1,000 tons. The statue originally depicted Rameses seated on his throne, rising to a height of about 60 feet. The collapse of this wonder of the ancient world may have occurred in the great earth tremors of 27 BC. Christian Copts may have furthered its destruction. Shelly's celebrated sonnet 'Ozymandias' (Greek for Rameses) captures to perfection the authority of this once great ruler of Egypt:

'My name is Ozymandias, king of kings:
Look on my works, ye Mighty, and
despair!'
(Roberts, British Library)

fragments of mummies'. They progressed and entered a narrow passage where they were obliged to grope on hands and knees. The confined space, and the heat from their torch, nearly stifled the party and some members had to return to the fresh air of the entrance. Denon, and those who continued, soon found evidence of the despoliation wrought by the tomb robbers:

Having crawled along nearly a hundred paces, over a heap of half-decayed bodies, the vault became loftier, more spacious and decorated with a considerable degree of care. We now found this tomb had already been searched. Those who had first entered it, not having torches, had used brushwood to give them light and these had set fire first to the linen and afterwards to the resin of the mummies. This had caused such a combustion as to split some of the stones, melt the gums and resins and blacken all the sides of the cave.

Denon filled his pockets with fragments of treasures the robbers had left behind. Some of these were small figurines that had accompanied the mummies. He examined some of the corpses from which the shrouds had been torn: 'From a number of bodies, that were not swathed up, I could perceive that circumcision was a constant custom among them and that depilation was not practised among the women. Their hair was long and flexible and the character of the head was in a fine style. I brought away with me the head of an old woman.'

Although Denon wanted to make more drawings, the conditions in the chamber were too confined and oppressive. The party was in need of fresh air and their torchlight was fading. In addition, it was growing late and the signal guns had already fired calling the party back to camp. When they returned to the valley 'they were reprimanded like truant schoolboys'. Denon didn't care. He was content 'with the booty acquired during this day'.

Denon remained for three more days in Middle Egypt and spent these at Luxor. It was here he found several fine medallions from the time of the Roman emperors Adrian, Augustus, Constantine and Trajan. These were worked in bronze and bore Greek inscriptions with the image of a crocodile on the reverse. In the court of a private house he had the good fortune to come upon a granite torso, displaying the two astrological signs of Leo and Virgo. He promptly purchased this from the owner of the house and had it carried to one of the French boats to be dispatched to Cairo.

While Denon was preparing his treasures for transport he heard that the detachment with which he was travelling had received orders to leave the district. And so Denon 'quitted forever the great Diospolis [Parva]' of Middle Egypt.

CHAPTER 21

Departure from Egypt

After completing his researches at Luxor, Denon returned to Qena with a number of sick soldiers who required medical attention. At Qena he found two boats awaiting his arrival, a reminder to him that he was to return to Cairo and await further instructions from Bonaparte. The Commander was in residence in the capital planning his departure from Egypt and return to France. Denon had mixed feelings at the prospect of leaving Egypt. For the last twelve months his thoughts had been occupied with the collection and illustration of interesting objects. He had become so absorbed with the antiquities of Egypt he had grown almost oblivious of his daily situation, taking each day as it came with little regard for what lay ahead. He reflected on his achievements:

> I had shrunk from no dangers in satisfying my curiosity. The apprehension of being obliged to quit Upper Egypt – without having seen all that was best worthy of remark there – would have induced me, without hesitation, to go through still greater perils. The circumstances arising from the unsettled state of the country, and my own obligations to comply with the military operations, had, in many instances, prevented me from taking more than a hasty glimpse of objects that would have amply recompensed a longer stay. But even if my researches have no other effect than assisting the future labours of those who may succeed me, in a time of greater tranquillity, I shall rejoice that my zeal has been thus at least serviceable to the arts.

On 5 July 1799, Denon set sail downriver. With some emotion he saw Dendera and Thebes recede from view. He had grown familiar with these regions of Egypt to the extent that 'the trees, the rocky eminences, the canals, the smallest monuments, everything had become so deeply imprinted in my memory that I was able to recognise and name each object within sight and their several distances from each other'.

As Denon progressed down the Nile he noticed the river had become more populated than ever with wildlife. There were pelicans that had inhabited it for the past month, together with storks, Numidian cranes, several species of wild duck, curlews and hens. These enlivened all the islands where he also saw large crocodiles as far downriver as Girga. In thirty-eight hours, Denon's flotilla reached this town that was already inhabited by the French. Here the party passed the day laying in provisions and waiting for a suitable wind. It soon become favourable and in two hours the boats reached Minchieh, the ancient township of the Ptolemies. Denon inspected a large quay that he considered to be of Greek construction. Near its ruins was a village inhabited chiefly by Christians but which contained nothing to stir his artist's curiosity.

Fruits and leaves of the doum palm. The French Commission reported sixty-two studies of the botany of Egypt, each accompanied with detailed illustrations. The palm tree was perhaps the most important of these subjects. In ancient Egypt, the imagery of the palm was an integral part of decorative art and design. Raffeneau–Delile undertook much of the botanical survey-work that was illustrated by Henri-Joseph Redouté, younger brother of Pierre-Joseph famous for his illustrations of roses. *(National Library of Scotland)*

Three miles lower down they came upon the remains of the site of Koptos, also called Akhmin. In the Ptolemaic era, this township was called Panopolis because of its associations with the Greek god Pan. In Egyptian mythology the equivalent god was Min, who was the symbol and embodiment of male fertility. Concerning this site and its lascivious associations, Denon remarks:

> I am informed there is still to be seen a building, buried up to the very roof, which no doubt is the temple formerly dedicated to Pan and consecrated to prostitution. A number of dancing girls, and women of the town, still subsist here. I was told that on a particular day in every week they assemble by a mosque near the tomb of the Sheikh Harridi where, mingling with the profane, they commit all kinds of indecencies.

The party journeyed further north and spent the night amid the remains of Antinoopolis, a halt which provided Denon with a brief opportunity to study the remains of this Roman town. By the side of the river could be seen the old city gates that took the

A Nile crocodile with its young – *Crocodilus niloticus*. Crocodiles frequented the banks of the River Nile at the time of the French survey of Egypt. Mature specimens were reported at more than 20 feet long. Crocodiles fascinated Denon who makes frequent reference to them in his *Journal*. The head of the crocodile was adopted in Egyptian imagery and the crocodile-god Sobek was venerated at the Temple of Kom Ombo. *(Saint-Hilaire/Redouté, National Library of Scotland)*

form of a triumphal arch. The main street of the town could still be made out. It appeared to have been adorned with a colonnade of Doric pillars under which people might walk in the shade. Some column shafts, and a few capitals, were visible amid the wind-blown sand.

Wishing to obtain a view of the whole of the ruins, Denon ascended a hill from where he perceived some inhabitants of the local village were assembling. They were suspicious of his intentions. No sooner had Denon made a hasty survey of the scene before him than he was fired upon. Unarmed and greatly outnumbered, he made a hasty retreat.

He returned to the security of his boat and took a further sketch of the ruins of Antinoopolis from the water. Resuming the journey, he and his party soon found themselves below the curiously named 'Monastery of the Chain' that was situated on a peak of the Mukattam hills. It was the custom of the monks who inhabited this retreat to swim into the river to supplicate for alms as the boats passed by. Denon's curiosity was roused by this information. It prompted him to find out more:

> From long tradition [the monks] seem to have acquired all the agility in the water of amphibious animals, advancing against the full force of the stream like fishes. They are burnt up by the rays of a vertical sun, unremittingly scorched on their dry and barren rocks and with difficulty – and by swimming – obtain a few occasional alms.

Their desolate retreat is called the Monastery of the Chain because they can only procure supplies of water and other necessities by means of a long chain attached to a windlass which they let down to the river. It appeared from the different groups of buildings, and of the monks we saw on the rock, that the monastery is of considerable extent and well peopled.

Passing the Monastery of the Chain, the party reached the township of Abu-Siefen. This location was the first, south of Cairo, where the French troops had billeted following the battle of the Pyramids. It afforded Denon a further opportunity to pass the pyramids of Saqqara.

At daybreak the following day, Denon and his companions found themselves between the townships of Alter-Anabi and Giza. They were now opposite El-Rôda with Cairo and Bulaq on their right. This situation presented to their gaze a rich combination of verdure that contrasted starkly with the bare and wild appearance of the mountain ridges on the horizon. Once more Denon's artistic temperament and inclination to philosophical reflection were stirred:

> I should have been glad to make a drawing of a view that shows, in so striking a manner, the relative situation of all these places. However, I was subject to fellow travellers who would sooner have granted me other favours than that of delaying our arrival for a few minutes. This little voyage fully persuaded me that it is a bad way to travel by water. The high banks intercept all view of the country and the fear of losing wind, or having it contrary, either changes or destroys all one's plans.
>
> You are hurried by places where you wish to stop and are delayed where there is nothing worthy of examination. Unsatisfactory, however, as this method of travelling is – to those who wish to make observations or drawings – to accompany the detachment of a military expedition is infinitely worse. Soldiers, ever active and restless, are constantly wishing to be on the march and, when on the march, they want to reach as soon as possible the end of their journey.

On arriving at Cairo Denon made straight for the headquarters of the Institute of Egypt. Since he was the first member of the Institute to arrive there from Upper Egypt, his fellow savants gathered around him enthusiastically and overwhelmed him with their questions: 'My pleasure was to find myself the object of their eager curiosity and to profit by the observations they made. I proposed to methodise my *Journal*, under their inspection, and then ask questions of them in return.' Subsequent events, however, dictated a different course of action. On learning of Denon's return to Cairo, Bonaparte also wished to see the fruits of the artist's hard-won labours. According to Denon: '[He] examined attentively all the drawings I had brought back and, satisfied that the object of my mission had been accomplished, he invited me to go to Alexandria and carry there my trophies to Abukir'. Thereby, Denon learned he would shortly leave Egypt to return with Bonaparte to France:

> My departure was fixed for the morrow. What at first I thought a dream proved to be a reality I found myself borne rapidly along in the very track of my most anxious wishes. Still, however, a feeling that I know not how to describe made me regret my departure from Cairo, a town that I had inhabited only by short intervals and which I never quitted without pain.
>
> It frequently happens that Europeans, intending to stay for only a few months at Cairo, suffer themselves to grow old there without being able to prevail upon themselves to depart.

The first stage in Denon's departure from Egypt was to travel to Alexandria. He embarked a small armed vessel that was waiting for him and his party at Bulaq. On the

Comparative studies of the viper. Venomous snakes abounded along the borders of the river Nile and were studied by the French Commission in their laboratory at Cairo. Above is a species found in the region of the Giza pyramids. Below is a mature specimen. *(Saint-Hilaire/Redouté, National Library of Scotland)*

passage downriver Denon, still eager to enrich his portfolio, took a drawing of the location where the Nile divides to form the Delta. On the third day following his departure he arrived at Rahmanieh. From there he and his companions set out the following morning on the landward part of the journey. For their security they were accompanied by a detachment of fifty armed men with a supporting retinue that

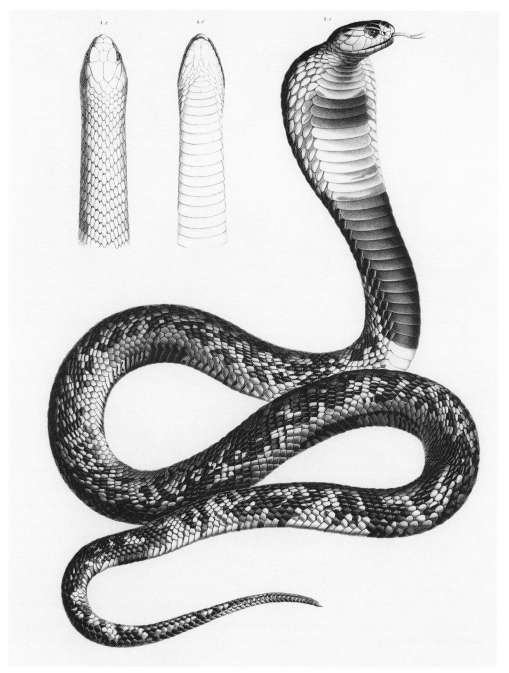

An asp, the Egyptian cobra. This is the highly venomous snake from whose bite Cleopatra chose her death. It had associations with the ancient sun-god Amun Ra. Ordinary Egyptian people were in terror of this serpent and held the snake charmers in awe – although Denon exposed them as tricksters and charlatans. *(Saint-Hilaire/Redouté, National Library of Scotland)*

included a train of camels. They headed for Demenhur. From there they followed the canal, traversed the province of Garbieh and arrived at Birket where they halted for the night. The next day the party breakfasted at the well of El Beydah and, the same day, reached their destination Alexandria, where they dined. From then on events moved rapidly as Denon's account reveals:

> General Menou came to inform us that Bonaparte was waiting for us on the beach. An hour later we had cleared the port and, at daybreak, we got under way with a north-east wind which, continuing to blow from this quarter for two days, carried us out of the track of the English cruisers. In order to avoid falling in with the enemy, we coasted along the arid shores of the ancient Cyrene [region of Libya] struggling against the currents of the gulf that remains, even at present, unexplored on account of its dangerous navigation.
>
> Nor was it without much difficulty, in this season of light and variable breezes, that we were able to double the Capes of Derna and Doira. In this latitude we were again befriended by an easterly wind that carried us across the Gulf of Cidre. Doubling Cape Bon we found ourselves at last opposite the friendly parts of Europe.

In making his departure from Egypt, Bonaparte and his small party were fortunate not to encounter the British fleet, as Denon himself was aware: 'During the whole of our coasting we had not descried a single [enemy] sail and, well convinced we were under the guidance of our lucky star, we indulged our joy in security. Bonaparte, as an unconcerned passenger, busied himself with geometry and chemistry or relaxed by sharing our mirth.'

The next stage of the voyage was to complete the journey to Corsica. They passed the gulf of Carthage and came in sight of the island of Lampedusa. The next day they saw 'at a distance of a league' the overhanging rock of la Pantellene. Soon after the mountains of Sardinia came into view. Corsica at length offered the party the first sight of a friendly shore and a brisk wind carried Bonaparte and his entourage to Ajaccio. There a boat was sent ashore to learn the latest intelligence concerning France and to inquire whether there were any hostile English vessels in the vicinity. News of Bonaparte's return to his native country soon spread among the local people:

> He was thought to have been lost when chance thus brought him home. Nothing could be more touching than the reception he experienced. The batteries saluted on all sides. The whole population rushed to the boats and surrounded our frigates. Public enthusiasm even triumphed over the fear of contagion and our vessels were immediately boarded by crowds crying out 'Bonaparte! – Bonaparte!'

When the French party disembarked, Bonaparte set about acquainting himself with the state of political and military affairs in Europe, of which he had received no direct information for many months. What he learned impelled him to hasten to Paris – France was at war with Austria. Within a few days he and his party set sail once more.

The wind was favourable and they got under way without difficulty. On the second day, urged on by a fresh breeze, they were in sight of the French coast. As they were congratulating themselves on their good fortune two English ships were sighted to windward, then five and afterwards seven. To reduce the risk of detection, the French

Species of catfish. The River Nile teamed with life and was a paradise for the French zoologists Geoffroy Saint-Hilaire and Jules-César de Savigny who classified numerous species of fish and vertebrates. Formidable and curious creatures were encountered such as *Malapterus electicus*, that could stun its prey, and *Synodontis* that swam with its belly uppermost. *(Saint-Hilaire/Redouté, National Library of Scotland)*

lowered their topmost sails. Then, fortunately, the moon was covered with thick fog. Denon was on deck, witnessing these events, and remarks:

> We could see nothing of the enemy's squadron but in the wind we heard their repeated signal guns as they formed in a semicircle between us and the coast. It was now debated whether or

A vulture. Vultures followed the French army to devour the animal carnage that occurred on the field of battle. Denon attempted to disect one of these voracious scavegers but had to give up because he could not endure the stench of its carcass. *(de Savigny/Redouté, National Library of Scotland)*

The Eagle of Thebes. The French naturalists gave the eagle this name since it frequented the Plain of Thebes and the Valley of the Kings. It is fitting to conclude this selection of images of Egypt with an engraving of this majestic bird since it was the emblem of the French army. *(de Savigny/Redouté, National Library of Scotland)*

not we should return to Corsica while the passage was still open to us. At this crisis, for the first time during the voyage, Bonaparte assumed command. He gave orders and committed himself to his fortune.

The French were once more lucky not to be intercepted by Nelson's ships. Sailing undetected they made for the coast of Provence. By midnight they were so near the shore as to no longer have any apprehensions concerning the English fleet. At daybreak they could see the ancient port of Fréjus. They had arrived safely at their destination. Denon relates the events that followed with a touch of patriotic fervour:

> Nothing could be more unexpected than our arrival in France and news of it spread with the rapidity of lightning. Scarcely had we displayed the flag of the Commander-in-Chief than the shore was covered with people who exclaimed 'Bonaparte!'
>
> The public enthusiasm became uncontrollable. All apprehensions of contagion were again forgotten and our two vessels were surrounded by boats filled with men whose only fear was lest they should be deceived in their hopes of the arrival of Bonaparte. Sublime emotion! France herself poured forth her thousands before him.
>
> Our hero was borne in triumph to Fréjus. An hour later he set out for Paris.

Once on shore, Denon allowed himself a few days of respite from his hazardous journey. He wandered about like a tourist:

> Delighted to become again my own master, I stole from the multitude and, for the first time since leaving France for Egypt, I enjoyed the sweet satisfaction of being no longer crowded nor hurried. Formerly I should have thought myself a traveller and stranger at Fréjus but, coming from Africa, I now seemed at home again – [like] one of the citizens of this little town with nothing more to do. I arose, I breakfasted at my full ease, I went to take a walk, visited the amphitheatre and the other ruins and looked with complacence at the frigates that had brought us – now lying at [their] moorings in the harbour.

It was not long after his return to French soil that Denon resolved to publish an account of his extraordinary travels. He takes leave of the reader with the following remarks:

> Here terminates my *Journal*.
>
> For my own part I shall esteem myself happy if, by my zeal and enthusiasm, I have succeeded in giving my readers an idea of a country so important in itself – and in the various recollections that are associated with it – if I have been able to portray, with accuracy, its characteristic forms, colours and general appearance and if, as an eyewitness, I have described with interest the details of an extended and singular campaign that formed [so] prominent a feature in the vast conception of this celebrated expedition.

Denon concludes his account of his travels in Egypt with this image of a man seated on a reed boat, for which he provides the following explanation:

This represents the manner in which the natives of Lower Egypt are seen to cross the Nile. Two bundles of reeds are tied together upon which the man seats himself with a paddle in his hand, his legs on each side hanging down in the water. With this simple and primitive means, he crosses fearlessly a river often more than half a mile wide. {And, one may add, alive with voracious crocodiles!}

POSTSCRIPT

The French Legacy

Denon returned to Paris on 16 October 1799. He immediately began work arranging the notes in his *Journal* and classifying the sketches in his portfolio with a view to publishing the results of his researches. News of his forthcoming publication was announced in the *Courrier de L'Égypte*:

> Citizen Denon has returned from Upper Egypt and has brought back a collection of over two hundred drawings . . . He made seven trips to the ruins of Thebes, ten to Tentyris [Dendera], four to Edfu . . . and as many to Philae . . . Citizen Denon has compiled in his collection everything that will serve to inform Europe about the ancient Egyptians, their deities, sacrifices, ceremonies, their lavish festivals and the triumphs of their heroes.

Denon worked tirelessly to raise a list of subscribers who would pledge themselves to purchase a copy of his majestic folios. Two hundred and eighty individuals responded. These included the crown princes of Germany, Italy, Russia and Spain; heads of state; noble persons of various countries including the Earls of Harrington and Aberdeen; generals who had participated in the Egyptian campaign; William Maclure, described as 'a citizen of the United States'; publishers; and booksellers. Also named among the many distinguished subscribers is Prince Franz Joseph von Lobkowitz, who supported Beethoven financially and in whose Vienna palace the *Eroica* Symphony was performed for the first time. This connection is of particular interest inasmuch as Beethoven dedicated his symphony to Napoleon Bonaparte in admiration of the man and his achievements – only later to rescind the dedication, in a rage, on learning that Bonaparte had been declared Emperor.

Denon's folios were available in two formats. A de luxe edition was printed on *papier vélin* – a fine, vellum-like paper – and a less expensive one on *papier ordinaire* – a coarser hand-made paper. Altogether 569 copies were purchased through subscription. Bonaparte headed the list of subscribers and ordered 46 copies (26 *vélin* and 20 *ordinaire*). The work was published in Paris in 1802 in two great folio volumes measuring 68 × 52 centimetres. One volume consisted of 265 pages of text, derived from Denon's *Journal*, followed by 94 pages of explanations to the accompanying plates (engravings), a two-page subject index and, finally, a four-page list of subscribers. The accompanying volume contains the plates themselves. The production is a masterpiece combining the art of engraving with that of book design. When opened, the folios are vast and assume the proportions known to antiquarians as double-elephant. This was the largest size adopted in publishing.

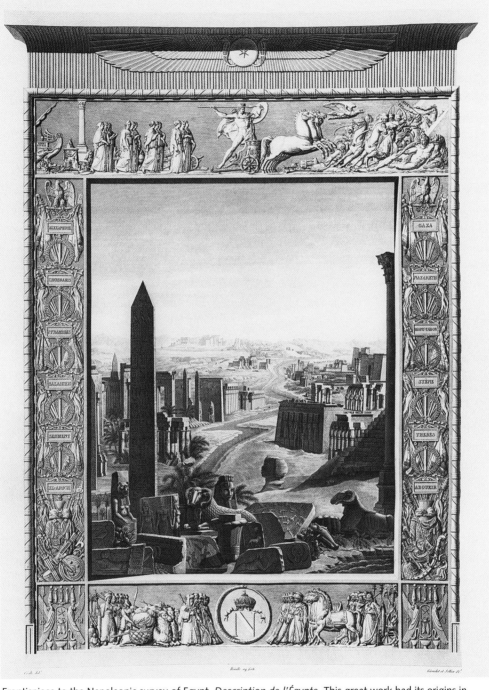

Frontispiece to the Napoleonic survey of Egypt, *Description de l'Égypte*. This great work had its origins in Vivant Denon's pioneering researches. The engraving depicts an Egyptian portal framing an imaginary scene illustrating many of the discoveries made by the French in their exploration of Upper and Lower Egypt. Bonaparte, deified in his chariot, scatters his foes. An eagle flies before him. Maidens march behind as symbols of the sciences and arts. The military campaigns, in which so many brave men lost their lives, are identified in the side panels. *(Cécile, Author's Collection)*

In the form described, Denon's book could only be purchased by the very wealthy – as can be inferred from the list of subscribers. In London, for example, the two volumes sold for 21 guineas. That was about the same cost, in early nineteenth-century values, as a contemporary Broadwood piano or a fine longcase clock. In order to reach a wider audience, Denon's publisher (P. Didot l'Aîné) brought out a two-volume edition in the more conventional octavo format. This sold rapidly and within a year Denon's *Voyages* (*Travels*) had been translated into several languages, including English (London, 1803). At least twenty more editions followed throughout the nineteenth century with as many more reprints and adaptations.

The success of Denon's work is testimony to the inherent interest of his subject. His book stirred the public's curiosity concerning one of the oldest civilizations in the world and about which little was known in the early nineteenth century. Denon opened the eyes of Europe to a culture that had long been shrouded in darkness and mystery. He brought Islam and the Orient closer to men's understanding. In addition, Denon's account reads like an adventure story. His descriptions are spontaneous, spirited, taken from life and are conveyed with the authority of an expert. Denon gives the reader an abundance of drawings that are the fresh and keenly observed productions of a gifted draughtsman. We are reminded also, throughout Denon's account, of the personal hazards he had to overcome in his enthusiasm to bring to the highest level possible the quality of his researches.

Denon dedicated his book to Bonaparte – styled with a touch of flattery:

To Bonaparte

To combine the lustre of your name with the splendour of the monuments of Egypt is to associate the glorious annals of our own time with the history of the heroic age; and to re-animate the dust of Sesostris and Mendes, who, like you, were conquerors, like you benefactors. When Europe learns that I accompanied you in one of your most memorable expeditions, it will receive my book with keen interest. I have neglected nothing in my power to render it worthy of the Hero to whom it is dedicated.

Vivant Denon

For his enterprise, Denon received his due reward. He was made a Baron and his book promoted Bonaparte's reputation. More importantly, for the history of art and design, his work began the process of a diffusion of awareness of Egyptian culture. Denon's own capacity to exert cultural influence was strengthened by his appointment in Paris as Director of the Musée Central des Arts (Musée du Louvre). His curatorial role exercised a direct influence on other French galleries and the collections displayed in the palaces owned by the state. Denon's artistic influence also extended into the provinces through his role as Director of the Musée des Monuments français. He also influenced the design of Sèvres porcelain and Gobelin tapestry work. Denon's advice was sought in civic architectural design: he contributed to the creation of l'Arc de Triomphe and to the design and ornament of a number of Paris's squares. In all of this work the Egyptian taste and style were pervasive. In Egypt, Denon had been Bonaparte's eyes. In France, his published researches were a wellspring for ideas ranging across the whole realm of design from grand architectural monuments through interior design and furnishing to the decoration of individual *objets de vertu*.

The influence on European art and design of the work of the French savants who accompanied Bonaparte into Egypt was as far-reaching as that of Denon. Working collectively as the Commission of the Sciences and Arts, the men of letters remained in Egypt to continue and extend Denon's pioneering researches. The artists and engineers (surveyors) followed in Denon's footsteps making their own surveys of Egypt's ancient monuments. Their work was published as the monumental *Description de l'Égypte – Collection of Observations and Researches that have been made in Egypt during the Expedition of the French Army*. This great work was published in several volumes: five volumes of engravings illustrate the antiquities of Egypt (1809–22); two volumes of engravings illustrate the architecture, arts and crafts of Egypt as portrayed by the French artists (1809–22); and three volumes illustrate the natural history of Egypt (1809–17). These folios contain more than 3,000 individual images and, together with their accompanying texts, constitute one of the great intellectual and artistic achievements of the nineteenth century. To house these great folios, a special bookcase was made by the cabinetmaker Charles Morel to designs by Edme-François Jomard, who had also taken part in the Egyptian expedition.

Just 1,000 copies of the *Description de l'Égypte* were printed and, because of their enormous cost, were destined only for the libraries of princes, noblemen and Europe's great institutions. To make the work more accessible, a second, cheaper impression was published known as the Panckoucke edition (after the name of the publisher Charles Panckoucke). Through its many beautiful illustrations, this work did much to increase the general public's understanding of the monuments of ancient Egypt and to establish a taste in design for all things Egyptian.

One of the great discoveries of the French expedition was the Rosetta Stone. This was unearthed in July 1799 when the coastal defensive works were being strengthened at Rosetta, under the direction of Lieutenant Pierre François Bouchard. He was struck by the appearance of three distinctive bands of characters inscribed on the stone and drew its attention to his commanding officer General Menou. A scholar by inclination, Menou realised the importance of the find and reported it to the Institute of Egypt at Cairo. The French were denied possession of the stone by the British, who seized it under the terms of the treaty of Alexandria in 1801. It now forms part of the Egypt Collection in the British Museum. However, the French were given a copy for scholars to study. Notable among these was the linguistic genius Jean François Champollion, the first professor of Egyptology. After intensive study, and benefiting from the work of the British polymath Thomas Young, Champollion made the vital connection between the stone's three bands of characters – hieroglyphics (top), Demotic (middle) and Greek (bottom). 'The door to the Egyptian mind now stood ajar.' The pioneering work of Champollion and Young made possible the future decipherment of all Egyptian hieroglyphic texts.

Bonaparte's Egyptian Campaign was a military failure. When Bonaparte departed Egypt for France he left behind him a much depleted army in the care of General Jean Baptiste Kléber. One out of every three soldiers perished. It was clearly impossible for the

French to hold on to their new territorial possessions. Kléber wished to vacate Egypt with his remaining men on the best terms possible – 'neither victor nor defeated'. The signing of a form of peace treaty with Rear Admiral Sir Sydney Smith prepared the way for this. Although not conclusive – hostilities were to continue for several more months – the French army of occupation was eventually evacuated under the direction of General Jacques Menou, following Kléber's death at the hands of an assassin on 14 June 1800. Interestingly, Sir Sydney Smith, who was a gracious and scholarly man, became one of the original subscribers to Denon's *Travels* in the first edition of 1802.

The enduring legacy of the French exploration of Egypt is to be found in the work of the savants, scholars and men of letters. Principal among them was Dominique-Vivant Denon. He remained active until the end of his life, spending his time amid his Egyptian collections, developing the art of engraving and pioneering the techniques of lithography. He died on 28 April 1825. His memorial simply bears his name without any epitaph. This was rendered by his friends, who announced his passing with the following words:

> An unforeseen and sudden death removed M. Denon from the arts and his friends. The range of his knowledge, the animation of his spirit and the aptitude of his intelligence were all fostered within him by a youthfulness whose source was in his spirit and in his heart and were rendered amiable and agreeable by the profound sensibility of his soul that nourished itself each day with his caprice and his taste and love of society.

The achievement of the French expedition into Egypt is well summarised in the words of Jean Baptiste Joseph Fourier, who is known principally for his work on trigonometric functions and the Fourier Series. In Egypt, he was an important member of Bonaparte's Commission of the Sciences and Arts and in recognition of his services was conferred upon him the splendid title of Governor of Egypt. At the Institute of Egypt, he was editor of its journal, the *Courrier de l'Égypte*, and supervised much of the expedition's scientific work. On his return to France he was one of the principal editors of the *Description de l'Égypte* and wrote most of its preface. His generous evaluation of the work of his scholar-companions, and his high estimation of the French exploration of Egypt, are expressed in remarks appropriate to our own conclusion to this daring and epochal enterprise:

> These works [engravings and texts], which give to Europe for the first time a just idea of the monuments of Egypt, will excite for all time an intense interest. They have a charm that is to them natural and surpasses all that could be achieved from the efforts and talents of a single man.

> No other country has been subjected to researches so extended and so varied. No other was more worthy of being the object.

Select Bibliography

This bibliography provides details of a selection of books concerned with the achievements of Dominique-Vivant Denon and the members of Bonaparte's Commission of the Sciences and Arts. It also lists a number of publications whose subject is the influence of the French legacy on architecture and design. Most of the books listed provide sources for further reading and aids to personal research.

THE WORK OF DOMINIQUE-VIVANT DENON:

Denon's researches were published, in French, in two large folios as: *Text – Voyage dans la Basse et la Haute Égypte pendant les campagnes du Général Bonaparte*. Par Vivant Denon. À Paris de L'Imprimerie de P. Didot L'Aîné, au Palais des Sciences et Arts. An X. [1802]; *Engravings – Planches du Voyage dans la Basse et la Haute Égypte* .The text volume consists of 265 pages describing Denon's travels to Egypt and his exploration of the ancient monuments. The account is written without headings or chapter subdivisions. The main body of the text is followed by: detailed descriptions of the plates (engravings), in their numbered sequence, I–CXLI (1–141); an alphabetical list of subjects; and, finally, a list of the names of the subscribers. The engravings volume consists of the presentation of the plates (engravings) in large folio format (66 × 50 cm). Some of the engravings are drawn in double-page format.

A contemporary edition of Denon's text is available, unabridged in French, as: *Vivant Denon Voyage dans la Basse et la Haute Égypte pendant les campagnes du Général Bonaparte*. [Paris, Pygmalion, Gérard Watelet, 1990].This includes an introduction by Raoul Brunton together with a map of Denon's travels in Egypt, reproductions of twelve engravings and a bibliography. The latter identifies many of the early editions of Denon's *Travels* and lists French-language books about Denon and the Egyptian Campaign.

An English-language edition of Denon's *Travels* was published as: *Vivant Denon Travels in Upper and Lower Egypt, In Company with Several Divisions of the French Army, During the Campaigns of General Bonaparte and Published with his Immediate Patronage*; tr. by Arthur Aikin. Two volumes (quarto) [London, T.N. Longman and O'Rees & Richmond Phillips, 1803].

THE WORK OF BONAPARTE'S COMMISSION FOR THE SCIENCES AND ARTS:

The first edition of the official French government publication of the work of the Commission of the Sciences and Arts in Egypt was published in several folio volumes of texts and plates (engravings) under the general title: *Description de l'Égypte ou Recueil des Observations et des Recherches qui ont été faites en Égypte pendant l'Expédition de l'Armée Française*, Publiée par les Ordres de sa Majesté L'Empereur Napoléon Le Grand. À Paris, de L'Imprimerie Impériale. MDCCCIX [1809]. The subdivision of this great work is as follows:

Antiquités, Text: two volumes in twenty-six parts published 1809–18

Antiquités, Mémoires: two volumes with twenty-one engraved plates, two folding maps, illustrations and tables which accompany the text, published 1809–18

Antiquités, Planches: five volumes containing 419 engraved plates, some coloured, published 1809–22

État Moderne, Text: two volumes published in three folios, portrait, four engraved plates, illustrations and tables which accompany the text, published 1809–22

État Moderne, Planches: two volumes containing 182 engraved plates, some coloured, published 1809–22

Histoire Naturelle, Text: two volumes, portrait, folding plates, published 1809–13

Histoire Naturelle, Planches: two volumes published in three folios containing 244 engraved plates and maps, some coloured, published 1809–17

A second edition of the *Description de l'Égypte* was published with the same title as that given above but without reference to Napoleon. The following text appears on the title page:

Seconde Édition, Dédiée au Roi, Publiée par C.L.F. Panckoucke. Volume I bears the date MDCCCXXI. The text, in twenty-six quarto volumes, was published between 1821 and 1828. The plates were published over the same period in the same three subject divisions as the first edition, namely, *Antiquités*, *État Moderne* and *Histoire Naturelle* but with the very large engravings folded so as to conform to the smaller format and binding of the standard-format engravings.

Contemporary editions of *Description de l'Égypte* include the following works:

Anderson, Robert and Fawzy, Ibrahim, *Egypt in 1800: Scenes from Napoleon's Description de l'Égypte*, (Barrie & Jenkins, 1987, London). This book reproduces a selection of engravings from the five volumes of *Antiquities* and the two volumes of *The Modern State* (of Egypt) derived from *Description de l'Égypte*. Commentaries are provided to each of the selected engravings.

Aufrère, Sydney H., *Description de l'Égypte* (Bibliothèque de l'Image, 2001). This book includes a preface with descriptions (in French) of the principal monuments surveyed and engraved by the artist-members of the Commission of the Sciences and Arts and reproductions of all the engravings in the five folios of *Antiquities*.

Benedikt Taschen, *Description de l'Égypte Publiée par les ordres de Napoléon Bonaparte* (Hohenzollernring, Benedikt Taschen, 1994). This book includes: a brief history of the Egyptian campaign in English, French and German; nine colour plates depicting Bonaparte; and facsimilies of all the engravings in *Description de l'Égypte* reproduced in small format (19 x 14 cm).

Gillispie, Charles C. and Dewachter, Michel, *Monuments of Egypt: The Napoleonic Edition* (Princeton, New Jersey, Princeton Architectural Press, 1987). This book reproduces all the engravings in the five volumes of *Antiquities* to the *Description de l'Égypte* together with short commentaries to each of the engravings. An historical introduction is given with portraits of several members of the Commission of the Sciences and Arts.

Russell, Terence M, *The Napoleonic Survey of Egypt: The Monuments and Customs of Egypt* (Aldershot, Ashgate, 2001). This book, in two volumes, includes: a short history of the Egyptian Campaign; the publication history of *Description de l'Égypte*; reproductions of 200 engravings; and translations of selected writings from the original texts.

THE FRENCH LEGACY

The following is a selection of books that describe the exploration and illustration of Egypt in the nineteenth century and the influence of the Egyptian style on decorative design.

Clayton, Peter A., *The Rediscovery of Ancient Egypt: Artists and Travellers in the Nineteenth Century* (London, Thames and Hudson, 1982).

Curl, James Stevens, *Egyptomania: The Egyptian Revival: a Recurring Theme in the History of Taste* (Manchester and New York, 1994, Manchester University Press). This book is a guide to the influence of ancient Egypt on architectural and ornamental design. It includes 151 illustrations, a glossary of Egyptian terms and an extensive bibliography.

Humbert, Jean-Marcel *et al*, *Egyptomania: Egypt in Western Art 1730–1930* (Ottawa, National Gallery of Canada, 1994). This is the official catalogue of an exhibition jointly organised by the Musée du Louvre and the National Gallery of Ottawa with the collaboration of the Kunsthistorisches Museum. The many scholarly essays and numerous illustrations collected in this book trace the dazzling influence of Napoleon's Egyptian Campaign over the whole realm of decorative art and design.

Reeves, Nicholas, *Ancient Egypt: The Great Discoveries: A Year-by-Year Chronicle* (London, Thames and Hudson, 2000). This book traces the history of the most significant Egyptian researches from the time of the discovery of the Rosetta Stone.

Roberts, David, *Egypt and Nubia from Drawings Made on the Spot (Vols 1–3)* (London, F.G. Moon, 1846–49). A facsimile edition, with extracts from Roberts's diaries combined with contemporary photographs, is published as: Bourbon, Fabio and Attini, Antonio, *Yesterday and Today: Lithographs and Diaries by David Roberts RA* (Shrewsbury, Swan Hill Press, 1996).

Russell, Terence M., 'Egyptian Antiquities: Monuments, Tombs and Excavations', in *The Built Environment: A Subject Index 1800–1960* (Gregg Publishing, Godstone and Brookfield, Vermont: 1987). This book lists several hundred published works relating to all aspects of Egyptian art and architecture and its subsequent influence on European architecture, art and decorative design.

THE FRENCH MILITARY CAMPAIGN

The serious researcher with an interest in Napoleon Bonaparte's military campaign in Egypt will find the following source invaluable: *Correspondance De NAPOLÉON I*, Publiée Par Ordre De L'Empereur Napoléon III, Imprimerie Impériale: Paris. This multi-volume work lists the correspondence of Napoleon Bonaparte together with the texts (in French) of his military commands and orders of the day. Volume III (1859) provides a record of the preparations for the invasion of Egypt; Volumes IV and V (1860) provide a record of the events bearing on the military campaign for the period 1798–99; and Volume VI (1860) provides a record of Bonaparte's departure from Egypt.

Chandler, David C., *The Illustrated Napoleon* (London, Greenhill Books, 1991). This book contains numerous images of Bonaparte's Egyptian and other military campaigns.

Herold, Christopher J., *Bonaparte In Egypt* (London, Hamish Hamilton, 1963). This book is an accessible account of Bonaparte's military campaign in Egypt and includes a detailed bibliography of related military studies.

Tracy, Nicholas, *Nelson's Battles: The Art of Victory in the Age of Sail* (London, Chatham Publishing, 1996). This book gives a detailed account of the battle of the Nile together with reproductions of contemporary nautical engravings and paintings.

Index

(Bold page numbers indicate illustrations and captions to illustrations.)